PIMLICO

83

THE IMAGE OF THE KING

Richard Ollard has written a number of books on seventeenth-century subjects, among them *Pepys: a biography* (recently reissued in an enlarged, illustrated edition), *Clarendon and his Friends, This War without an Enemy: a history of the English Civil Wars* and *The Escape of Charles II.*

He is past Vice-President of the Navy Records Society and his most recent book is *Fisher and Cunningham: a study in the personalities of the Churchill era.* In 1992 he was awarded the Caird Medal by the Trustees of the National Maritime Museum.

THE IMAGE OF THE KING

THE KING

Charles I and Charles II

RICHARD OLLARD

PIMLICO

PIMLICO

An imprint of Random House
20 Vauxhall Bridge Road, London SW1V 2SA

Random House Australia (Pty) Ltd
20 Alfred Street, Milsons Point, Sydney
New South Wales 2061, Australia

Random House New Zealand Ltd
18 Poland Road, Glenfield
Auckland 10, New Zealand

Random House South Africa (Pty) Ltd
PO Box 337, Bergvlei, South Africa

Random House UK Ltd Reg. No. 954009

First published in Great Britain by Hodder & Stoughton Ltd 1979
Pimlico edition 1993

1 3 5 7 9 10 8 6 4 2

Richard Ollard 1979

A CIP catalogue record for this book is
available from the British Library

Printed and bound in Great Britain by
Mackays of Chatham PLC, Chatham, Kent

ISBN 0-7126-5698-7

TO MICHAEL AND FAITH

Acknowledgments

———◆———

I am most grateful to all those who have allowed me to reproduce the portraits without which this book would lose its savour. They are individually acknowledged in the list of illustrations. In this field I owe much to Sir Oliver Millar not only for the exhibitions he has arranged and the catalogues he has written but for allowing me to draw yet again on his knowledge and judgment. I am similarly indebted to Mr Richard Walker for information, suggestions and encouragement. Their kindness and learning have put me in the way of much that I would otherwise have missed but they are of course not in any way responsible for the use that I have made of it.

Contents

———◆———

Illustrations

———◆———

ACKNOWLEDGMENTS

1. Reproduced by gracious permission of Her Majesty the Queen.
2. Crown copyright. The Victoria and Albert Museum.
3. From the collection at Parham Park, Pulborough, Sussex.
4. Reproduced by kind permission of Galeria Sabauda, Turin.
5. Cliché des Musées Nationaux, Paris.
6. Ashmolean Museum, Oxford.
7. Reproduced by kind permission of Madame de Paepe.
8. From the Charles Cottrell-Dormer Collection. By kind permission of the Courtauld Institute of Art.
9. By kind permission of the Cleveland Museum of Art.
10. By kind permission of the Trustees of the Hinchingbrooke Estate.
11. From Goodwood House by courtesy of the Trustees.
12. By kind permission of the Duke of Grafton.
13. Reproduced by permission of the Syndics of the Fitzwilliam Museum, Cambridge.

Preface

Tattle . . . pray spare me their titles; I'll describe their persons.
Scandal Well, begin then: but take notice, if you are so ill a painter, that I
    cannot know the person by your picture of her, you must be con-
    demned, like other bad painters, to write the name at the bottom.

The writer who attempts to explain what his book is about must be
liable to the reflection on his articulacy so pointedly expressed in this
exchange from Congreve's *Love for Love*. But the reader has some right
to know what he is being offered.

The main subject matter of this book is the character, personal and
political, of two Kings and the representation of that character during
their own time and after. It thus swings between the interpretation
and examination of evidence about what they were actually like and
the criticism of the various forms in which their image was projected,
either by themselves or by other interested parties. Masques, pictures,
statues, medals, poems, histories are among the most obvious sources.
The seventeenth century did not need to be told that the eye has
quicker and stronger apprehensions than those afforded by the printed
page. On the other hand when it is a matter of diffusion and duration
the written word comes into its own.

The idea of the book presented itself from a Winterhalter sketch of

Prince Albert and Queen Victoria in Restoration dress. The self-
consciousness of the Prince, his serious concern for matters far
transcending the frivolities of fancy dress, were admirably rendered as
he sat there, somewhat stiffly, looking out from the dark luxuriance of
ringlets cascading onto his shoulders. The incongruity first made one
laugh and then made one think. If Queen Victoria and Prince Albert,
of all people, could find themselves in thrall to Charles II his spell
must reach far.

Two other ideas quickly entwined themselves round this. First the
obvious but curiously neglected fact that Charles I and Charles II
were father and son. Why were they never, or practically never,
considered together? It has been well observed that historians are as a
profession too apt to accept or impose lines of demarcation that do not
correspond to the contours of events. Thus a diplomatic historian
occupies himself with, say, the causes of the First World War, a
military historian takes over on its outbreak, to be succeeded, when
the guns fall silent, by colleagues who will consider its consequences,
diplomatic and political, social and economic. This excessive division
of labour has been under increasing challenge in the last decade or so
to the manifest advantage of the study.

It seemed to me that it might be interesting to examine the
character and the image of the two Kings, usually kept apart, in the
relation to each other that history, if not historians, had in fact given
them. To do so from the distance of the twentieth century must involve
placing their likenesses from time to time in the different perspectives
in which they were first seen; and this leads naturally to a further
inquiry into what effects the original artist or writer was trying to
convey and why. How did they themselves wish to appear? How far
did this correspond with, how far was it influenced by, the development of their characters in real life? How and why has their
representation changed at the hands of historical partisanship?

The tracing of the image of Charles I suggested itself in a number of
ways. The portraits in the Age of Charles I exhibition at the Tate
Gallery in 1972 offered a fascinating study in character and interpretation; indeed in portraiture and propaganda. The Inigo Jones
exhibition at the Banqueting House focussed this more sharply.
Looking through a large part of the Sutherland Collection in the
Ashmolean Museum in connexion with a book on the Civil War, I was
struck by the heightening of Charles I's romantic qualities in the
hands of the eighteenth-century engravers. All this seemed to offer a

coherent theme. Whether it does, or more strictly whether I have conveyed it, is for the reader to decide.

The book is therefore a study in the character of two historical figures. It is not in the proper sense a biography, still less a history though I have, where it seemed necessary, supplied some biographical and historical detail. Historiography and iconography are also highly relevant, though no specialised or technical knowledge of these subjects is claimed or required. Since the interest of the book is in the character of Charles I and Charles II, I have tried my best to disengage it from the difficulties of historical detail and, where I could not, to narrate and explain, to identify and describe, as occasion demanded. The brief chronological table that follows will supply, if nothing else does, a degree of continuity and coherence.

Note to the Pimlico edition

I have taken the opportunity of this new edition to rewrite a passage on page 70, removing the story of Charles II as Prince of Wales promising *carte blanche* to his father's judges in exchange for his life. Dame Veronica Wedgwood first discredited this in her *The Trial of Charles I* (1964) and I am grateful to Lady Antonia Fraser for pointing this out to me.

Richard Ollard

Chronological Table

1600	19 November	Charles I born at Dunfermline.
1603		Accession of James VI of Scotland to throne of England as James I.
1612		Death of Henry, Prince of Wales, Charles I's elder brother.
1623	March-August	Charles I and Buckingham in Madrid.
1625	March	Charles I succeeds his father.
1625	June	Charles I marries Henrietta Maria.
1628		Assassination of Buckingham.
1629	March	Charles I dissolves Parliament, which is not summoned again until April 1640 (the Eleven Years Tyranny). The decade of the King's attempt at personal rule is the decade of the Van Dyck portraits and the Inigo Jones Masques.
1630	29 May	Birth of Charles II.
1639		The First Bishop's War. Military humiliation of Charles I following his attempt to impose the Laudian system of Church government in Scotland.
1640	April-May	The Short Parliament meets but is dissolved when it

refuses to vote money and expresses alarm at the King's Church policy.

	August-October	The Second Bishop's War. The Scots occupy Newcastle and impose severe economic terms on the King.
	November	The Long Parliament meets.
1641		The machinery of Charles I's personal rule is dismantled.
	May	Strafford executed.
	October	Outbreak of Irish revolt and massacre of English and Scottish protestants in Ulster.
1642	January	Failure of Charles I's military coup against the Long Parliament (the arrest of the five members).
	February	Henrietta Maria sails for Holland.
	July	First skirmishes in the war between King and Parliament.
	August	The Royal Standard raised at Nottingham.
	October	Battle of Edgehill. First major action of the Civil War. Result indecisive.
1643		The Court at Oxford. A year of Royalist successes.
1644		The Scots ally themselves with Parliament and enter England.
	July	Defeat of the Royalists at Marston Moor.
1645	March	Crumbling of the Royalist position leads Charles I to send the Prince of Wales to the West with Hyde as his principal adviser.
1646	May-June	End of the First Civil War. Charles I surrenders to the Scots at Newark. They withdraw to Newcastle with him as their prisoner. Hyde and the Prince of Wales escape first to Scilly and then to the Channel Islands. Against the advice of Hyde the Prince finally joins his mother in Paris.
1647	January	Charles I, handed over by the Scots to the Parliament, moves to Holmby House, Northamptonshire.
	June	Charles I taken into Army custody by Cornet Joyce. Imprisoned at Hampton Court.
	November	Escapes but is recaptured and imprisoned at Carisbrooke Castle.
1648	May-June	Outbreak of the Second Civil War. The Prince of Wales takes command of the ships that revolted from Parliament and sailed to Holland.

	August	The Second Civil War ends in Royalist defeat. Charles I negotiates with Parliamentary commissioners at Newport, Isle of Wight, while secretly trying to divide his enemies. The Prince of Wales remains with his sister and brother-in-law in Holland.
	December	Charles I moved to Hurst Castle, Hampshire, and then to Windsor in preparation for his trial.
1649	30 January	Execution of Charles I. Monarchy abolished in England. Charles II proclaimed King in Scotland. Charles II rejoins his mother in Paris.
	September	Charles II moves to Jersey.
1650	February-March	Leaves Jersey to meet Scots commissioners at Breda.
	June	Sails for Scotland.
	September	Cromwell's victory over the Scots army at Dunbar.
1651	January	Charles II crowned at Scone.
	August	Leads Scots army into England.
	September	Final defeat at Worcester. The King a fugitive.
	October	Escapes to France.
	November	Hyde rejoins the King at Paris and thenceforward remains his principal adviser during the remaining eight and a half years of exile.
1660	May	Restoration.
1667		Dismissal and exile of Hyde, now Earl of Clarendon.
1685	6 February	Death of Charles II.

I
The Stuart Touch

———◆———

Charles I and Charles II are not often brought before the public in a double bill. One is tragedy, the other comedy. One personifies principle, the other cynicism. One was long venerated as a martyr, the other admired as a man of the world, cool, rational, tolerant. Looking down at them in the dock of history their judges have rarely denounced them for the same crimes. Charles I brought disaster on his realm by asserting too high a view of his rights and duties. Charles II by his frivolity and idleness exposed the country to disgrace and humiliation. The antitheses are familiar and could easily be multiplied.

Yet besides the far from negligible fact that they were father and son, they have one immense and overwhelming quality in common. Both Kings created images of themselves which had a power and durability that outrange all competition. Our own century might be thought to have surpassed all others in this field of endeavour, and in the gross this is no doubt true. What are mass-marketing techniques but the projection of an image? And have not the national leaders of the last fifty years shown a sometimes alarming mastery of these potentialities? Hitler and Stalin, Baldwin and Roosevelt, Kennedy and de Gaulle, all these very different men succeeded in imposing on their compatriots—or at least a great part of them—a vision of themselves, to which their style in speech and writing, their public attitudes, their policies, their tones of voice, their taste in dress, their modes of relaxation all seemed integral. *Le style c'était l'homme même.* It was not with them as it was with Gladstone or Lloyd George or Joseph Chamberlain who might at any given moment be identified with a single contentious political issue such as Home Rule or Tariff Reform. Their personalities appeared to evolve organically, to move in response to the deeper underlying rhythms of history, submerged far beneath the choppy water of the episodic and the everyday. 'My thoughts grow in the aroma of that particular tobacco.' 'Do not disturb the President of the Republic except in the case of a world war.' Can the management of affairs in a twentieth-century state really have been conducted with such unconcern? It is easy to expose the inanities of detail in any style: the point is, does it work?

In the instances from recent history here cited the question answers itself. The style created, the image projected, was sufficient to its purpose. A few decades, or even a few years, later the magic may have lost its power. What is remarkable about Charles I and Charles II is that to an astonishing degree their highly distinct projections are still clear and pristine on the screen of national consciousness, hardly, if at all, impaired by the passage of generations. This is not to belittle or neglect the historical scholarship of the last three centuries in which criticism, interpretation and perspective have changed as they will for ever go on changing. The historiography of the subject will be considered in its place. Historians approach the past in a critical spirit that is at once the motive and the effect of their study. It is by the unquestioning, seemingly instinctive, assumptions of ordinary people that a nation's view of its history is defined.

Charles II provides an excellent example of the distinction. Historians have in the past and do at this moment differ widely in their estimate of him, not only as a King, but as to what sort of man he was. The national consciousness has never had any doubt. Charles II was the best of company, gay, carefree, pleasure-loving, tolerant. He possessed the wit and charm of Falstaff without his contemptible grossness. No wonder that he should be the first choice of every woman since his time (including, it has been alleged, though on no discernible authority, Queen Victoria) invited to pick an English monarch to sit next to at dinner. The image has, if anything, expanded in its own warmth. A hundred years after Queen Victoria's accession in George Bernard Shaw's *In Good King Charles's Golden Days* we are presented with a King whose cool distaste for fanaticism has grown into a compassionate horror of cruelty and vindictiveness, whose sceptical pragmatism has developed into a self-denying acceptance of the supremacy of Parliament. How far, if at all, this amiable portrait can be reconciled with what we know of the sitter will be the business of this book to establish. In the process it may be that we shall glimpse the origins and development of the two images. And it may be pertinent to inquire whether, in spite of appearances to the contrary, there may not have been more in common between the two Kings than is generally supposed. That their ages were very different seems indisputable.

To compare two men who though intimately connected by relationship and function lived apart in space and time, common points of reference are required. In the case of Charles I and II similarities sometimes take on the appearance of identity. The experience of the father coloured the son's apprehension of events. It would not be possible to live through the twenty years that followed the meeting of the Long Parliament in 1640 and to feel as Sir Henry Wotton wrote in his *Panegyrick to King Charles* (1633):

> . . . we know not what a Rebel is; what a Plotter against the Common-weal: nor what that is, which Grammarian[s] call *Treason*: the names themselves are antiquated with the things. . .[1]

Charles II reigned in the shadow of his father's scaffold. Names and phrases lurking near the surface of consciousness leapt unbidden to the minds of men whose lives had been wrenched out of shape by civil war. In the opening stages of the great struggle to exclude James, Duke of York, from the succession to the throne, the King refused his assent to a bill transferring his control of the militia to Parliament 'though but for half an hour'.[2] The choice of words could hardly have been accidental. On the eve of the Civil War his father had refused a similar proposal with a vehemence no one would have forgotten: 'By God, not for an hour. You have asked that of me in this, was never asked of a King.'[3] In every age people draw historical analogies from the immediate past, often inappropriately. The opinion, so widely expressed, as the Exclusion Crisis deepened, that 'Forty-one is come again' had a frightening coherence. Some of the Opposition leaders were the sons of men who had then confronted Charles I.

There were other close personal connexions between the two Kings

besides those of blood and family. Charles I had chosen his son's tutors
and governors. He had, when the danger of defeat and capture began
to loom over him, detached his ablest minister Sir Edward Hyde, later
Earl of Clarendon, to advise and guide his heir and to accompany
him, if necessary, into exile. Clarendon, the best servant of the Stuarts
who was also through his daughter's marriage to become the grandfather of the last of the dynasty, knew both Kings intimately and has
left abundant evidence of his opinions. Out-distancing even Clarendon in the length of high and distinguished service to both monarchs
James Butler, Duke of Ormonde, has also provided materials for a
double portrait. Court and Government were still in the seventeenth
century so inextricably mixed that a man who served the King in the
one probably did so in the other. Clarendon and Ormonde stand, as it
were, on their own legs. But a little lower down the scale one might
instance Sir Philip Warwick as a man who had served the father as a
courtier and the son as a Treasury official. Many of the churchmen
who were so closely identified with both Kings, Archbishop Juxon for
instance or Brian Duppa, qualify under both categories. It is in this
circle of Court and Church and Government that the people who
knew and served both masters are to be found. This statement is not
quite the tautology that it sounds. Some of the people who were the
intimates of one but not the other did not belong there. Those who
were close to both did.

The evidence of such witnesses is of the first importance in any
attempt to establish resemblances and discrepancies between the two
characters whose historical projections are in such striking contrast.
But the witnesses themselves cannot escape the flux of existence so
neatly summed up in the Greek axiom that it is impossible to step into
the same river twice. The young Mr Hyde who passed from the
brilliant intellectual world of Selden and Falkland to become the
speech writer and constitutional adviser to King Charles I is not
equivalent and interchangeable with the much-tried, much-enduring
elder statesman, racked with gout and intolerant of jumped-up Court
spaniels, who returned to Whitehall with Charles II in May 1660.
That he saw both men closely and saw them in relation to each other
gives his judgments a rare value but does not sterilise them in the sense
that a surgeon's instruments are sterilised. He was a part of all that he
had met, and like Ulysses in Tennyson's poem felt no satiety in his
appetite for experience and understanding. Hyde, like Pepys, continued to evolve. Perhaps that is why their personalities come through

so fresh and clear. No projector of images could achieve such wholeness: no *trompe l'œil* such solidity. The men who knew both Kings were for the most part young or in the prime of life when they knew Charles I, and older and wearier when they knew Charles II.

There are exceptions. Many of the churchmen who collectively formed so strong a link between the two reigns were in the afternoon of life at the time of their association with the father and late into its evening when the son came into his own again. This is especially true of that trusted and intimate circle who attended Charles I in his captivity, Juxon, Duppa, Hammond and Sanderson. Hammond who had done more than any other single person to maintain the character and position of the Church of England in the days of its adversity did not live to see the Restoration, dying exactly a month before Charles II rode into London. Juxon and Duppa survived only long enough to say their *Nunc dimittis*. Duppa had been the first of the clergymen chosen by Charles I to act as tutor to the heir apparent. His successor Dr Steward had died in exile in 1651 and his deputy, John Earle, lived only till 1665. Yet it is probable that these three had a greater influence on Charles II's notions of religion, faint and fugitive though these appear, than the real architect of the Restoration settlement of the Church, Gilbert Sheldon. Sheldon had succeeded Juxon as Archbishop of Canterbury early in the reign and had effectively discharged the duties of the post from the beginning. He held the primacy till 1677 and stamped his character, fearless, authoritarian and combative, on the policy and institutions of the Restoration Church. The force of his mind had impressed Charles I: the strength of his character brought him under Charles II's displeasure. He was one of the few churchmen who dared to reprove the King for his open immorality and to refuse him the sacrament.

The Church was the cornerstone of Stuart kingship. James I had elaborated his theory in *The Trew Law of Free Monarchies* and summed it up in his famous epigram 'No bishop, no King'. Charles I had embraced his father's teaching with his whole heart. And as the Civil War and its aftermath were to show even those who opposed him at every point still accepted the view that society was held together by the cement of revealed religion. There were limits to everyone's toleration, however tender a man might feel to the scruples of another's conscience. It was not essentially a question of religious ardour or philosophical liberalism. The cohesion of any society must derive from some agreed principles of right and wrong. For Cromwell as for Charles I, for Hyde as for Sir Henry Vane these were to be found in Christianity, variously interpreted. By the time of Charles II this view was still general but neither so tenaciously maintained nor so universally accepted. The harsh treatment of Dissenters which Sheldon championed was no longer the expression of a confident educated and articulate opinion. Much more it was orthodoxy whistling to keep its spirits up.

Charles II, as is well known, was in sympathy with the changing spirit of the age, a change which in his case at least seems to have been prompted more by a general scepticism than by any belief in toleration. As his ministers no less than his opponents were to find the King was not inhibited by an over-solicitous concern for the rights of others. Unlike his father and paternal grandfather he seems not to have thought his moral and philosophical position through to the certitudes on which they rested. By all accounts he was without their intellectual eagerness. Most of those who saw him in his more serious moments have contrasted his physical energy, exemplified in his fondness for long and fast walks, his early rising, his love of riding and sailing, with his extreme mental indolence, combined as it was with obvious intellectual capacity. No wonder he was often bored 'not knowing how to get round the day' as Burnet put it: and no wonder if he had not subjected himself to the severe and rigorous labour of organising his moral, political and religious ideas into a coherent system.

Perhaps in this he showed his superior genius. Perhaps the Stuarts and their gorgeous palaces, their solemn temples, melt, under rational criticism, into air, into thin air. Perhaps it was their nature, like Prospero's, to cast spells rather than to formulate political philosophies. From first to last how they defy sobriety and probability. Through the half-shut eyes of imprecise historical recollection what a stir of colour and movement, what drama, what pathos, what inexorability. Mary, Queen of Scots and Bonnie Prince Charlie are but two of the major luminaries in this constellation. Escapes, pursuits, imprisonments, disguises, sudden reversals of fortune, plots, betrayals, loyalty and courage, how their story has differed except in the last two particulars, from that of the dynasty that has supplanted them. This no doubt goes a long way to explain why Charles I and II are more vividly present to the popular historical consciousness than monarchs whose achievements were more lasting or whose personal qualities were more remarkable.

That both Kings had a lively instinct for projecting an image of themselves can hardly be contested. Charles I, after all, was commemorated by a book whose title literally translated from the Greek means simply The Image of the King. *Eikon Basilike or the Portraiture of His Sacred Majesty in his Solitudes and Sufferings* became one of the best sellers of the seventeenth century. Hume in the next century expressed the highest admiration for it:

> The Eikon . . . must be acknowledged the best prose composition which at the time of its publication was to be found in the English language.[4]

Since the work was published posthumously the King can hardly have had the final word in the choice of title, though the work itself purported to be from his own hand. The attribution was, from the first, disputed.

To the creation of such an image, physique, maturity and appropriate means of projection necessarily contribute. The young are too tender, in appearance if not in heart, to afford material for such a stereotype. Both Kings looked the parts they were to create. The ethereal quality of Charles I was enhanced by his slightness and fragility. His face, particularly as rendered by the genius of Van Dyck, has continued to touch the imagination and excite the pity of succeeding generations as it is said to have done from Bernini. Receiving the famous triple portrait that Van Dyck had painted for him so that he could model the King's bust 'he exclaimed that he had never seen a portrait whose countenance showed so much greatness and such marks of sadness: the man who was so strongly charactered and whose dejection was so visible was doomed to be unfortunate'.[5] Thus the image consummated by the King's execution was already palpable before the events of January 1649 stamped it on the mind of romantic Toryism.

How far it is open to a man to choose, how far his physical equipment and impact dictate, what impression of himself he can impose on his fellows is an unanswerable but perhaps not a meaningless question. Actors and casting directors are keenly aware of the limitations that build, height and habit of body place on the expression of character. In real life is it mind and temperament that conform to antecedent physical causes or is it the flesh that expresses the spirit? As with the authorship of *Eikon Basilike* the best available opinion may be a mumbled reinsurance against too categorical an answer. But certainly both Kings express in their persons, or at least in the likenesses that have come down to us, that aspect of themselves that they attempted to project. Small wonder, perhaps. Who paid the painters, sculptors and the medallists? But many instances might be given where the most extensive patronage has failed, visually at any rate, to embody a desired conception. Caesar and Napoleon, Queen Victoria and Frederick the Great disappoint expectation. May it not be that characters of real and unmistakable force offer the greatest difficulties to those whose business it is to establish a desired image? The more insipid the person, the easier the task. The artist has a freer hand, the subject less recalcitrance.

Such questions may throw some light on the relation of appearance to reality in the images of Charles I and II. But before advancing to that point it is necessary first to consider the formative influences, personal and other, that shaped the two men and to see what can be established from the evidence of those who knew them. From there the next step is to examine their treatment at the hands of historians. The image of the Stuarts cannot have come out of nothing. Its influence has certainly been a power in our history.

2

Charles I: Man and Majesty

There is no explaining the historical appeal of Charles I without acknowledging the depth of affection he inspired in those about him. The loyalty he commanded there was personal and protective, rather than political and dynastic. The attraction of that delicate, grave, retiring nature was by no means confined to those who shared his beliefs and opinions. Aubrey tells us that his Republican friend James Harrington, one of those appointed by Parliament to attend on the King during his captivity, '. . . passionately loved his Majestie . . . and I have oftentimes heard him speake of King Charles I with the greatest zeale and passion imaginable, and that his death gave him so great a griefe that he contracted a disease by it; that never anything did goe so neer to him'. The most persistent and the most nearly successful of those who attempted to contrive the King's escape from imprisonment in the Isle of Wight had himself fought for the Parliament during the Civil War.[1] If this was the effect produced in opponents what might not be expected from his friends?

Sir Philip Warwick wrote that when he thought of dying it was one of his comforts that when he parted from the dunghill of this world he should again meet King Charles I. Clarendon who had many reservations about the King's policies had none about his personality. 'Mr Hyde was so entirely devoted to his majesty . . .'[2] The Duke of

Ormonde in 1680 nearing the end of a long life filled with assignments to disaster and calls on a loyalty that was proof against despair lost the son on whom his hopes rested. To a correspondent who reported the insincere condolences of a courtier he wrote:

> My loss, indeed, sits heavy on me and nothing else in the world could affect me so much: but since I could bear the death of my great and good master King Charles the First, I can bear anything else: and though I am very sensible of the loss of such a son as Ossory was, yet I thank God my case is not quite so deplorable as that nobleman's; for I had much rather have my dead son than his living one.[3]

Ormonde had more reason than most to reproach the memory of a King who had rewarded his own unswerving honour with deceit. To those who had seen King Charles both in prosperity and adversity there was, it seems, a truth of heart that transcended his untrustworthiness.

The contradictions of the King's character are concealed by his composure. This quality, in such striking contrast to the excited, undignified manner of his father James I, is the essence of his regality.

> His deportment was very majestick; for he would not let fall his dignity, no not to the greatest Forraigners that came to visit him and his Court; for tho' he was farr from pride, yet he was carefull of majestie, and would be approacht with respect and reverence. His conversation was free, and the subject matter of it (on his own side of the Court) was most commonly rational; or if facetious, not light . . . His way of arguing was very civil and patient; for he seldom contradicted another by his authority, but by his reason: nor did he by any petulant dislike quash another's arguments; and he offered his exception by this civill introduction, 'By your favour, Sir, I think otherwise on this or that ground' yet he would discountenance any bold or forward address to him. And in suits or discourse of business he would give way to none abruptly to enter into them, but lookt that the greatest Persons should in affairs of this nature addresse to him by his proper Ministers, or by some solemn desire of speaking to him in their own persons.[4]

Sir Philip Warwick describes what Van Dyck painted. His evidence is confirmed by those not of the Court circle who witnessed the King's reception of public disasters and private sorrows during the Civil War.

The trial and execution have immortalised this image of him.

Here, at any rate, appearance and reality, the projection and the person, are indistinguishable. The reason perhaps is that both are works of art. The tranquillity, the rare self-command that Charles I showed in his maturity were achieved by rigorous self-discipline. As in the fairy story the face had grown into the features imposed by the mask. Nothing came easily to the King except his purity of taste. As a boy he had been handicapped by weak joints and a defect of speech so severe that his father was ready to expose him to the hazards of surgery. He never grew into a tall, well-built man as his sons and his elder brother did, but his will-power triumphed over his disabilities. He mastered the art of horsemanship and was almost as fond of hunting as his parents, although some judges noted a certain doggedness in these activities rather than the ease of the natural horseman. He was active and energetic, tough and wiry, in spite of his physique, not from bodily endowment.

The shyness and diffidence consequent to such difficulties were perhaps made keener by the grace and success of his brilliant and handsome elder brother. Prince Henry was the favourite not only of his adoring parents but also of those who for a variety of reasons felt no enthusiasm for the Stuarts. Once the mute resentment flared into fury when the elder boy teased the younger that when he was King he would make his brother Archbishop. Charles was only eleven when Henry's death suddenly made him heir to the throne. But the struggles of childhood are not easily smoothed away. The tension and seriousness of a character formed by tenacity and self-discipline expressed themselves in dignity and restraint.

Neither of these qualities were conspicuous in his parents. Anne of Denmark was widely censured for her frivolity, her extravagance and her love of pleasure. Her open and friendly nature, attractive in itself, did not help her to establish the reputation of august virtue her position demanded. James I in appearance, manners and habits was grotesquely unfitted to personify the high monarchical doctrines he expounded. His unimpressive physique was embarrassed by disabilities he could not help. His tongue was too large for his mouth and he dribbled like a baby. His imperfect control over his bodily functions and his indifference to personal hygiene revolted the none too fastidious sensibilities of contemporary Englishmen. His manners were those of an overgrown spoiled child. Thwarted or alarmed he would sob and bawl, amused he would laugh with the same tedious excess.

Aubrey tells the story of a courtier whose moderately witty verse 'made his Majestie laugh so that he was ready to beshitt his Briggs'.[5] His intellectual abilities were exercised with the same lack of discretion. On a visit to Cambridge one of the contestants in a public disputation overcome by his own intellectual exuberance fainted away. The King, excited by the dialectical chase, vaulted into the empty saddle and continued the argument.[6]

Charles I only received the full warmth of his mother's affection after the death of her first and favourite son. James had not perhaps been quite so prepossessed in favour of Prince Henry. Indeed his general popularity combined with his personal friendship among the survivors and heirs of the Elizabethan tradition are said by some to have irritated the King's jealousy. With Charles there was no such obstacle. His relations with both his parents were henceforward happy and affectionate. But the discipline that early circumstances had imposed on him perhaps prevented him from following the example of his father's self-indulgence. Neatness, order, decorum, moderation were, and remained, the notes of his personal life. Sir Philip Warwick's account of his diet is of a piece with that of his manners.

> His appetite was to plain meats and tho' he took a good quantity thereof, yet it was suitable to an easy digestion. He seldom eat of above three dishes at most, nor drank above three: a glasse of small beer, another of claret wine, and the last of water; he eat suppers as well as dinners heartily; but betwixt meales, he never medled with anything. Fruit he would eat plentifully; and with this regularity he moved as steddily as a star follows its course.[7]

The clockwork regularity of his habits was observed by others in the Civil War. An officer who was with him in Oxford during the winter of 1644-5 wrote:

> . . . he kept his hours most exactly, both for his exercises and for his dispatches, as also his hours for admitting all sorts to come and speak with him. You might know where he would be at any hour from his rising, which was very early, to his walk he took in ye Garden, and so to Chapple and dinner; so after dinner, if he went not abroad, he had his hours for wrighting and discoursing, or chess playing or Tennis.[8]

Both these accounts come from friendly sources. They are confirmed from a hostile one. 'King Charles', wrote Lucy Hutchinson, the widow of one of the men who signed his death-warrant

> was temperate and chast and serious; so that the fooles and bawds, mimicks and Catamites of the former Court grew out of fashion, and the nobility and courtiers, who did not quite abandon their debosheries, had yet that reverence to the King to retire into corners to practise them. Men of learning and ingenuity in all arts were in esteeme, and receiv'd encouragement from the King, who was a most excellent judge and a greate lover of paintings, carvings, gravings, and many other ingenuities . . .[9]

A certain authority stands out from all these descriptions of the King. Yet the earliest portraits show a diffidence that however well concealed in public was to reveal itself in his most secret and intimate correspondence and most fatally in his conduct of affairs. His own self-scrutiny at last forced him to recognise it. 'Never repose so much upon any man's single counsel, fidelity and discretion, in managing affairs of the first magnitude [that is, matters of religion and justice] as to create in yourself or others a diffidence of your own judgement, which is likely to be always more constant and impartial to your crown and kingdom than any man's.'[10] This parting message to his son was delivered to Juxon the day before his execution. In its sentiments he was drawing a moral from his own misfortunes that his truest friends were to echo.

It seems a strange contradiction that a man so ready to listen to conflicting opinions and to adopt inconsistent policies should remain so tenacious of his principles and so impervious to the virtues of those who questioned them. Issues lost themselves behind people. Once the King's emotional loyalty was engaged the carefully constructed barriers of reason and judgment were swept away. Two such loyalties dominated his life: the first to the Duke of Buckingham and the second to his Queen, Henrietta Maria. In both cases their ascendancy was preceded by an initial period of distrust and dislike. In both cases the capitulation that followed was total.

George Villiers, first Duke of Buckingham was a court masque in himself. In his beauty, his magnificence, his centrality to his age and his meaninglessness to any other he partakes of that most characteristic expression of Stuart Court imagery. He might have been an allegorical figure invented by Ben Jonson and plumed by Inigo Jones.

Buckingham was everything and he was nothing. He brought off, without apparent effort, the extraordinary feat of doubling as favourite to King James and Prince Charles, carrying his supremacy unchallenged into the new reign. In war, in administration, in diplomacy he was entrusted with the direction of affairs without having given any proof of outstanding ability and certainly without any depth of knowledge or breadth of experience. No Stuart minister had such immense opportunities or such slender qualifications. Villiers brought no accession of strength to the Crown. He was not rich: he was not well connected: he was not popular; indeed, he was not known. James I shocked his supporters and delighted his enemies by the violence of his infatuation for this splendid-looking young man. The riches and offices that he heaped on him brought him overnight his own patronage and thus his own following. His grace of manner and person fitted him for life at court and made it easy for him to conciliate, to win over and finally to enslave the awkward, diffident boy who had at first resented his position. As Prince and King, Charles was approved, by an age that valued formality, for the standards of deportment that he expected and set. The contrast with his father was extreme. But his relations with Buckingham show an altogether uncharacteristic lack of restraint. On their expedition to Spain in 1623 to negotiate a marriage with the Infanta, a half-baked scheme deplored by the English ambassador, the Prince and his mentor behaved with a skittishness hardly suited to an important diplomatic initiative. Even before leaving England 'setting out with disguised Beards, and with borrowed names of Thomas and John Smith' they seem to have regarded themselves as characters in some chivalric romance, jumping their horses across country instead of following the high road and overtipping the ferryman at Gravesend because they had not brought any silver.[11] Measure and gravity, the disciplined qualities of the King's style, are absent from all his dealings with Buckingham. In the series of letters that he wrote to the favourite after his disastrous mismanagement of his own ill-conceived expedition against the Ile de Rhé, Charles's anxiety to take the whole blame on himself is abject.[12]

In only one other relationship is there any sign of the same self-abasement, that with the Queen, Henrietta Maria. But that was itself an echo, a reflection. Buckingham had contrived the French marriage out of pique at the predicted failure of the Spanish one. It was his creation. Nonetheless it was widely remarked that the King only fell in love with his wife after Buckingham's death. In July 1626 Charles wrote him a long letter recounting his quarrels with the Queen and specifying the causes of them '. . . her eschewing to be in my company . . . her neglect of the English tongue and of the nation in general'.[13] Whatever was the secret of the Duke's fascination it seems to have been in no degree erotic. In the commodious sewers of Stuart court scandal there is no suggestion that Charles I had homosexual inclinations. It seems more probable that the explanation lies in the splendid insubstantiality, the glittering, beckoning illusionism for which the King's spirit hungered. Images attracted Charles I, reality repelled or bored him.

Nowhere is this better illustrated than in the sumptuous masques mounted by Inigo Jones at Whitehall in the 1630s.[14] From first to last the twofold theme is the triumph of Charles I as the hero king, the adored father of his people and a celebration of the divine beauty and virtue of Henrietta Maria, fit consort for such a paragon. The essence of the masque is spectacle. It is part pageant, part ballet, part opera, part *tableau vivant*. There is verse to be spoken or sung, there is music and dancing. But it is in the splendour of the design, of costume, of scenery, above all of special effects that the Court masques of Charles I seek their achievement. The King, personating his own allegory, descends from a heavenly chariot. The Queen floats above the stage in clouds that part to reveal her radiance. The capstan and the windlass that hoist or lower these glorious figures of true constitutional doctrine are, like the mechanics of all finished art, hidden from the spectator. Yet the masque involves and embraces its audience more closely than the theatrical forms with which we are familiar. The masquers come down from the stage and mix with the court who join like the chorus of a Greek play in the affirmation of truths emblematically expressed.

To these productions the King devoted care and expense on a scale that is only explicable on the hypothesis that he regarded them as regal acts of the deepest significance. That he himself inspired the content of the masques, that he collaborated with Inigo Jones more as a fellow artist than as a patron seems in the highest degree probable. Magnificent and beautiful though Jones's drawings show them to have been, fugitive and ephemeral though we know they were, the masques were not in the King's eyes the seventeenth-century equivalent of a fancy-dress ball. The King, as Lucy Hutchinson emphasised, was serious. And about nothing was he more serious than his concern with projecting his image. Stephen Orgel and Roy Strong have well written 'No other English monarch has ever been so intensely concerned with his own iconography, and in the masques and court plays of the 1630s we may observe the royal imagination fashioning, through the art of Inigo Jones, as of Van Dyck and Rubens, a Kingdom and a self.'[15]

It was to this that the King was drawn by his own extraordinary talents and sensibilities. The bias of every man of unusual gifts lies towards the field in which he knows he can excel. In the masque *Albion's Triumph*, performed in January 1632, Charles is allegorised as a triumphant Roman Emperor. For a monarch whose military exploits had been uniformly humiliating the concept might appear absurd. But it is explained that the nature of Albanactus's triumph is higher than anything so ordinary as winning a war. He has conquered himself and continues to do so. '. . . this brave Albanactus Caesar . . . daily conquers a world of vices . . . no vice is so small to scape him, nor so great but he overcomes it, and in that fashion he triumphs over all the kings and queens that went before him. All his passions are his true subjects . . .'[16] Defiance of historical reality by this flattering moral self-portrait may well have been for the King a sufficient answer to the reproaches of Cadiz and the Ile de Rhé. It is certainly consistent with his passionate resentment against the critics of Buckingham, who conceived both these rash projects and himself commanded the second.

If the defeat of English arms was no impediment to the King's readiness to cast himself in the allegorical role of a triumphant Roman Emperor, it cannot be imagined that the murmurs and snarls of the Puritans, the menacing growth of political opposition, even the occupation of part of England by the Scots, could shake his tranquil certainties. In the winter of 1639-40 when it was clear that the King's expedients for governing without recourse to Parliament would work no longer, the last of Inigo Jones's great series went into production. In this piece the King exhibited himself in a favourite rôle, that of the calming, soothing, civilising philosopher-King who brings his re-calcitrant subjects to a realisation of their happiness under his benevolent rule. Nobody has his ears cut off or is made to feel the distasteful necessities of discipline. The King and his fellow masquers were soaring in an empyrean where such earthbound considerations had no place. In the masque the Genius of Great Britain pleads with Concord not to forsake the realm:

> Stay then, O stay! if but to ease
> The cares of wise Philogenes

To which Concord agrees in special recognition of the King's wisdom and virtue, a sentiment in which the Good Genius joins:

> O who but he could thus endure
> To live and govern in a sullen age,
> When it is harder far to cure
> The people's folly than resist their rage.

At the end of the spectacle they lead the people, now happily brought to a better frame of mind, in a song to the King:

> Murmur's a sickness epidemical
> 'Tis catching, and infects weak common ears.
> For through those crooked, narrow alleys, all
> Invaded are and killed by whisperers.
> This you discerned, and by your mercy taught
> Would not, like monarchs that severe have been,
> Invent imperial arts to question thought,
> Nor punish vulgar sickness as a sin.[17]

At this point Henrietta Maria and her ladies were to be seen approaching in a cloud of surpassing beauty and the proceedings concluded with a general recognition that life on earth did not offer sufficient opportunity to sing the praises of the royal couple, a debit that must be carried forward into the columns of eternity.

We know that within a few months the King was to summon and dissolve one Parliament, that before the end of the year its successor was to impeach Laud and Strafford, the chief executants as well as the chief designers of the King's policy of personal rule. We know that a bare two years later Henrietta Maria was to leave England in fear of her life. The hindsight of history must not mislead our attempts to understand character and motive. It is not reasonable to expect Charles I or anybody else to have known what was going to happen. But equally it is not reasonable for Charles I to expect his contemporaries or the generations that have succeeded them to accept such a picture of a mild and healing prince. But did such a thought ever enter the King's head? It seems doubtful. Charles was not by his understanding of his position called on to inquire into the minds of his subjects. As he said on the scaffold, 'A subject and a sovereign are clear different things.' What mattered was to fuse image and reality, to create a work of art. A sovereign was an artist in a medium no one else could work in.

Such high and mystical conceptions exist in a rarefied air. A clear idea, said Burke, is necessarily a small idea. Part of the deviousness, even the readiness to deceive, that Clarendon and his closest colleagues deplored in the King may be attributed to the difficulty of formulating his deepest perceptions. The twentieth-century reader is satiated with explanations of failure, personal or social, political or economic, that reduce every problem to one of communication. Yet artists, and the King whatever he was was surely that, find precise definitions imprisoning or insufficient. It is to his wider artistic apprehensions that we must now turn.

3

Charles I: the Trial of Faith

Charles I, it is agreed on all hands, was the greatest connoisseur of the arts in general and the most discriminating patron of contemporary artists ever to reign over us. Rubens was a diplomat as well as a painter but there is no reason to suppose that he was speaking in the first capacity when he described the King as '*le plus grand amateur de peinture du monde*'. If this is translated in its strict sense of having the best taste in painting of any patron and collector then alive the catalogue of his pictures would go far to justify it. To reassemble the collection dispersed after the King's execution would strip the principal galleries of Europe and America of some of their greatest treasures. His supremacy in this field, at least, would seem to be incontestable, resting as it does on the judgment of one of the greatest masters in the history of European painting and on the evidence of the pictures that he possessed and loved.

A devil's advocate challenging the King's title to a place among the immortals of connoisseurship might argue that he came by it as he came by his throne, by inheritance and by entering into other men's labours. His mother and his elder brother had both made considerable collections to which he was the heir. The Duke of Buckingham had himself bought pictures on the lavish scale that he affected in everything. His preference for the Venetian school probably in-

fluenced Charles's growing taste even before the visit to Madrid in
1623 revealed the full glories of Titian. Buckingham's pictures were
enthusiastically praised by Rubens in a private letter written after the
Duke's death. The man on whose taste and advice the collection had
been formed, Balthasar Gerbier, was one of those who acted in the
same capacity for the King. But unquestionably the most original and
scholarly collector and patron was Thomas Howard, Earl of Arundel,
who spent several years in Italy acquiring his connoisseurship at first
hand. It was in Arundel's service that Inigo Jones became a citizen of
the Italian Renaissance, breathing its air and thinking its thoughts,
seeing through its eyes and feeling along its nerves. Besides Gerbier
and Jones, Charles inherited the expert advice and knowledge of
diplomats such as Sir Henry Wotton and Sir Dudley Carleton, and
courtier-virtuosi such as Nicholas Lanier, musician, artist and connoisseur, who was responsible for buying the Duke of Mantua's
collection in its entirety, perhaps the greatest coup of the reign. Even
Rubens and Van Dyck, the greatest of the many painters whom
Charles I patronised, could hardly be said to be his discoveries.

All this is true. But it does not of itself vitiate the claims made for the
King. In the arts as in the politics of his time he did not create his
inheritance. But there is abundant evidence that in the arts he made
his inheritance his own. He understood, he enriched, he enjoyed
unfeigned admiration, as his masques would have us believe that he
did in the whole sphere of kingship. It was not only in the visual arts of
painting and sculpture, architecture and design that his cultivated
sensibility was remarked. He was musical and he had an ear for the
cadences of English prose that was as much admired as his eye for a
picture. Dr Fell, the formidable Dean of Christ Church in his son's
reign, described him as 'the most accurate judge and greatest master
of English rhetorick which this age hath given'.[1] Charles himself
thought that his chaplain Dr Henry Hammond 'was the most natural
orator he ever heard' and warned him against the parsonical in-
tonation that he had fallen into in a country parish.[2] That the King
did not confuse style with content is plain from his judgment in
another of his favourite chaplains: 'I carry my ears to hear other
preachers, but I carry my conscience to hear Mr Sanderson, and to act
accordingly.'[3]

The arts were not for Charles I a mere adornment of life. They
were, in their minor expressions, no doubt an addition and extension
to its pleasures. But their real function was to bring order and truth to

the confusion of experience and actuality, to elicit its meaning, which must if correctly interpreted be nothing other than the will of God. The great portraits commissioned from Van Dyck were not intended simply to record or to flatter in images pleasing to the eye. They were meant, just as much as Inigo Jones' masques, to project an image of kingship locally personified in Charles and his Queen. The style in painting and architecture and sculpture which the King favoured was identified with the Renaissance courts of Italy and of the Spanish and Austrian Habsburgs. Puritan susceptibilities were immediately excited by the taint of Catholicism. Had not the King tried to marry a Spanish Habsburg and had he not soon afterwards brought home a Catholic Queen? Was there not an only too plausible association between Henrietta Maria's aggressive Catholicism, the King's extravagant and propagandist use of the arts most deeply-expressive of un-English ideas, and the political and legal search for ways of governing without recourse to Parliaments? That Charles I, a monarch unrivalled in our history for his devotion to the Church of England, should be seen by many of his subjects as the promoter of a Popish conspiracy or, at the least, a dupe of Popish wiles is ironical. But once granted the proposition, widely accepted in seventeenth-century Britain, that the Pope is Antichrist it is easy to trace the ultimate source of everything that one fears and dislikes. The King's image-building, unlike that of modern commercial operators, was not based on any consumer research. He neither knew nor cared what prejudices, what traditions, what passions he might antagonise.

The irony is intensified by the fact that the King's religious life and the spirit that informed it were in many respects closer to the Puritan than to the Roman Catholic. He was a man of prayer, of an ardent and a simple faith, and of great strictness of life. So much might be said of the sincerely devout in any sect or Church. But Charles I like his Puritan subjects extended the rigour he professed and personally practised to his judgments of others. Not for him the consolation found by Charles II in the reflection that God would not make a man miserable only for taking a little pleasure out of the way. And not for anyone else either. Henry Marten, according to Aubrey,

> was a great lover of pretty girles . . . King Charles I had a complaint against him for his wenching. It happened that Henry was in Hyde Parke one time when his Majestie was there, goeing to see a Race. The King espied him, and sayd aloud, Let that ugly Rascall be gonne out of the

Parke, that whore-master, or els I will not see the sport. So Henry went away patiently, *sed manebat alta mente repostum* [but it lay stored up deep in his heart]. That Sarcasme raysed the whole Countie of Berks against him.[4]

The favourite contrast between the laughing licentious Cavalier and the chaste censorious Puritan would put the King on the side that history did not.

Largely the confusion arises from the ambiguous use, then as now, of the term Puritan. Most often but by no means always in the seventeenth century it means those who adhered to the doctrines of John Calvin, the arch-theologian of Presbyterianism. Most often now, and sometimes then, it means people who insist on strictness of life and simplicity in worship. The lines of conflict were drawn when Laud's High Churchmanship collided head on with Scottish Calvinism. The two Bishops' wars with Scotland were the immediate cause of the two Parliaments of 1640 and coloured the events that flowed from them. Yet Laud and Strafford, the two execrated architects of the policy of 'Thorough', had been called to the King's service by his political necessities rather than by his personal inclinations. That he felt affection for Archbishop Laud seems clear, but it was an affection born of gratitude and respect, not of natural affinity. Strafford he needed, more perhaps than he needed Laud, but he does not appear to have liked him. Their relationship had got off to a poor start with the King's insulting dismissal of his future minister from a minor but honorific administrative post in his native Yorkshire coveted by one of Buckingham's henchmen. Matters had then gone from bad to worse. Strafford had been imprisoned for refusal to pay a forced loan. He had, worst of all, taken a prominent part in the attempt to impeach Buckingham. No one who had offended this the most passionate loyalty of his life could enjoy the King's unreserved approval. The authoritarianism of the two men drew them together in the conduct of affairs but their springs of action were different. Strafford's whole nature was consumed with a passion for executive efficiency; the King's was essentially visionary. And Strafford's power to repel is as clear across the centuries as the King's power to attract.

With Laud, one of the few men in public life to achieve intimacy with Strafford, it was another story. He had made his entry as the client not the critic of the great favourite. His devotion to a religious view of kingship was patent. His clumsiness in handling people aroused Charles's protective instincts, as Clarendon records. His liberal patronage of learning, his brusque determination to impose measure and order on public worship and to centre it on the altar rather than the pulpit were after the King's own heart. But fond as he was of the Archbishop the King did not confine his choice of spiritual advisers or model his own very real piety on that of Laud or the Laudians. Juxon and Sheldon, the one a protégé of Laud, the other his most sympathetic successor in the see of Canterbury, were certainly among the divines for whose attendance Charles I petitioned during his captivity. It was Juxon who attended him in his last hours. But Juxon was a most un-Laudian Laudian, on good terms with everybody, charitable, gentle and courtly. This was the type of clergyman whose ministrations Charles preferred for himself and whose instruction he chose for his son. The three divines who were at one time or another charged by the King with the religious education of the Prince of Wales—Brian Duppa, Richard Steward and John Earle— would have been more at home in the world of George Herbert and Little Gidding than in that of the High Commission and the Star Chamber. Like Herbert and his friend Nicholas Ferrar, the founder of the Little Gidding community, all three were men of wide and well-digested reading and all of them had seen something of life at Court or in great houses without having their heads turned.

Duppa indeed had been born into the royal service. His father had been master brewer to James I's Court: other members of the family were employed in the Royal Navy and the royal dockyards. A successful academic career opened the door to a wider world. He learned Hebrew as a schoolboy at Westminster and was elected a Student of Christ Church at the age of seventeen. Three years later he was elected a Fellow of All Souls and spent five years travelling in Europe. A chaplaincy in a noble household led to his appointment as Dean of Christ Church in 1628, where he caught the eye of Laud on the look-out for a tutor to the Prince of Wales in the middle 1630s. His churchmanship was in Stuart eyes impeccable but it is the flavour of his personality, its simplicity, courtesy and cultivation that perhaps explains his standing with both Kings. He had been made Bishop of Chichester in 1638 and was translated to Salisbury in 1641, but the outbreak of the Civil War and the abolition of episcopacy brought him back to Oxford where both the King and the Prince kept their court until the danger of defeat made it prudent for the heir apparent to retire to the West and, eventually, overseas. Duppa stayed with the King and after his execution lived quietly in Richmond. During the

long years of the Commonwealth he kept up a correspondence with
his few surviving and aging brethren of the episcopal bench and was
clearly one of the most trusted informants of the exiled Court. His
house was several times raided and ransacked by the Cromwellian
authorities but so skilfully did he manage affairs that nothing was ever
found that incriminated him or anyone else. How discreet he was may
be judged by the letters he exchanged with another prominent
Royalist of a younger generation, Sir Justinian Isham. Both men knew
that they were objects of suspicion to a government that ran a first-
class intelligence service. To exchange political information or even to
express an opinion on the tendency of current affairs would have been
to invite arrest. But they were free to discuss books and writers and to
reflect on the mysterious providence that had brought them and those
who thought as they did to so ruinous a condition. Duppa thus
expressed his reading of experience:

> . . . for though I am no such stoick as to have no affections left, yet I shall
> strive to be so much a Christian as neither to please nor displease my self
> too much with whatsoever shall happen. Those few words 'Thy will be
> don' settle the soul more than the loadstone can possibly operate upon the
> needle which still varies and hath the motion of trepidation.[5]

This is the quietism of George Herbert and his circle. To hear it
from the man chosen by the King to be his son's guide in all vexed
questions of religion is perhaps unexpected. Duppa remembers the
Court of Charles I without censoriousness but without regret. One of
its most conspicuous members, Lady Carlisle, who betrayed the
King's attempt on the five members to Pym, is now his neighbour at
Petersham:

> You would hardly believe that this great lady formerly waited on by all the
> great persons of the Court, should now walk single and alone to the seat on
> top of the Hill, and enjoy herself more in this retiredness than in all her
> former vanities . . .[6]

Though unworldly, he has the insights of a man who has read and
travelled. '. . . Reading of good authors is like walking in the sun,
which will leave a tincture upon us, though unawares of it.'[7] He
retains his intellectual curiosity. He goes to meet Hobbes at Roehamp-
ton, and brings away his *Elements of Philosophy* and his *Six Letters to the*

Professors in the University of Oxford with deep misgivings about their contents.[8] And he is without vanity. Pressed by Sir Justinian for fair copies of his sermons to be collected and printed, he excuses himself

> . . . nothing of mine was ever yet printed by my consent and I must grow much more in love with myself than yet I am, when I give way to it for the future.[9]

There is nothing here of the loud, assertive, bullying tone with which the leaders of the High Church party in both reigns are generally and not unjustly associated.

Duppa was a very old man when his pupil suddenly found himself restored to the throne. In spite of his infirmities he was translated to the bishopric of Winchester but his gallant efforts to play the part to which the King invited him were soon over. He died at Richmond in 1662. Charles II visited him on his death-bed and knelt to receive his blessing. For all his cynicism the King was not indifferent to the Christian virtues in his higher ecclesiastics. When as Prince of Wales he had gone into exile his father had chosen a rather more combative figure to uphold the position of the Church of England in his son's counsels. This was Richard Steward who was much admired by both Evelyn and Clarendon for his learning and his preaching. Westminster and All Souls had in his case led to a country parsonage, but his powers as a controversialist had drawn him to the King's notice and to high preferment. Clarendon tempers his praise for his character and abilities with a hint that he lacked a sense of proportion. Steward died in 1651 and was succeeded by John Earle, a wit and a scholar who had all Duppa's gentleness and grace. He had been one of Lord Falkland's circle and thus an old friend of Clarendon's who remembered him as

> . . . a man of great piety and devotion, a most eloquent and powerful preacher; and of a conversation so pleasant and delightful, so very innocent and so very facetious, that no man's company was more desired and loved. No man was more negligent in his dress, and habit, and mien; no man more wary and cultivated in his behaviour and discourse . . . He was amongst the few excellent men who never had nor ever could have an enemy . . .[10]

He was the man of all the Clergy for whom the King [Charles II] had the greatest esteem: he had been his subtutor and had followed him in all his exile, with so clear a character that the King could never see or hear of any one thing amiss in him. So he, who had a secret pleasure in finding out anything that lessened a man esteemed eminent for piety, had a value for him beyond all the men of his order.[11]

Earle was made Dean of Westminster at the Restoration and soon promoted to a bishopric. He was a steady opponent of Sheldon's persecuting policies against Dissenters. In this he was very much in sympathy with his pupil. If Charles I wanted to bring his son up a bigot he went an odd way about it.

Perhaps his concern to project his conception of monarchy and to identify it with High Churchmanship has tempted those who dislike the second to colour it with the first. Thus both can be made to appear like a failed imitation of the absolutism and intolerance of the triumphant Counter Reformation. Archbishop Laud's arrogant and arbitrary methods of enforcing his own wishes brought him into conflict even with his own natural supporters. Quite apart from antagonising the nobility, whether well or ill disposed towards the Court, by his high-handed and officious behaviour the Archbishop did not hesitate to break the very rules he was tireless in asserting against others. Among his many claims to the gratitude of the University of Oxford was his reform of its statutes. Yet in 1635 he pressed on the Warden and Fellows of All Souls the election of a candidate for a vacant fellowship whose qualifications did not satisfy the requirements of the College statutes. The Warden civilly pointed out the illegality. But the College had been founded by an Archbishop of Canterbury and the Visitorship is still vested in the occupant of that see. Laud exerted his rights as visitor, claiming, with perfect truth, that the election was disputed since most of the Fellows lacked their Warden's courage, and declared his candidate elected. What makes this story still more revealing of the contradictions in Laud's character is that the Warden in question was Gilbert Sheldon, a rigorist after his own heart, and the candidate was Jeremy Taylor, whose *Liberty of Prophesying* he would hardly have approved if he had survived to read it. The Archbishop had a strong streak of the sergeant-major but there were other and gentler sides to him.

This is even more true of the pre-Civil War High Church party to which his name is so often attached. In the University of Cambridge relations between the two parties in the Church were generally more friendly and tolerant. Joseph Mead, Milton's tutor at Christ's, refused to quarrel with people because they differed from him in opinion, an example which if it eluded his most famous pupil was followed by the admired philosopher and theologian Henry More. Not indeed that these virtues were only compatible with Anglicanism on the banks of the Cam. The King's favourite chaplains already mentioned, Hammond and Sanderson, were Oxford men. Anyone less like the storm-troopers of ecclesiastical absolutism would be hard to imagine. Izaak Walton recalls a chance meeting with Sanderson outside a book-shop in the city during Cromwell's time. It was raining so they sheltered under an overhanging roof but finding they had so much to say to each other they adjourned to a warm and cheerful inn. Looking back on his life Sanderson blamed his own diffidence and lack of enterprise as his chief's fault. It was that which had prevented him from accompanying Sir Henry Wotton as chaplain on his embassy to Venice and had thereby lost him the opportunity of meeting Wotton's great friend Paolo Sarpi 'a man whose fame must never die, till virtue and learning shall become so useless as not to be regarded'. Such admiration for this most formidable critic of papal pretensions to political authority hardly squares with the crypto-papism so often attributed to the King's intimates.

The King's religion was most deeply his own. It is here, if anywhere, that the lines of his personality are to be traced. It is here that the characters of his spiritual counsellors may throw some light. His court, like his masques, like his great State portraits, is less a guide to what he was than to what he wished to be taken for. And the characters of his favourites, first Buckingham and then the Queen, so much more distinct than his own are more clearly reflected there. The tendency that he deplored in himself towards allowing his judgments to be formed for him was predictably exploited by Henrietta Maria, self-willed and self-confident in everything. The moving spirits of the Court, Lady Carlisle and the Earl of Holland, were her favourites and became his by virtue of that. Only his cousin the Marquis of Hamilton owed nothing to the Queen.

> . . . the King used him with so much tender kindness that his carriage to
> him spoke more of the affection of a friend than of the power of a master; he
> called him always James, both when he spoke to him and of him, as an

expression of his familiarity with him; and it was presently observed by all that none had more of the King's heart than he possessed.[12]

Hamilton shared the traits of his royal cousin without his serious convictions. He was anything but straightforward. His readiness to intrigue and to deceive with false hopes was not constrained by loyalty to any clear principles. Yet as Clarendon emphasises it was to him more than to anyone else that the King listened when Scottish affairs were all important and it was to him that Charles wrote from Oxford in December 1642:

> I will either be a glorious King or a patient martyr, and as yet not being the first, nor at the present apprehending the other, I think it now no unfit time to express my resolution to you. One thing more . . . the failing to one friend hath indeed gone very near me; wherefore I am resolved that no consideration whatsoever shall ever make me do the like . . .[13]

Here are brought together the two images, that of Van Dyck and Inigo Jones with which the reign opened and that of the *Eikon Basilike* with which it closed. Shadowing both is the King's conviction that he had sinned by signing Strafford's attainder and that God would punish him for it.

Both these projections of the King's rôle have succeeded in acquiring historical substance in their own right, irrespective of truth or falsehood to the figure who conceived and perfected them. In the closing scenes of his life, at his trial and on the scaffold, he rose to the part. But in the long examination to which defeat and imprisonment subjected his character it is the diffident hangdog figure of the early portraits that shows through. Defeat was a confirmation from the ultimate court of appeal that he was guilty in the matter of Strafford's death. Yet except for brief and poignant moments when the King faced the facts of his situation in all their hopelessness and all their menace, he was ready to accept schemes that combined clear dishonour with obvious futility. Self-delusion had become addictive. The patience and loyalty that Ormonde showed when his royal master repeatedly denied that he had gone behind his back, broken his most solemn undertakings and jeopardised the lives and estates of his most faithful followers stand out in strong contrast against the King's behaviour. He has left no censure. What he must have felt may be gauged by the outburst of Hyde, perhaps his closest ally in the divided counsels of the Royalists.

> . . . Yet I must tell you, I care not how little I say in that business of
> Ireland, since those strange powers and instructions given to your
> favourite Glamorgan, which appear to me so inexcusable to justice, piety
> and prudence. And I fear there is very much in that transaction of Ireland,
> both before and since, that you and I were never thought wise enough to
> be advised with in. Oh Mr Secretary, those stratagems have given me
> more sad hours than all the misfortunes of war, which have befallen the
> King, and look like the effect of God's anger towards us . . .[14]

Was the King equally conscious of bad faith? Everything points
against it. His great adversary, Cromwell, has freely and vociferously
been accused of hypocrisy, and his accusers number many contemporaries not a few of whom fought on the same side as he. Charles I
however has scarcely, if at all, been so attacked, except in the
indiscriminate abuse of pamphlet warfare. That he was on occasion
underhand, sly and downright dishonest only his hagiographers and
the rationalist David Hume would attempt to deny. That he was
conscious of so acting is a different proposition. It is a fact of common
observation that high-minded persons are frequently unscrupulous. A
constant concern with the ultimate sometimes breeds a contempt for
the obvious. If Charles had been simply a pious fraud someone among
the excitable and quarrelsome crew of courtiers, soldiers and poli-
ticians who swarmed round him would have been found to say so. And
his fortitude would scarcely have been possible to a man who was not
clear in his own conscience.

Having thought his position through in the great scheme of things
Charles I was content with a less rigorous examination of particular
proposals and expedients. Where their probable consequences came
home to him was in the world of symbol and appearance. Many
examples could be cited from his conduct of the Civil War, such as the
decision, against the advice of Prince Rupert, to sit down before the
city of Gloucester when dash and bluff had failed, or the belief that
Montrose's brilliant successes as a guerrilla leader in the Highlands
could reverse the total defeat of the Royalist armies everywhere else.
When the war was over it was the same with his projects of escape. The
gesture was what mattered, the style, even perhaps the costume. The
King initiated the series by his midnight departure from Oxford in

1646. 'Farewell, Harry' said the Governor, as he opened the east gate for the King and his two companions. The careful deception, the covering of traces, the choice of disguise, the well-kept secret of the destination were all that they should have been. What was lacking was realism. The King had no plan. He made for London, but after looking at his capital mournfully from the high ground to the north-east turned away northwards, hoping to hear from the Scots army or from the French diplomat through whom he was seeking an accommodation. He then turned east into Norfolk with a vague idea of taking ship—but how and why and whither were points that had not yet been considered. A highly unsatisfactory verbal assurance, at third hand, from the Scots brought him back again to the Midlands to throw himself into their hands. He had obtained nothing. The symbolic associations of the performance were no doubt rich. Lear in the storm, Odysseus received by the swineherd when he returned in disguise to his own kingdom offered suggestive images. But the episode struck an observer such as Hyde with less edifying reflections. In February 1647 he wrote to his old friend John Earle.

> . . . I would rather (and it is known I would so) he should have stayed in Oxford, and after defending it to the last biscuit, been taken prisoner with his honest retinue about him, and then relied upon his own virtue in imprisonment, than to have thrown himself into the arms of the Scots, who held them not fairly open . . . I thought it an unkingly thing to ask relief of those who had done all the mischief, which it may be, had more of Philosophy or Metaphysicks in it than practical reason. And I hope that God hath disappointed all his other expectations to shew that Christian Princes can safely rely on nothing but their own [?virtue] and the integrity of their consciences to him; and that he shall owe his redemption purely to that; and that, when the people shall see how constant and tenacious he is of what is just and right (without the council, support or comfort of one honest man about him) they will so much abhor their jealousy and disesteem of him that they will conclude him the only fit Sovereign to preside and govern any Reformation.[15]

The justness of this perception leaves little to say. The fact that it was made before the Second Civil War and the trial and execution of the King renders it all the more remarkable.

Left. Charles I when Duke of York by Isaac Oliver. Probably painted in 1612.

Portrait of Charles I as Prince of Wales in grisaille by Sir Balthasar Gerbier, signed and dated 1616. Gerbier, besides being a painter, was one of the agents employed by Charles I on the continent in his purchase of works of art.

Right. Miniature by Peter Oliver of Charles I as Prince of Wales, signed and dated 1621.

Charles I by Mytens. Painted in 1627 for the King's sister-in-law, the Duchess of Savoy. The architectural background is by Steenwyck. The King's approval of this official image was marked by the grant of a fresh sitting in the following year and emphasised by the retention of the stance in several subsequent portraits, all of which were painted for recipients overseas.

Opposite. Mytens portrait of Charles I as Prince of Wales in 1623, painted soon after his return from Spain. His slight stature and his immaturity are skilfully disguised in a painting that prefigures the dignity of the later state portraits.

The famous Van Dyck portrait now in the Louvre. No other picture expresses such overt consciousness of sovereignty.

Marble bust of Charles I by Le Sueur, signed and
dated 1636.

Hoskins miniature of Charles I.
Perhaps painted about 1647-8,
the expression has the sadness
and resignation of the famous
Lely portrait at Syon with
perhaps more of the gentleness
that so endeared the King to his
close servants.

The Three Heads of Charles I by Van Dyck painted in 1635-6 for Bernini. Every aspect of the sitter's character from obstinacy and shiftiness to a pensive nobility and a visionary religious conviction can be discerned in this triumph of portraiture.

Opposite. The Van Dyck of Charles I in robes of state painted in 1636. The kingly authority of the head should be compared with the Simon engraving overleaf.

Dobson portrait of Charles I in armour. Painted in Oxford during the Civil War but unfinished and perhaps completed by another hand in Queen Anne's time. This portrait marks an interesting stage on the road from the regality of Van Dyck to the pathos of the late portraits and the martyrology that follows.

An engraving by Beckett from a Van Dyck portrait of Charles I in armour. The tranquillity and benignity are those of a soul that has conquered in no earthly fight.

Engraving by Simon from the Van Dyck of Charles I in coronation robes. Innocence and martyrdom have been added to the hauteur of the portrait.

The King's captivity in the hands of the Scots was a period of acute misery.

> Now, for myself, know that none are suffered to come about me but fools or knaves (all having at least a tincture of falshood), every day never wanting new vexations, of which my publick devotion[s] (which ought and used to be a Christian's greatest comfort) are not the least. This being my condition, and (as I have already shewed thee) not like to mend, I believe that thou wilt not think it strange that I desire to go from hence to any other part of the world . . .[16]

The Scots had removed him at once to the safe distance of Newcastle on Tyne from where this letter was secretly despatched to the Queen. Sir Robert Moray, later to be one of the Foundation Fellows of the Royal Society, was charged with smuggling the King out of prison in disguise and conveying him to Tynemouth where a ship had been provided for him.

> . . . and it proceeded so far, that the King put himself in the disguise and went down the back stairs with Sir Robert Murray. But his Majesty apprehending it was scarce possible to pass through all the guards without being discovered and judging it hugely undecent to be catched in such a condition, changed his resolution and went back; as Sir Robert informed the writer.[17]

Escaping, one might have thought, was of its nature a furtive and undignified activity. Too nice a sense of public occasion was hardly to be reconciled to it.

The welcome liberality with which first Parliament and then the Army treated their prisoner when the Scots exchanged him for a down payment on their arrears at once revived the King's illusions of political prosperity and removed the incentive to escape. His chaplains were restored to him, he was allowed to hunt, he was served with the deference due to a King. At Hampton Court he was even allowed to receive visitors and to enjoy the company of his children. Old courtiers and honoured veterans of the Royalist cause were permitted to take lodgings in the neighbouring villages of Richmond and Kingston. The monarchy to all appearances was once again in bud after the cold bare winter of defeat and humiliation. Lely's portrait of the King with his strikingly handsome younger son shows a face harrowed, perhaps hardened, by suffering but abates no jot of regality. While it was being painted the King was playing the old game, the only game he knew, of encouraging each of the conflicting parties amongst his opponents to believe that he was seeking their exclusive alliance. It seems highly probable, that it was Cromwell's discovery and demonstration of the King's bad faith that knocked away the stage scenery and tore up the lines of this last Court masque. Intimations of an assassination plot prompted yet one more secret flight. This time the proprieties could be perfectly maintained. The King left his palace by a door into the garden, he was rowed across the river, he found horses waiting for him at Thames Ditton. Decent, even leisurely, as his departure was, pursuit was strangely slow. Once again as at Oxford the stage management was beyond criticism: all that was wanting was a play. The King and his two companions arrived undetected at the safe house, Titchfield, near Southampton. But nothing had been done to obtain a ship, if the King's intention had been to rejoin his wife in France, his daughter in Holland, his mother's family in Denmark, his loyal subjects in the Channel Islands or, as Hyde and others urged, to seize the now ungarrisoned, superbly fortified frontier post of Berwick-on-Tweed. The appearance of seizing the initiative was object enough. One of the King's companions John Ashburnham was sent to the Isle of Wight to sound out the allegiance of its military commander Colonel Hammond, on no safer ground than that he was the nephew of the royal chaplain whose sermons the King so much admired. Ashburnham, who had accompanied the King on the Oxford escapade, followed his master's practice rather than his precept. Despite clear instructions not to divulge the King's whereabouts until he had obtained Hammond's sworn protection he blurted out everything without being given an unambiguous undertaking and ended by bringing Hammond in person to Titchfield. 'What! Have you brought Hammond with you? O you have undone me!' The King's words vary slightly as reported in the earliest authorities but their sense is too congruent to admit of a doubt.[18]

Hammond's treatment of him again encouraged him to think of himself as a King in fact as well as name. He was, to a great extent, given the freedom of the island: he visited the well-affected gentry and received their courtesies at his Castle of Carisbrooke. His diet, his clothing, his style of life were those of a great personage. But the Second Civil War which resulted from his secret diplomacy changed all that. Even before it broke out the exasperated Parliament had voted in January 1648 that no more addresses should be made to the King. Once again it was time to think of escaping.

And once again the King found capable and courageous assistance. Harry Firebrace, a young man of good family who had served with the Parliament in the war, had been appointed to attend the King on his journey from Newcastle. The grace of Charles's personality, never more evident than in misfortune, won a deep and lasting loyalty. It was logical that Firebrace should apply for a page's place in the Carisbrooke establishment and that the post should be given him. In spite of the close watch now kept on the King, Firebrace established swift and secure communications and put together a plan of escape that took account of everything and left no opportunity for indecision. That Charles's shilly-shallying was likely to prove the greatest hazard Firebrace seems to have appreciated. The King was to climb down from a window in his lodgings into the great courtyard that at night would be empty and unguarded. Firebrace would be waiting there with a longer rope knotted at one end round a rough seat by which he could lower the King from the battlements of the curtain wall. That only left the outer works from which the drop was a mere nine feet. Two local gentlemen would be waiting on horseback with a mount for the King ready saddled. They would escort him at once to the point on the coast where a vessel belonging to the island was waiting for him. The movements of the patrols and the habits of the castle guards were all known and allowed for.

Firebrace had brilliantly prevented the King's temperamental vacillation. He had even provided a method of escape that might commend itself to his sense of style. The descent from the castle walls, the night ride to the coast, there was nothing here to offend the most fastidious taste. But he was defeated by the King's obstinacy. On the night of March 20th, 1648 Charles started to climb out of his window and got stuck. A quarter of a century later Firebrace recalled 'Whilst he stuck, I heard him groane, but could not come to help him; w^ch (you can imagine) was no small affliction to me.' The affliction must have been the more intense because Firebrace had foreseen this very difficulty and had proposed means of overcoming it.

> I told him I feared it was too narrow. He sayd he had tried with his Head; and he was sure, where that would passe, the Body would follow. Yet still I doubted, and proposed a way to make it a little wyder, by cutting the plate the Casement shut to at the bottome: which then might have been easily put by. He objected that might make a discovery; and commanded me to

prepare all things else; and that, he was confident would not impede him.[19]

There were to be other projects of escape contrived by Firebrace, miraculously avoiding the detection that the King's indiscretion seemed certain to bring about. It seems highly probable that he passed on more than he should to Lady Carlisle. Certainly he was still in secret correspondence with her. The silent persevering purposefulness required for an escape was not in his character. But the rôle envisaged by Hyde in his letter to Earle was to give Charles I the highest expression of himself and to fix an image of monarchy in which feebleness and vanity could have no place.

4

The Heir Unboyed

The execution of the King was as far-reaching in its consequences as it was dramatic in its impact. On the scale of European history it set a precedent that monarchs could never dismiss from their consciousness. Assassination of reigning Kings, murder of those captured in battle, elimination of rivals for the succession, all these were occupational hazards as old as monarchy itself. The assertion of a right inherent in the people to punish a king for levying war against his own subjects was uncompromisingly new. Charles I's equally uncompromising denial of this claim formulated a view of authority grounded in religion and buttressed by law that is forever associated with his dynasty. On the scale of English history it epitomises the Stuart monarchy, deriving its theory from James I and drawing after it the practical result of Charles II's restoration. The Whig historian Burnet concedes the point as freely as the most reverent of Tories could desire: '. . . the death of King Charles the first whose serious and Christian deportment in it made all his former errors be entirely forgot, and raised a compassionate regard to him, that drew a lasting hatred on the actors, and was the true occasion of the great turn of the nation in the year 1660.'[1] On the scale of the King's closest, most persistent concern it perfected the image he had in life so dishearteningly failed to establish.

To the King himself the event had other meanings. Clearest among them was divine retribution for consenting to Strafford's attainder. To the son who succeeded him this made itself felt in a more directly political, less religious sense. Charles II as a boy of ten had watched the impeachment of his father's great minister from the royal box. In the later years of his own reign when his government had its back to the wall over the Exclusion Bill he walked one day into the House of Lords and, finding Lord Keeper North 'sitting upon the Woolsack (as the King thought) pensive, his Majesty came and clapped himself down close by him, and "My Lord," said he, "be of good comfort; I will never forsake my Friends, as my Father did"; and rose up, and went away without saying a word more'.[2] Charles II was an acute interpreter of experience. Like his father he read little, but his great intelligence enabled him often to surprise, even to disconcert, his servants by his grasp of difficult and technical matters, particularly when his interest was aroused. But the tone of their minds differed markedly. Charles I explained events, or sought to explain them, by reference to first causes, his son by reference to immediate ones. History to Charles I as to Cromwell was the slow, partial unfolding of God's judgments, to be prayerfully scrutinised in the hope of finding there light and leading but in fear, too, of recognising divine chastisement. Charles II's view was by contrast secular, his analysis rational. His father had made bad worse by yielding to pressure that he should have withstood and had thus demoralised his supporters. The error was tactical: the hypothesis of divine retribution unnecessary.

Not all his servants would have endorsed the favourable comparison he drew between himself and his father. In a tight corner he had a steadier nerve, a cooler head and a shrewder understanding. But whether he had deeper loyalties and greater staunchness is quite another question. The curt dismissal of Clarendon after a quarter of a century's service 'Bid the Chancellor be gone' might well have given his successor on the Woolsack cause to be pensive. If the Stuarts had any truer friend, history has been remiss in not recording the fact. The story of the relations between the young King and his elder statesmen, particularly Clarendon and Ormonde, offers the deepest insight into the character of Charles II. But his upbringing and early life have a logical priority. How did Charles I and Henrietta Maria understand their parental responsibilities? What were the effects on the young Prince of the events that flowed from the meeting of the Long

Parliament in the autumn of 1640?

There seems little doubt that the upbringing designed for Charles II was almost the exact opposite of that which he actually received. The Van Dyck picture of the five eldest children of Charles I painted in 1637 shows the Prince as quietly confident of majesty as his father. Although only seven years old the magnificence of the dress proclaims him no ordinary child. The negligent ease with which he rests his left hand on the head of a boarhound several times his own size and weight shows that brute force is naturally subordinate to him. Perhaps the demonstration is even more telling than the equestrian portrait conventionally favoured for this communication, and employed to notable effect by the same painter in his portraits of Charles I. The boy had the advantage over his father in being exceptionally tall. We may be sure that this great picture expressed the King's aspirations for his son and stated the means by which they were to be attained. The choice of governor for the young Prince, the magnificent Earl of Newcastle, one of the greatest landowners and the supreme authority on horsemanship in England, was entirely consistent. The future Charles II was to begin where his father left off; he was to embody the idea of kingship, to sustain the image of monarchy. Knowledge of men and affairs, direct contact with subjects and an understanding, at first hand, of their concerns, belonged to a secondary order of reality. An apprentice to kingship must preserve his integrity from such mundane intrusions.

Charles II's experience was very different from Charles I's theory. Few monarchs could rival his first-hand knowledge of low life, of the shifts of debtors, the humiliations of the cadger. Before he was into his teens he had seen the splendours of his father's vision rudely dispersed, his palaces abandoned, his capital closed to him, his Queen seeking asylum in France. The Prince's governor had left London for his northern estates, resigning his charge to another great nobleman of a very different type, the Marquis of Hertford.

> . . . In many respects [wrote Clarendon] he wanted those qualities which might have been wished to be in a person to be trusted in the education of a great and a hopeful prince, and in the forming his mind and manners in so tender an age. He was of an age not fit for much activity and fatigue, and loved, and was even wedded so much to his ease, that he loved his book above all exercises . . .

But if he was not so well suited as the dignified riding-master who had preceded him to be the companion of an active and high-spirited boy he had other and as it turned out more useful qualifications. Apart from his wealth and position, he was widely respected. 'A man of great honour . . . and of an universal esteem over the country.' Part of this feeling arose from his independence of royal favour: '. . . he had received many and continued disobligations from the court, from the time of this King's coming to the Crown, as well as during the reign of King James.' The Parliamentary leaders felt that the heir was in safe hands. Hertford was married to the sister of the Earl of Essex, to whom the command was to be entrusted on the outbreak of war. It was thus something of a shock when Hertford brought the young Prince to join his father at Greenwich and accompanied the King north to York. His subsequent appointment to command the Royalist forces in the West meant that he had little opportunity to influence the Prince's character. His supreme service had been to prevent his young charge from being used as a hostage.

Prince Charles was twelve when the war broke out. The notion that this was too tender an age for battle is very recent. In August 1914 the Prime Minister's daughter wrote in incredulity to Winston Churchill, then First Lord of the Admiralty, to ask if it were really true that midshipmen of fourteen then serving in capital ships would be ordered to sea.

It seemed to me unthinkable that these little boys should be plunged into the inferno of a naval battle. I shall always remember the gentleness and understanding of his immediate reply:

My dear—it is true. But you must remember and remind their mothers that they belong to a great Service. This ordeal is an honour of which they would not wish to be and should not be deprived. I know that it is harder to face these ordeals for others than for oneself. We shall both have many in the days to come. We must help each other. W.[3]

This exchange took place in living memory. During the Revolutionary and Napoleonic wars of a century earlier Sir Winston's explanation would hardly have been thought necessary. Nelson went to sea when he was twelve and one of his contemporaries was serving afloat at the age of seven and saw his first action at eight. In Charles I's time his nephew Rupert had been present at his first siege at twelve and had served his first campaign as a cavalryman at fifteen. War was traditionally the business of princes. A start could hardly be made too early.

It was therefore natural that the Prince of Wales should be given the command of a troop of lifeguards formed from volunteers of noble family, though the appointment should be seen more as that of a Colonel-in-Chief than the conferring of operational control. He and his brother were nearly captured at the battle of Edgehill which doubtless caused more care to be taken thereafter. This introduction to military experience is commemorated in Dobson's portrait of him in which the battle, conventionally rather than realistically represented, is taking place in the background. The Prince's military attire carries magnificence to the point of dandyism. The lace cuffs, the lawn sleeves, the embroidered breeches, the extravagantly knotted knee-ribbons assert the glory of regality against the confusion of rebellion and war. None the less there is a sturdiness and force and, in marked contrast to the die-away beauty of Charles I, an earthy, level-headed plainness about the boy in his breastplate and buff coat.

And a boy, of course, he still was. The martial excitements of Edgehill were succeeded by an attack of the measles. On rejoining his father in Oxford he found that a new governor had been provided for him, or rather, had insinuated himself into the post. This was the Earl of Berkshire, 'a man,' says Clarendon 'of any who bore the name of gentleman, the most unfit for that province, or any other that required any proportion of wisdom and understanding for the discharge of it.' The King and Queen were, apparently, well aware of his inadequacy.

> But it was the unhappy temper of the court at that time to think that it was no matter who was employed in that office . . . since the King and Queen meant to be his governor, and firmly resolved that he should never be out of their presence, or of one of them: when, within little more than a year after, the King found it necessary to sever the Prince from him, and lived not to see him again: and then he found and lamented that he had deputed such a governor over him.[4]

Even granted the proximity of his parents, Oxford during the Civil War was not the best school for manners or morals. John Aubrey, who was an undergraduate at the time, bears vivid witness to the indiscipline of the soldiery and the indecency of the men and women of fashion who thronged there. His evidence is convincing because he

was himself so uncensorious. After the restraint and decorum that
Charles I so sincerely preferred, the volatility of wartime Oxford must
have had its attractions for the young and the frivolous. Drinking,
duelling and whoring, the common amusements of the displaced
noblemen and soldiers of fortune who had offered their swords to the
King, do add colour to life, even if in tones that the fastidious would
reject. A taste for the crude and the raffish is more easily acquired than
the refined aestheticism of Charles I. Charles II certainly acquired it.
Whether or not his time in Oxford contributed to it must be a matter
of conjecture, but it can hardly have bent the twig the other way.

The setting up of his own court and council in the West in 1645 had
one momentous consequence for the shaping of his mind and character. It brought him within the orbit of the most intelligent, the most
articulate and the most intellectually self-confident of the Royalists,
Edward Hyde. The opening of this relation set a pattern that persisted
through all the mutations that time and circumstance were to bring.
One of the objects the Prince's father had in view was, in Hyde's
expressive word, to 'unboy' him. Presiding over his own council he
would learn the habits of business. He would have to listen to
argument, to weigh advice and to endure boredom. To supply the
deficiencies of the Earl of Berkshire the King surrounded his son with
the soberest and most capable of his servants, Hyde himself and the
Lords Hopton and Capel. Education in kingship was second only to
the preservation of the heir in the scale of their duties. And given the
characters and aptitudes of the men involved this in effect meant that
Hyde would have to bring up the Prince in the way he should go.
Hopton and Capel were both field commanders who would have their
hands full holding the Royalist position in the West. Hyde would draft
the letters, advise on appointments, evaluate intelligence and, above
all, safeguard the public and private character of his charge. He was to
be in effect tutor and governor although Duppa and the Earl of
Berkshire, the respective holders of these offices, accompanied the
young Prince as members of his household. The traces of this first
relationship were to prove ineffaceable.

The situation in the West in the spring of 1645 was hopelessly
unstable. The endemic diseases of Royalism, indiscipline and dis-
loyalty, raged unchecked. The personal quarrels of the local commanders made co-ordinated action all but impossible. The ablest of
them, the dissipated George Goring, was employing his tactical
mastery to the end of obtaining a command independent both of

Prince Rupert and of Hopton. The atrocities and corruption of the Royalist administration were as bad as anything England had to suffer during the whole Civil War. The military position was crumbling and the political situation ruinous. The Prince and his Council therefore found themselves forced to abandon their intended capital of Bristol and to move further west, partly for safety and partly to attempt to bring order out of chaos by personal intervention. This had the unfortunate effect of bringing the Prince into contact with the first of the many tiresome women to whom he was to allow liberties as great as any he took with them. This was Christabel Wyndham, wife to the governor of Bridgwater, one of the great beauties of her day, who had been the Prince's nurse. What those duties had involved is not entirely clear. She could hardly have undertaken the work of a nanny or a governess. Probably she helped to look after the boy and keep him amused. Whatever their past relationship had been the Prince had 'an extraordinary kindness' for her. To Hyde's annoyance

> he was not only diverted by her folly and petulancy from applying himself to the serious consideration of his business, but accustomed to hear her speak negligently and scornfully of the council . . . She had besides many private designs of benefit and advantage to herself and her children, besides the qualifying her husband to do all acts of power without control upon his neighbours, and laboured to procure grants or promises of reversions of lands from the Prince.

Hyde of course obstructed her purposes. In revenge she built up her own party at the council table headed by the futile Earl of Berkshire. Thus the dissensions it had been intended to compose were increased, and the Council itself brought into contempt.

> Lastly, being a woman of great rudeness and country pride, [having nothing womanly about her except her body] she valued herself much upon the power and familiarity which her neighbours might see she had with the Prince of Wales: and therefore, upon all occasions, in company . . . would use great boldness towards him; and, which was worse than all this, she affected in all companies . . . a very negligent & [disdainful] mention of the person of the King; the knowledge of which was the true reason that made his Majesty not willing that his son should go farther west than Bristol; since he knew Bridgewater must be a stage in that motion.[5]

Pepys's friend Captain Cocke was, it seems, wide of the mark when he told the Diarist that she was 'as a minister of state, the old King putting mighty weight and trust upon her'.[6]

Where Mrs Wyndham led Lady Castlemaine was in due course to follow. Hyde's refusal to countenance impropriety of conduct was all the fiercer when the offence was compounded by levity towards the persons or institutions that embodied the political continuity of the nation. It was his misfortune that at the very beginning of his association with his future master he found himself cast not only as tutor to an adolescent quite unaccustomed to discipline or to habits of application but worse, much worse, cast in the necessarily unpopular part of a moral teacher prefacing his instruction with the words 'Thou shalt not'. This element, unhappily for both, was never to vanish completely from their intercourse. Faults and virtues on both sides domesticated it. Hyde was eminently qualified to form the mind and character of a ruler. Beyond his obvious honesty, intelligence and courage he had a breadth of cultivation, a depth of political judgment and a largeness of mind rarely united in a statesman. But these qualities cast their shadow. He was didactic to a degree intolerable to any who did not enjoy the warmth and humour of his friendship. He was an intellectual, on intimate terms with the most learned and the most original minds of the age of Charles I, many of whom had chosen the Parliamentary side. Far from concealing his contempt for those he found loutish, provincial or unlettered, he had a quick and wounding wit. He was intolerant of the slipshod. He was self-satisfied. In short he was a difficult colleague. As tutor to a bright but indolent pupil, more than a little spoilt, he was likely to be resented.

The Prince's character if it was yet unformed could hardly have been without the two complementary aspects so often remarked in his maturity, the readiness to dissemble and the desire to please. A more pliant nature, or at least a more pliant manner, than Hyde's might have recommended itself to him. Hyde for all his splendid virtues was not well-bred, as Duppa and Earle were, though of humbler family than he, and as Ormonde was, a great aristocrat whose behaviour supported that description. He was not cut out for a courtier. To the Prince whose friends and associates of necessity were and had always been courtiers this precluded an easy intimacy. And what was not easy was antipathetic.

How carefully Hyde studied the handling of his charge we do not know. Certainly he was a shrewd observer of humanity and had as Sir

Charles Firth well said a genius for friendship. But he was an active politician and a speculative thinker at the height of his powers in the front rank of a struggle without parallel in the history of his country. He knew that he was taking part in great events. His mind was constantly occupied with the problems of historical causation, of interpretation of motive and understanding of character, of political analysis and constitutional argument. When a year later he took advantage of his enforced leisure on the island of Jersey to write the first books of his great *History of the Rebellion* he did not come to the subject unequipped by previous reflection. In 1645 the war was to so realistic an eye visibly approaching its climax. What would the King do in the event of a Royalist defeat? What should he do? Hyde had a great deal to think about. It would be surprising if he devoted much time to the unfamiliar and uncongenial problems of measuring his words to the taste and understanding of a fifteen year old.

The pace of events in any case kept the Prince's Court in a state of anxious evasion. The King issued instructions that his son was to go to Denmark, that he was to join his mother in France, that he was to obey her in all things except matters of religion, that he was to conduct himself by the advice of his council. For the moment the last was his only practicable policy and it was largely thanks to Hyde and Hopton that the Prince escaped to Scilly, and entirely thanks to an opportune dispersal of the Parliamentary fleet by a violent storm that he escaped from there to Jersey. In that most secure fragment of Royalist territory, whose governor Sir George Carteret maintained com-munications with Ireland and Scotland by means of a large and thriving fleet of privateers, he was urged by Hyde and Hopton to remain. His mother however commanded him to join her in Paris and her voice, reinforced as it was by his father's strict injunction, carried the day. Hyde resigned his commission and settled down thankfully to reading and writing.

The Prince was just turned sixteen when he came to Paris. It would be difficult to imagine a more extreme contrast than that between the worlds he was entering and leaving. The poverty and hugger mugger of Royalist England reeling to defeat was hardly the school for the most polished and formal metropolis in the world. The solid four-square masculinity of Hyde's dominating intelligence was a strange preparation for life in a capital ruled by women. Congenial though the change might be Charles was at something of a loss for his inability to speak or even understand a word of French. The elaborate formalities of welcoming the heir to the English and Scottish thrones who was also first cousin to the King of France were thus made impossibly stilted. When Charles at last was officially received by Louis XIV, himself aged six, the child and his English cousin were incapable of exchanging the simplest civilities. The Queen Regent, Anne of Austria, was better able to smooth over the embarrassment of her nephew's social deficiency but for his mother, Henrietta Maria, it was a serious obstacle. She had brought him to Paris in order to complete her control of Royalist policy, too long influenced by Englishmen like Hyde whom she neither liked nor understood. Now at last with her husband a prisoner in the hands of the Scottish army and her son committed to her governance in Paris she could impose her panacea, the re-creation of the auld alliance between France and Scotland. The King must knuckle under and accept Presbyterianism. What could it matter? It was only exchanging one heresy for another. That would give him an army. And the Prince was to marry her niece, Mademoiselle de Montpensier, la Grande Mademoiselle as she was called, the greatest fortune in Europe, possessing in her own right lands and revenues sufficient for the needs of a seventeenth century state. Once these two matters had been attended to a Royalist rising under her favourite courtier the Earl of Holland could be set in motion et voilà tout.

Her attempts to force the King's conscience added to his loneliness and his distress. In June he had written to her from Newcastle:

> Indeed I have need of some comfort, for I never knew what it was to be barbarously baited before, and these five or six days last have much surpassed, in rude pressures against my conscience, all the rest since I came to the Scotch army: for . . . nothing must serve but my signing the covenant (the last was, my commanding all my subjects to do it), declaring absolutely, and without reserve, for Presbyterian government . . .[7]

The Queen turned the screw tighter, threatening to abandon all her efforts and enter a convent if he did not give in. He withstood this cruel attack with a restraint and a gentleness to her that show only part of what his firmness cost him. To her favourite adviser Jermyn he wrote more openly. 'This, if it fell out, which God forbid, is so destructive to all my affairs—I say no more; my heart is too big, the rest being fitter for my thoughts than for my expression. In another way I have mentioned this to the Queen, my grief being the only thing I desire to conceal from her.'[8] The words answer to the pathos Bernini saw in Van Dyck's portrait.

The Queen's project for her eldest son took equally little account of realities. Mademoiselle de Montpensier was three years older than the Prince, fashionable, lively, flattered by everyone, fully aware of her own cash value and determined to obtain the best marriage in Europe. A Protestant, a boy without a word of French, let alone the *bon sens* requisite in a husband, would have had to be at least a reigning monarch to merit her consideration. As a fugitive from a lost kingdom he was almost disqualified to pay his addresses to her. Almost, but not quite. He was after all her first cousin and heir to two kingdoms, however dubious his prospect of enjoying his inheritance. And though unfitted at present for polite society by his ignorance of the language and habits of France he was tall and well-formed and notably graceful in his movements. That he was handsome no one could claim. His own later judgment 'Odds fish, what an ugly fellow I am,' was then, and would have been earlier, a true one.

But even if Mademoiselle did not dismiss the possibility out of hand, there were other obstacles so formidable as to relegate the scheme to the scrapheap of Henrietta Maria's political inventions. The first of them was that neither the Queen Regent nor Mazarin had the slightest intention of losing control of so vast an asset. In spite of the fact that Mademoiselle was nineteen they had by no means ruled out the possibility of marrying her to the infant Louis XIV. Most decisive of all was Charles's obstinate refusal to court his cousin. In so humiliating a situation the last thing he could afford was a rebuff. To decline the opportunity of so dazzling a prize was perhaps a small but much needed fortification of his self-esteem.

He spent nearly two years in the orbit of the French Court, sometimes in Paris itself, sometimes at Fontainebleau, but mostly at St Germain-en-Laye, on the outskirts of the capital, where Henrietta Maria had been granted the use of a royal château. Charles rapidly assimilated the tastes and standards of his hosts. Even after his restoration he preferred the Parisian style in tailoring. In the later stages of his exile, laden with debt and surrounded by men who out of loyalty to him had exchanged prosperity for shabbiness, he continued to order dress swords from the best shop in the Palais Royal. The Court of the Queen Regent formed his taste. The gaiety, the cynicism, the factiousness, the easy manners of Restoration Whitehall reflect Paris on the eve of the Fronde rather than the Versailles of Louis XIV.

A few months after the Prince had left Jersey Hyde was aroused early one morning by an English traveller fresh from·Paris. 'He told me my Lord Jermyn said the Prince was here at Jersey like a school-boy, no distance kept, but all suffered to be as familiar with him as if they were his fellows. I asked him whether that were mended; he said, yes, the English were kept at a great distance but the French were as familiar with him as could be imagined.'[9]

Amongst the English who still played some part in his education were John Earle and the philosopher Thomas Hobbes. 'The Prince gives good Dr Earles (who is a most worthy man) leave to read to him an hour in a day; and Mr Hobbs to teach him the Mathematicks another. What progress he makes I know not, but without doubt he hath a sweetness of nature not easy to be corrupted.'[10] Hyde's opinion of the two instructors is easily perceived. Hobbes' teaching, if Aubrey is to be believed, included matters not generally included in any academic syllabus. Did he awake in his pupil that pleasure in repartee for which in later life Charles acquired a reputation superior to his own? It is certain that the Prince liked him and enjoyed his company. Unfortunately not many of his circle were as stimulating. Even the time allotted to his tutors was readily sacrificed to more inviting pursuits. And why not? Apart from what might come of Henrietta Maria's overbidding in the dynastic marriage market, the Prince had no part in the scheme of things. By obedience to his parents he had lost the independent Court that might have drawn him into serious affairs in his own right. His mother was indeed anxious to prevent this. She knew very well that the solid weight of English Royalism would always be found on the opposite side to France, Catholicism and Scotland, the elements she was trying to recombine. Hyde, Hopton and Capel were, to her eye, scarcely distinguishable from Hampden and Pym. This implacable resentment was a powerful influence, sometimes on one side sometimes on the other, in the shaping of her eldest son's political character. For the moment we may be sure that the less time he spent listening to Hyde's old friend Dr Earle or to the dangerous unorthodoxy of Hobbes the better she would be pleased. His preferences may be easily imagined.

In the early summer of 1648 this interlude of idleness came to a sudden end. The Prince's younger brother, James, Duke of York, escaped to Holland, disguised as a girl. A few days later the Parliamentary fleet in the Downs mutinied and sailed for Helvoetsluys where they put themselves under the orders of the Prince of Wales.

James, however, was on the spot, while Charles was still in Paris. The professional intriguer who had contrived his escape was quick to see the immense opportunity. Encouraged by him James offered himself to the sailors as their Admiral and was cheered to the echo. Almost simultaneously Royalist revolts broke out in Wales and in Kent, Sir Marmaduke Langdale seized Berwick, Sir Philip Musgrave Carlisle. The two northern routes were opened for the Scottish army that Charles I's favourite cousin the Duke of Hamilton was, after so many windings and turnings, to bring to the rescue of his master. Henrietta Maria's favourite the Earl of Holland was preparing, ineffectively, to seize London. The Second Civil War had broken out.

For the Prince of Wales the path of duty was clear. He must go at once to his sister's Court in Holland, assume the command of the fleet and employ it to supply the insurrectionists with arms and stores. Since he was also under strict instructions from his father to recall Hyde to his service if ever he should leave France he sent off an express to Jersey summoning him to Paris. Communications were so bad that by the time Hyde had received the message and crossed to Normandy he reckoned that the Prince would be on his way to the Channel ports even if he had not already arrived there. Meeting other old colleagues from the council of Charles I at Rouen he waited there with them for further news of Charles's movements. This it had been Henrietta Maria's prime objective to deny him. The war was to be won by her favourites and hangers-on while Hyde and the others were out of things in some provincial town or following uselessly several jumps behind the race. In this part of her objective she was entirely successful. Although the Prince, who loyally tried to carry out his father's orders, wasted several days in Calais, news of his being there did not reach Rouen until the urgent need for his presence with the revolted fleet induced him to risk the voyage up channel to Helvoet-sluys. As soon as they heard, Hyde and his friends hurried to Dieppe to take ship though three hours at sea, even in calm weather, made him so ill that three days on dry land were insufficient to restore him to health. In the event seasickness was the least of the evils the poor man endured. They were captured by privateers, robbed, cheated and lost all their papers. Worst of all, these disasters kept them from their place at the Prince's side.

The situation that faced him would have taxed the skill of an old political hand. The key to the whole success of the far distant and ill co-ordinated Royalist efforts obviously lay in the revolted fleet. This was a wholly unexpected accretion of strength, transforming the prospects of Royalism. But what the seamen had done, apparently in a fit of pique at the displacement of a popular and experienced commander in favour of a militant ideologue, they could as easily undo. The true grounds of their exasperation no doubt was that their pay had fallen badly into arrear and was anyhow beneath that of the soldiers. The penniless exiles of the Prince's Court were hardly in a position to outbid the Parliament with the whole financial resources of the city under their hand. Clearly the greatest care would have to be taken not to offend the seamen. In the all-important matter of command Charles had been put at a disadvantage by the accidents of time and distance. The chance that his young brother happened to be on the scene had led to the seamen acclaiming him their Admiral. Fourteen and a half was not an impossible age at which to fight but it was too young to command in chief. The arrival of an undistinguished Parliamentary commander, Lord Willoughby of Parham, alarmed by the growing power of Radicalism in Church and State, and anxious to offer his services to the Prince, was seized on as a solution. Willoughby was made Vice-Admiral. It was a pity he had arrived so promptly as the next defector, William Batten, was far better qualified to command the fleet. Indeed he had commanded it and it was his supersession by Colonel Rainborough that had touched off the mutiny. Batten was the only principal figure to make his entry after Charles, who promptly knighted him and appointed him Rear-Admiral. It only remained to persuade his younger brother to discharge the responsibilities of Admiralty from his sister's palace while Charles himself took immediate command. This was achieved not without difficulty. The fleet then set sail for the mouth of the Thames, intending to pay the sailors and victual the ships out of the proceeds of the rich prize money that should be there for the taking. On the important questions of whether and how far to support towns and castles captured by Royalists or whether to seek or decline action against warships still loyal to the Parliament no clear resolution had been taken.

In this extraordinarily difficult command Prince Charles had two professional advisers of superior quality, Batten who probably knew more about ships and sailors than anyone else on either side in the Civil War, and Prince Rupert, who had accompanied his cousin from Paris where he had been on leave from the French Army. Rupert was to prove himself at sea as on land a daring and skilful commander. It was still quite natural to regard the two forms of military experience as interchangeable. Rupert certainly considered himself the obvious choice for Commander-in-Chief. That his cousin probably agreed with him is strongly suggested by the fact that he was so appointed after this first and all-important cruise was over. But Charles had anything but a free hand. He was surrounded by his mother's côterie one of whom, Lord Jermyn, himself ludicrously coveted the post of Lord High Admiral and all of whom hated Rupert, hated Hyde and thought that Batten, so far from being knighted, ought to have been strung up from the yard-arm. The fact that he had fired on Henrietta Maria after she had landed at Scarborough in 1643 was not to be forgotten. To help matters along Rupert also detested and despised Batten and was on bad terms with the old, steady, commonsense Royalists of the Hyde and Hopton school.

It is not surprising that this viperous crew achieved nothing but the deepening of personal feuds. A young man of eighteen, however gifted, can hardly teach sense and discipline to a clutch of seniors accustomed to command. Love of the sea and mastery of naval affairs were to be often remarked in Charles II even by those who were cool to the point of hostility. This was to be his only opportunity of commanding a fleet. If the strategic result was the collapse of the Second Civil War into defeat in detail it might be argued that the want of elementary forward planning and operational control had made that inevitable from the start. The tactical failure, to win over or to isolate the Parliamentary naval forces, to relieve the besieged port of Colchester or the forts in the Downs, to take prizes that would pay and victual the fleet, was humiliating. But the negative consequences were to prove valuable to Charles. He had not caused his future subjects to spill each other's blood. He had not looted or pillaged, or even interrupted the foreign trade by which London lived. He had not left his country naked to her enemies by destroying her navy in a fratricidal holocaust. There were grounds here for an image distinct from that of his father. And his release of captured shipping was to pay an unexpected reward when he himself was a fugitive with a price on his head.

5

First Steps to a Style

———◆———

The sweetness of nature that Hyde had found so hopeful an element in the Prince's character was to be tried beyond its strength in the months that followed. Back on dry land the squabbles of his seniors became ever shriller, their behaviour more childish and unruly. A duel between Prince Rupert and the Lord Treasurer, Colepepper, was only avoided by the combined weight of Charles's prohibition and Hyde's strenuous diplomacy. By the standards of the age even a duel between two of the Prince's privy counsellors would have been less disgraceful than the street punch-up in which the incident culminated, leaving Colepepper so knocked about that he could not appear in public for several days. The humiliation of the Prince was intensified by the dilatoriness of the Dutch authorities in dealing with the misdemeanour.

This had been merely a clash of personalities. There were far more serious and not less heated divisions over which the Prince was called on to decide. To resolve them was beyond the power of any man. To calm them was hardly possible. The various parties contending for control of Royalist policy had no use for the proposition that the umpire's decision is final. The two most pressing practical questions were interlinked: first, what was to be done with the fleet? second, should the Prince go to Ireland or to Scotland? With a Scots army under Hamilton actually invading England there were strong arguments for this last course. But the envoy of the Scots Parliament whom Charles found waiting for him at The Hague almost as soon as he had disembarked put his case in so aggressive a manner, declaring that the Prince had no right to consult his English council on a purely Scottish matter, that the young man for all his agreeable and conciliating temper felt obliged to assert himself against such overbearing behaviour. As always the Scots were imperious on the matter of religion. The Prince was not only to take the covenant himself, he was to impose Presbyterianism on the Church of England and he was to leave all his Anglican chaplains behind him. To Hyde as to Charles I the acceptance of such conditions would have been the betrayal of the Royalist cause. The Prince did not share this passionate commitment but he certainly disliked the Presbyterian style and resented the roughness of approach.

The Scotch case was anyhow weakened by the swift and total defeat at Preston and by the withdrawal of Henrietta Maria's tireless championship. She now favoured Ireland to which Ormonde, who had been for some months in Paris, was preparing to return. The southern ports would provide an excellent base for the fleet and he was confident that not only the Prince but the Queen too might follow him there. This gradually gained ground with the Prince. But there could be no question of a sudden move. His father's situation in the Isle of Wight now that the last throw had failed was one of acute danger. To move either to Scotland or to Ireland was to extend the time taken for an exchange of letters from a few days to two or three months. There were also strong personal inducements to stay where he was. His sister Mary and her husband William II of Orange were the kindest and most generous of hosts, providing not only accommodation but funds to pay for a liberal household. And in Lucy Walter, alias Barlow, Charles had acquired the first of the celebrated *poules de luxe*, as distinct from a mere mistress, with which his name is imperishably associated. To attach him yet more securely to his quarters he was laid low by a severe attack of smallpox. By the time he had recovered, his father's affairs were evidently moving to a crisis. He had been taken from the Isle of Wight across the Solent to Hurst Castle and from there to Windsor. In January the curtain was to rise on the last act set in Westminster and Whitehall.

In this extremity the Prince acted both against his father's express instructions and against the cool recognition of self-interest that was to distinguish his own policy as King. He acted impulsively and from affection. Not content with glavanising the States General into sending over an embassy to plead for the King's life, promising his own person as surety for any conditions that might be imposed, he wrote a letter of personal appeal to Fairfax, the Commander in Chief of the Army. He even addressed an appeal directly to the Council of War of which Cromwell was of course the animating power. He wrote, surely the slenderest of hopes, to his boy cousin Louis XIV and to Mazarin, imploring their intervention. There can be no question of his affection and distress, emotions rarely disclosed in his maturity. Charles was at this time at the centre of an affectionate family. Besides his hosts, for whom he certainly felt a close attachment, his aunt Elizabeth of Bohemia and her lively and attractive daughters made part of a Christmas circle very different from the polished formalities of St Germain or the strains and anxieties of civil war. He believed, too, that Lucy Walter was carrying his child. He began to recognise in his youngest palatine cousin Sophie, a girl of wit and spirit with the good looks of her family, attractions enough to stir throughts of marriage. He was young.

His father's injunctions to Henrietta Maria had been categorical:

> I conjure you . . . by all that you love, by all that is good, that no threatenings, no apprehension of danger to my person, make you stir one jot from any foundation in relation to that authority which Charles is born to. I have already cast up what I am like to suffer . . . Only I desire that consolation, that assurance from you, as I may justly hope that my cause shall not end with my misfortunes, by asseuring mee that misplaced pittie to mee do not prejudice my sone's right . . . No man's person ought to be put in ballance with this cause.[1]

The Prince's generous efforts achieved nothing. By one of those twists of everyday relationships with which the drama of history is brought home the man to whom it fell to tell him of his father's execution was the brother of one of the Cromwellian colonels who had signed the death warrant. Dr Goffe, a Royal chaplain and one of Charles I's favourite confidential agents, was at a loss how to break the news. Finally he resorted to addressing the anxious young man as 'Your Majesty'. Charles, overcome with emotion, rushed from the room.

The reality of his distress marks a point both in the arrest of his
character and in the development of the face he was to turn to the
world. Two or three years later his father's old ministers were to be
shocked by the freedom the young King allowed to the second Duke of
Buckingham, son to the earlier favourite, in mimicking and making
fun of Charles I. Bishop Burnet who first met Charles II a decade and
a half after the execution and who was anything but an admirer of
Charles I says of the Duke, 'he had the art of treating persons or things
in a ridiculous manner beyond any man of the age: he possessed the
young King with very ill principles both as to religion and morality,
and with a very mean opinion of his father, whose stiffness was a
frequent subject of his raillery.'[2] In the years 1649-51 most of the
tenderness perceived by early students of the King's character
hardened. Spontaneity and warmth of heart were replaced by an
indifferent agreeableness that sought only the reflection of itself. The
King contracted into a colder, cannier figure though his manner
remained deceptively open.

The fact of his succession altered the balance of the alternatives
between which he must choose. Of the first and most fundamental
choice, that between action and waiting on events, there could be
even less doubt than before. He must go somewhere and do something
if he was to appear as the champion of his cause and the instrument of
divine judgment on his father's murderers. As to where to go and what
to do, Hyde still counselled Jersey as a springboard for an attempt on
an England now horrified and repentant; Ormonde had left for
Ireland where Rupert had taken the revolted fleet, already somewhat
diminished and seriously undermanned; Montrose was planning to
raise another Royalist army in Scotland while his sworn enemies,
Argyle and Lauderdale and the leaders of the Kirk were urging
Charles to enter in person into the kingdom where he had already
been proclaimed. The price of this last and most compelling invitation
was, as it always had been, adherence to Presbyterianism, body and
soul, an adherence which comprehended the forcible Presbyterianis-
ing of England and the condemnation of Montrose to exile if not to the
scaffold. It would also involve denouncing Ormonde's authority in
Ireland and undoing the peace settlement between the Royalists and
the Irish rebels.

Leaving aside all questions of religious conviction, an exercise that
did not then or later present any insuperable difficulty to Charles II, a
true grandson of Henri IV, was it tolerable to start by throwing over

the two most loyal, most chivalrous champions of the Royalist cause, Montrose and Ormonde, supported as they were by the steady core of the young King's most trusted advisers, Hyde, Hopton and Nicholas and by the brilliant Prince Rupert? The King thought not. He would go to Ireland, taking ship from Jersey. This decision was exactly contrary to the wishes of his Orange sister and brother-in-law and of his mother who had reverted to her earlier preference for the auld alliance. To gain their objective the surest tactic was to play for time and to detach the various members of the unstable coalition ranged against them. Hyde was appointed to accompany the veteran Lord Cottington on an embassy to Madrid with the avowed object of raising money but the real one of getting him out of the way. Hopton, who was the commander-designate for a proposed Royalist rising in England, was sent to Cologne to see what money could be raised there. Montrose was despatched on a similar errand to the northern courts of Friesland, Denmark and Sweden.

During their absence the Royalist position in Ireland began to disintegrate. Rupert, determined to man his ships in Kinsale, attempted to raise a thousand landsmen and had Mass said in the seaports where it was expressly forbidden by Ormonde's articles of peace. Impatient as always of political necessity he attempted to form a party among the Irish Catholic Confederacy to oppose Ormonde. One of the colonels who joined it revealed its existence in a letter to Ormonde who simply forwarded the document to Rupert.[3] To intrigue against a man of such courtesy and ingenuousness would seem to be almost as difficult as to quarrel with him, but Rupert did his best. No effort was made to co-ordinate the activities of the fleet with Ormonde's attempt to secure Dublin for the Royalist cause. The Commonwealth understood these things better. The Irish squadron was strongly reinforced in the early summer and was soon able to blockade Kinsale. Even before Cromwell landed at Dublin to burn his name into the flesh of Irish history Ormonde's forces had suffered a serious reverse. The scene had darkened before the lurid atrocities that followed the capture of Drogheda threw the perils of Royalism into sharp relief. At that low point in the fortunes of his cause Ormonde still urged the King to sail for Ireland: '. . . it will be . . . to your Majesty's infinite honour to have attempted it with such disadvantage, whatever the event may be.'[4]

By the time that letter, written on September 27th, reached the King Ireland was plainly lost. In October Rupert had seized the opportunity offered by a spell of rough weather to slip out of Kinsale while the Commonwealth ships had been blown off station. He made for Portugal, abandoning the attempt to maintain any naval presence in home waters. How seriously Charles had ever contemplated the Irish venture must remain doubtful. He had certainly shown none of the dash that so hazardous an enterprise demanded. He did not leave Holland until the beginning of June and then decided to visit his mother in France before embarking. His progress through the Low Countries was attended with more ceremony than might have been thought appropriate to an exile bent on regaining his rights. Once arrived in Paris his mind was easily engaged in familiar pre-occupations. His mother was still indefatigably pressing the Montpen-sier marriage. His wardrobe needed attention. To these and other such concerns was added the desire to assert his new position, particularly against his mother's pretensions and to a lesser extent against the elder statesmen who might presume too far on his youth and inexperience. His firm refusal to make appointments to his council at Henrietta Maria's direction was generally approved. But there were many who shared her consternation when the King showed signs of passing once again under the domination of his earliest favourite, Mrs Wyndham. Her influence had been reinforced by the marriage of a daughter to one of the King's boyhood friends who had now reappeared on the continent and been made a groom of the bedchamber. Disapproval of this friendship had been one of the reasons why Charles I had sent his son to the West in the closing stages of the war. Naturally the young King wanted to show that he would choose his friends for himself but it was taking matters a great deal too far when he revealed his intention of creating an unknown and ignorant country gentleman, the husband of his old nurse and father-in-law of his friend, Secretary of State. The Queen stormed. Hyde remonstrated. But it was the elaborate mockery of the aged Lord Cottington, whose teasing of the infuriated Archbishop Laud had once elicited a smile from Charles I, that turned the trick. Ridicule, Charles II's own preferred weapon, succeeded where reason failed.

Hyde and Cottington had taken in Paris on their way to their joint embassy in Madrid. Soon after their departure Charles himself left for Jersey, accompanied by James, Duke of York. The parting with his mother was cool: the hospitality of the French Court cooler still. It was mid-September when the King arrived in the last of his possessions to offer him unqualified loyalty. Sir George Carteret, the Lieutenant

Governor (it was characteristic of the Stuart monarchy that the Governorship should have been bestowed on Henrietta Maria's favourite, Lord Jermyn, who tried to sell the island to France for ready cash) was one of those whose career of service to the Crown was almost equally divided between father and son. After long and varied service as a sea-officer he had joined the Navy Board as Controller five years before the Civil War. A Jerseyman himself he had reconquered the island from the Parliament at the end of 1643 and had made it into a privateering base of great importance. The King, when he left Jersey in the spring of 1650, had good cause to write

> Carteret, I will add this to you under my owne hand that I can never forgett the good services you have done to my father & to me and, if god bless me, you shall find I doe remember them to the advantage of you and yours; and for this you have the word of your very loving freind. Charles R.[5]

This promise was fully honoured. At the Restoration Carteret was rewarded with the Treasurership of the Navy, one of the most lucrative posts in the government. When the disasters of the Second Dutch War exposed the Navy Board to the avenging fury of the House of Commons the Treasurer was enabled to exchange offices with the Deputy Treasurer of Ireland, another of the most coveted jobs in the administration. The ingratitude so often charged against the Stuarts is notably absent from Charles II's treatment of this brave and loyal servant. Pepys, a sharp and often malicious critic of his colleagues, praises Carteret for his good nature, his diligence and his honesty. As host to the young King and his brother he was as generous as his credit and the profits of his privateers would allow. Best of all no doubt was his lack of political standing or ambition. His sympathies lay with Hyde and Hopton to whom he had given shelter four years earlier, but he was essentially an executive, content to carry out a policy rather than frame one. For the winter of 1649-50 Charles was thus free from pressure. Ireland had fallen through. Rupert was in Lisbon, Hyde in Madrid, Montrose in Scandinavia, the Queen in offended dudgeon. There was nothing much to do, a situation by no means disagreeable to his taste.

Unfortunately matters could not stand still, or saunter, to use the word so often chosen by contemporaries to describe Charles II's preferred tempo. Scotland demanded a straight answer to the questions Charles I had equivocated over. The activities of Montrose in the northern courts had alarmed the ruling party. The exiled King was to be forced to choose between this romantic firebrand and the leaders of government and kirk whom, if successful, Montrose would supplant. If he chose the established authority and disavowed Montrose the reward would be his immediate restoration to one of his kingdoms. He would have an army and a state committed to him. On the other hand the asking price was high and all the indications were that once he had burnt his boats and accepted, it would be raised higher still. The very title-deeds of Royalism, the Church of England and the law that established it, the religious sanction of monarchy, would have to be pawned. Charles II, unlike his father, was not inhibited by strong and serious convictions from entertaining any such idea. Father and son had in common their dislike of Presbyterianism and their instinct to avoid a clear, consistent, single-minded policy. It was thus inherently probable that the young King would go much farther down the road Charles I had taken first at Southwell and again in the Isle of Wight, the road of apparent concession and fair words. The probability was strengthened by the absence of Hyde, the most formidable, the most eloquent and the most resolute opponent of this policy.

At a meeting of the Council in Jersey Hopton and Nicholas, supported by the young Duke of York, stood out for Royalist principles. They were overridden by the soldiers and courtiers and Queen's friends. To their way of thinking Charles had nothing to lose. If the Scots beat Cromwell and restored the King to his own, he would be the man on horseback. The Presbyterians would meet a very different reception from an English King in Whitehall than from a penniless refugee in Jersey. If Cromwell won, well, things would be no worse than they were at the moment. What this argument, seductive in its simplicity as in its worldly wisdom, failed to take account of was the grave danger of the English Royalists rallying to the Republican government. The terms they were offered for submission were conciliatory. If they continued to reject them the financial penalties were severe. All of them had already suffered for their loyalty. What inducement was there to risk the future of their families and their estates if Royalism meant nothing after all? On the merely pragmatic level the policy was worse than dubious. On that of principle and loyalty it was contemptible.

Yet to turn down the thrilling possibility of transforming the situation, to refuse to set the match to the powder train and see what would happen, to decline the first opportunity of exercising the arts and powers of kingship would have been a hard decision to take at the age of nineteen. The men who advised rejecting the offer out of hand were the sober and the serious. The gay, the adventurous, the men of the world were for following it up. James, Duke of York was the only exception and at nineteen one is not to be taught prudence by one's juniors. No doubt Charles II was aware of the principles and personal loyalties that were at risk. His continued encouragement of Montrose· shows that he still did not accept the necessity of choosing between irreconcilables. Perhaps his charm and good temper inclined his counsellors to believe that he might win the harsh, granitic leaders of the Covenanting party to a more pliant frame. He made a promising start by achieving a unanimous vote of the deeply divided council in favour of a treaty with the Scots 'on honourable terms'. As Nicholas had made clear, this meant that nothing was to be agreed to the prejudice of Ormonde or Montrose.

The King arranged to meet the Scots Commissioners at Breda in March. In the last week in February he left Jersey and travelled across Normandy to Beauvais where Henrietta Maria was waiting for him. She was still sure that if only Montrose were recalled an arrangement could be made with the Kirk that would not require the humiliation and hypocrisy of taking the Covenant. Charles once again refused to be drawn into making her a party to his plans. Once again they parted coldly, she to return to Paris, he to meet the Commissioners.

The negotiations were long and distasteful. The Commissioners began by turning the screw so tight that nobody thought the King could possibly agree. Hyde though still in Madrid had expressed himself in the most emphatic manner. Charles himself was deeply affronted by the lack of consideration shown for his position. If the Commissioners were bent on forcing him to humiliating terms they might have left him a rag or two of self-respect. Left to himself he would far have preferred Montrose, a European figure with manners and cultivation that matched his courage and gifts of leadership, to the sour, grey, schoolmasterish nobodies who so clearly relished wielding the tawse. There was no chance, he saw now, of uniting all the Scottish parties under the Crown. But might not Montrose be a valuable counterweight to these domineering Covenanters who required him to do penance for his own beliefs and those of his father and mother?˙ Might it not even be possible to escape and join

Engagers.

Montrose once he had landed? Such considerations induced him to play for time rather than break off relations. Yet this in itself sealed the fate of Montrose. Had he been, as he once was, the single focus of loyalty, the King's man in Scotland, he would have commanded support that now was withheld. But if the King was on the point of doing a deal with the powers in possession, Argyle and the Kirk, who would want to risk identifying themselves with a guerrilla leader that both hated mortally? Charles, no doubt, was unaware of the danger to which he was exposing the most heroic of his supporters. He had sought and, as he thought, obtained private assurances from Argyle that whatever the Commissioners might publicly demand neither Montrose nor Ormonde should suffer for their loyalty. But he was playing poker out of his class. The people he intended to deceive knew that they were successfully deceiving him.

Events moved fast, communications were slow. The contrast heightens the horror. The day before Charles at last agreed in principle, if principle be the word, to the terms he had so long baulked at, Montrose's little army had been routed in a bare Highland valley where broom and birch were all the cover that the wretched fugitives could find. The slaughter was almost total. Nonetheless Montrose's extraordinary power of will enabled him to survive a journey over the mountains, without a guide and with no food, which killed one of his two companions. He arrived in the country of a clan he believed his friends on the very day that the King signed the Treaty of Breda. On May 4th, three days later, he was surrendered by his hosts. On May 8th the King wrote to the authorities in Edinburgh requesting them to grant conditions to Montrose's forces whom he was now ordering to disband. On May 9th he wrote a private letter to Montrose granting him discretion to disregard his official instructions. On May 10th the bearer of these missives left for Scotland. On the day that he landed at Leith Montrose was being paraded up the High Street of Edinburgh, his hands tied behind his back so that he should not be able to protect his face from the stones it was hoped that the crowd would throw. Three days later he was executed, proclaiming from the scaffold his love and veneration for the late King and, with the magnanimity and charity that have raised his name above the corrosion of time, absolving Charles II from the least taint of responsibility for his own death.

Whether it was possible for the King himself to form so consoling an opinion we do not know. Of the compunction that he may have felt there is no evidence, but that is far from saying that it is not reasonable to suppose that he may have felt it. What is certain is that he was deeply mortified by the contempt that had been shown him and by the realisation that his new allies had made a fool of him. Immediately on hearing of Montrose's defeat he had sent an urgent letter to the Scots Parliament demanding an explanation and deploring the shedding of blood among his loyal subjects. The Parliament did not deign to take cognisance either of this or of the earlier message from their sovereign until four days after Montrose was dead and dismembered. The humiliation bit deep.

Worst of all was that the King's first independent initiative in high policy had proved immediately disastrous. Hyde and his party of elder statesmen had warned him, even, so far as they could, opposed him. There could be no argument as to who had been in the right. The Queen, whose advice he had made plain he did not require, had encouraged him. But the minute she learned that he had actually agreed to take the Covenant and to commit himself and his family to Presbyterianism she denounced the act with the same fervour that she had promoted it. The solid English Royalist gentry were appalled. They hated the Scots. They disliked, on the whole, Presbyterianism. The Presbyterian party, as such, had led the struggle against Charles I and were only recent and grudging converts to the support of his son as a lesser evil than Army radicalism and its ecclesiastical eccentricities. All these loyalties had been weakened if not alienated and what had been gained? To hobnob with Montrose's killers was disgusting even if they had shown any signs of wanting any such thing. The only self-respecting course was to break with them. But having pawned self-respect in order to equip oneself as a buccaneer would it not seem the part of a hot and shamefaced adolescent to ask for it back again? Men of the world do not do that kind of thing. And to be a man of the world appears to have been Charles II's most abiding concern.

He was not short of exemplars. From the early days of the Civil Wars the soldiers of fortune that England, Scotland and Ireland had exported so liberally to earn their living and learn their profession in the armies of France, Sweden and the United Provinces came flocking back to take service in their own country. Indeed the balance of the trade was reversed: some distinguished foreign officers such as Prince Rupert and his chief engineer Sir Bernard de Gomme, or the Tuscan Bernardo Guasconi found ready employment. Polite society, so long without the tincture of military style added by a standing army, found itself inundated by professional officers. Morals, manners and fashion could hardly remain uninfluenced. The footloose glamour of a style of life where pleasure is to be taken, money to be spent, youth to be enjoyed while they are available has a powerful appeal. No wonder that the young King found the company of men like Wilmot and the Berkeleys more congenial than that of the prudent counsellors and learned divines who belonged to the slow, steady peacetime establishment of Church, law and landowning. These companions were the men who had urged him not to have too nice a conscience about the promises he made to the Scots. What would they think if he were to turn back now? On the other hand it would not do for the Kirk and the Parliament and their sermonising Commissioners to think that he was going to kow-tow. He defied them by attending a celebration of the Holy Communion according to the rites of the Church of England and receiving the sacrament on his knees. He shocked them by going every night to balls and every entertainment that was offered. Yet in spite of this gaiety it was remarked that he often seemed melancholy. The pressures he was under would have tested a character fully formed and sure of itself. As a young man anxious to please and ambitious to succeed, conscious of great abilities and that great things were expected of him, he could see no clear way ahead. He was for the first time facing severe censure for having acted against principle and honour. If he drew back, would not that amount to an acceptance of guilt? To be able to admit to having behaved badly is one of the marks of a strong and mature person. In a man set in authority it calls for a degree of self-confidence such as is mostly developed by experience. Several years and many disappointments later Charles wrote to an unknown correspondent (the letter was intercepted by Cromwell's secret service):

They who will not believe anything to be reasonably designed, except it be successfully executed, had need of a less difficult game to play than mine is. And I hope my friends will think I am not too old [he was at the time of writing just twenty-five] and have had too much experience of things and of persons to be grossly imposed upon.[6]

The bitter acquisition of this experience might explain his present melancholy.

6

Escapade

◆————

That the young King had been unfairly left to face, on his own, forces
that he could not be expected to master was generously conceded by
at least one man who had a right to grumble at the overriding of his
own advice. Sir Edward Nicholas was emphatic in his letters both to
Hyde himself and to their common friends that he had no business to
go off to Madrid when he should have been at hand to repel dangerous
counsels:

> Sir Ed. H. censured by all for deserting the K at such a time when his
> personal service was most necessary, for an employment which most men
> believe might have been performed without his help.

Thus wrote Nicholas to his errant colleague. He was alarmed and
horrified by the levity and cynicism of the people round the King. 'I
much doubt your friend Sir John Berkeley hath no greater proportion
of Religion than a creature of Ld Jermyn's is obliged to have.' 'Mr
Long will serve all turns and says honour and conscience are
bugbears'.[1] Defeat and demoralisation were the two principal educa-
tive influences on Charles II. He could not be expected to draw from
them the stoicism and the fortification of purpose that Hyde so
magnificently expressed when things were at their blackest. What
purpose had he to fortify, beyond the regaining of a throne which he

was not responsible for losing but whose loss was a reproach to his self-esteem? Hyde and Ormonde and Carteret and Nicholas and Hopton were all rooted in a society that had formed their standards, nourished their loyalties and rewarded their talents. Civil War and exile were aberrations, dreadful, painful, embittering, but for all that increasing and intensifying the value of 'the old, loved prints' on which they looked back. For Charles II civil war and exile was all he had known since boyhood. Eight years is an eternity at nineteen.

The young King embarked for Scotland early in June. In defiance of the Kirk he took with him an Anglican chaplain and several boon companions whose tastes and conversation were not such as to commend them to his hosts. During the voyage, which was protracted by bad weather, he was pressed to make further concessions, even to the extent of prohibiting Roman Catholics throughout his dominions, a measure that went far beyond the harshest measures of the Reformation and ran counter to the agreements entered into by Ormonde. Charles at first refused but after a month at sea, with Scotland at last in sight, he gave in. His pliancy was not reciprocated. It was made plain that no undertaking had been given to restore him to the throne of England by force of arms. Even his admission to that of Scotland was probationary. His Anglican chaplain was sent back to the continent. His friends were warned that they too had no right of access except by permission of the Kirk and the Committee of Estates. Those Scottish noblemen who did not belong to the strict Covenanting party were dismissed to their homes. The English Royalists were reduced to single figures. The King was permitted neither to take part in the conduct of affairs nor to choose his own amusements. Even cards were strictly forbidden him. He was constantly required to express contrition for his own and his father's acts and beliefs and to proclaim his especial detestation of his mother's religion. Above all he was to be kept away from the army in case his appearance should provoke a spontaneous demonstration of loyalty and thus make him a power in his own right.

From this public and pitiless humiliation, predicted by his sober English advisers, Argyle appeared in the carefully contrived rôle of deliverer. The King became his guest and lived, once more, like a gentleman; lived, indeed, much better than he had been accustomed to in the shifts of war and foreign hospitality. He was spared interminable and insulting lectures and spent his days hunting instead. He was even for a time at the beginning of August allowed to join the Army outside Edinburgh, where his reception was all that he had wished and the Kirk had feared. Argyle was himself the linchpin of the alliance between Parliament and the General Assembly, so that when he assured Charles that he would not in the end be held to the strict observance of all the promises that had been exacted from him he was gladly believed. Or at least it was easy for the King, who wanted to believe him, to appear to accept what this most plausible and well-bred politician wanted him to believe. Argyle was anxious to cement his position by marrying his daughter to the King. But Charles was quick to learn the dance-steps of diplomacy and required time to obtain his mother's views on so important a question. There seems no reason to suppose that he himself regarded the proposal with any enthusiasm.

During the few days that Charles spent with the army it was manoeuvring under Leslie's deft generalship against Cromwell who had come hotfoot from Ireland. Cromwell's aim was to force a battle, Leslie's to deny one. At last Cromwell's army, weakened by hunger and disease, retreated towards Berwick and were cornered at Dunbar. The annihilating victory that should have been Leslie's went to Cromwell. Just as the Pope is said to have offered a requiem for Gustavus Adolphus, the great Protestant hero of the Thirty Years War, so Charles, with equal lack of probability, is reported to have fallen on his knees to give thanks for the destruction of his insufferable ally. 'It's probable', wrote Cromwell laconically reporting the event, 'the Kirk have done their do.' His judgment proved correct. As their political star sank, so Charles's rose. He was crowned at Scone in January 1651 and took a steadily more effective part in the operation of government. By the summer he was ruling over a country, or more accurately the central and eastern highlands, where his own policy of religious and political comprehension had been adopted and commanding an army whose officers were no longer subject to theological commissars. His energy, his tact, his resource were admired by his own people and acknowledged by his opponents. He had shown that he had the talents needed for kingship and the will to use them. Could he not claim that his great gamble had come off?

Perhaps he could. Power can neither be won nor kept by those who stickle for absolute justice and perfect honour. The test of leadership is whether men will follow. That, at least, he had now put himself in a position to establish. His own extraordinary buoyancy, the banishment of that listlessness and melancholy so often remarked at earlier and later stages of his life, suggests that he had no doubts. Yet the charges to be set against whatever he had won were no less formidable for being more familiar. He had broken faith with true friends to win favours from false ones. The worthlessness of the bargain had been obscured by the wider disasters that had followed but the transaction was not rendered thereby either wise or politic, still less honourable. A few days after landing in Scotland Charles had been entertained in Aberdeen where Montrose's hand was nailed up opposite his lodging. The dishonour and the desire to humiliate could hardly have been more brutally expressed. In so far as he had been emancipated it had been the pressure of Cromwell's victories not the emergence of his own kingly qualities. His masters had been forced to relent in strictness because they no longer had the strength to compel. Two or three times there had been a move to hand him over, as his father had been handed over, to the English Army. Even now Cromwell was the real ringmaster at whose whipcracks troops and assemblies wheeled this way and that. It was Cromwell's crossing of the Forth that set Charles in sudden motion for England, knowing that his base had been cut off, his forces divided, and hoping that England would rise to welcome him.

The result vindicated everything that Hyde and Nicholas had said. Although the Commonwealth Government was unpopular, not yet confident of its own authority and well aware of the strength of Royalist sentiment, the little army that crossed the border in August grew no larger, as it made its way down the north-western counties, traditionally sympathetic to old ways and established institutions. That there were no sympathetic risings in other parts of the country was largely to be explained by the wholesale breach of Royalist security. Most of the men who were to lead it were behind bars and some of the most active conspirators had been executed. Yet the groundswell of revulsion against the régime that had been caused by Charles I's execution should surely have broken with waves of shattering force. What had stilled the movement of the waters if it were not that Charles II's betrayal of the identifying principles of Royalism had provided a moral justification for inertia and that his bringing in the hated Scots offended the patriotism of all Englishmen?

The King did not lack evidence of how slim his chances were. The refusal of Carlisle to open its gates to him was the foretaste of what was to follow. Proclamations and promises brought in no recruits. His principal commanders, Hamilton, the brother of the unfortunate favourite of Charles I, and Leslie were certain that disaster lay ahead, the one with candid, even cheerful resignation, the other in disgruntled taciturnity. Charles himself continued, to all appearances at least, in high spirits. He was, after all, well used to the headshakings of his older advisers. He had the company of Wilmot and Buckingham and some others of congenial disposition. He was leaving Scotland behind him and had the world in front. Like his father he seems to have enjoyed the open-air life of an army on the march. He was all his life an excellent horseman and a tireless walker. And all his life he was at his best when the prospect was threatening. He had lived long enough to see the uncertainties of politics and war. A stake on a long-priced horse was more exciting than no bet at all.

The campaign, if it deserves that title, was a fiasco. At the battle of Worcester in which it ended on September 3rd, the anniversary·of Dunbar, the King's army faced overwhelming superiority in numbers, quality, generalship and firepower. Defeat was no dishonour. Charles won high praise for the carriage and dash he displayed in this his only battle. In the confusion of defeat he showed a notable coolness and grasp of essentials. No plans had been made for his escape. The quickness and decision, so unlike the hesitations of his father, were his own. His first concern was to distance himself not from the enemy but from his own troops as they fled in disorder to the north. To remain in the path of the main pursuit was to invite capture. His second resolve, to make for London, again showed sound judgment. The obvious course would have been to regain Scotland or to make for Wales, much nearer and, throughout the Civil War, a stronghold of Royalism. London was a bolder and a cleverer choice. The movements of strangers in the countryside of the seventeenth century were likely to be conspicuous. People did not travel much in the ordinary course of life. A great port and a centre of commerce such as London or Bristol was a notable exception. The roads to them were in constant use. A large town has always been the easiest place to hide in. When there were no police it was easier still. The incessant traffic on the river made it the best place to find a passage for the continent. Finally he determined, as he told Pepys nearly thirty years later, to keep his plans to himself. Only to Wilmot who had also decided to make for London did he reveal his intention and arrange a rendezvous.

In the event he was denied the opportunity of carrying out his scheme. It proved impossible to detach himself from the crowd of gentlemen and officers who were escaping from the city. Indeed it was some little time before this group managed to detach itself from the Scots cavalry. Leslie had kept them out of the action and they were thus well placed to head the rush northwards, the only side on which escape lay open. The royal party turned east off the main road but by then it was much too late to make the wide sweep that would have been necessary to get behind the Cromwellians and make for London. The King was told of a secure house in Brewood Forest, north-west of Wolverhampton, that had sheltered Lord Derby who had been wounded in a skirmish before the battle itself. He agreed to make for it in the hope of lying up until the heat of the pursuit was past. They arrived just before daybreak after a night ride in which the way had been lost at least once. There had been no time or opportunity for anything to eat beyond a hunk of bread and a can of beer while the horses got their breath back outside an inn near Stourbridge.

Here at last the King's luck turned. The household were Roman Catholics to a man, accustomed to sheltering priests and passing them on to the next safe house. Conspiratorial habits were instinctive. In a moment they had the King's horse inside the house where no passer-by could report it, they had replaced his fine clothes with those of a woodman, cut his hair short and helped him to blacken his face with soot from the chimney. Best of all they had found a pretext for getting rid of his mounted entourage by reporting the presence of the main body of Leslie's cavalry only three miles away. They might join them and force their way back to Scotland. For the first time the King was on his own.

The six weeks during which Charles II was on the run were as important to his view of himself as the masques of Ben Jonson and Inigo Jones had been to his father. Once it was safe to talk about his adventures without compromising the men and women who had helped him, his escape after the battle of Worcester became his favourite topic of reminiscence. In exile he maintained a discreet silence. But the moment that his restoration removed the shadow of reprisals he began to discourse on the subject and, in the view of some of his courtiers, was all too ready to revert to it throughout the twenty-five years of his reign. Pepys set down in his diary what he could catch of the King's account given to the company on board the *Royal Charles* as she bore him across the channel in his hour of triumph in 1660. He recorded a full version, taken down in shorthand in two private interviews with the King at Newmarket in October 1680. Charles took pains to establish the history and the iconography of the subject.

He commissioned his Sergeant Painter, Robert Streater, to represent the story of his first days in Brewood Forest in a painting which is still in the Royal collection. He gave exclusive rights in the story to the careful and critical author of *Boscobel* (the house near which he took refuge in the branches of an oak tree) and then, dissatisfied with the result, pronounced it inaccurate in unspecified details and withdrew its official status. He long intended to found a new order of chivalry, to be called the Knights of the Royal Oak, to commemorate this picturesque event. Oakapple Day became an important feast in Restoration England and is still observed by the Pensioners of Chelsea Hospital.

The story of his adventures lent itself to the projection of an image identifying the monarch with the profoundest loyalty of his people. It was not the courtiers or the nobility who saved him in his hour of danger: it was a cross-section of the nation. The family to whom he owed the most when the pursuit was at its hottest, the Penderels, were poor country folk. Butcher's meat was a luxury they might expect to enjoy perhaps half a dozen times in their lives. Between them and the Wyndhams of Trent, substantial country gentry of the same family as the King's nurse, every sort and condition played a part: churchmen, innkeepers, merchants, indoor servants, seamen, ex-Royalist officers and minor gentry. Charles, it seems plain, hugely enjoyed the element of romantic disguise. Was there not, for all the risk involved, something in common with the exploits of his ancestor, James V of Scotland, who conducted his own surveys of public opinion incognito in the character of the Gudeman of Ballinbreich? He could and did realise the scene Shakespeare imagined for Henry V before Agincourt, discussing the character and even the appearance of the King with blacksmiths, ostlers and the like. Except for his great height and graceful carriage, both of which made him conspicuous, he was perfectly equipped to meet the demands of his situation. He was a born actor, a good mimic. He was quick and observant. He had a cool nerve and an easy temper.

It was said of Charles II in later life that he was at his best with strangers. Unkind courtiers suggested that this was because he recognised with delight a new and therefore appreciative audience for the anecdotes in whose repetition he took such pleasure. But there are people who prefer multiplicity of casual acquaintance to a more intimate and continuous relationship. Charles was easily bored and disliked sitting still. The variety that came his way during this passage of life was the more highly spiced because it was unpredictable. This is not to say that the experience of being a hunted man can have been a pleasurable one. There were moments, sometimes long moments, of intense fear, particularly in the first few days. When the maid called up the stairs of Moseley Hall, 'Soldiers! Soldiers are coming!' and his host hurriedly secreted him in the Priest's Hole, his feelings can hardly have been agreeable. When an hour or so later he was let out he took a little time to recover his self-possession. But most of his sudden dangers drew his self-command into the instant reflex of self-preservation. When Pope, the butler at Abbots Leigh, recognised him, when the promised boat failed to meet the night rendezvous on Charmouth beach, when the ostler at Bridport opened his conversation with the inauspicious words, 'Sure, sir, I know your face', there was a challenge to be met that left no time to be frightened.

The temptation to tell again in detail this best of stories must be resisted, the royal precedent to the contrary notwithstanding. For the development both of the King's character and of his sense of identity these few weeks are worth several years. At a time when his very existence depended as never before on the courage and discretion of others the greatest gain was paradoxically in self-reliance. He had to rely on other people to provide ways and means, to feed and clothe and protect him, to secure intelligence, to suggest courses of action. But he had to rely on himself to choose and carry out the plans so arrived at. His performance gave him solid grounds for self-respect.

The second great gain was that the company he kept was self-selected by loyalty, by courage and by honour. All the considerations that usually determined the style and character of his entourage—his own preference for the meretricious, the nagging of faction, the feuds and the jealousy inseparable from a Court—were inoperative. He met all sorts of people whom he would never have come across if the choice had been left to him and to his ministers, and he met them in a way that precluded falseness and flattery. He gained some real insight into the springs of human action outside the world he knew. He discovered ordinary life. At the same time he was cut off from his habitual pleasures. No hunting, no womanising, no sauntering. He was forced in on his own resources. He was among strangers, devoted, loyal, admirable strangers, but strangers still. He had to satisfy their expectations, so different from the flippancy and cynicism of his own circle. Of those who had accompanied him to Worcester, Buckingham and Wilmot were fugitives like himself. Buckingham made his escape

to the continent on his own but Wilmot was never long out of contact
with the King and shared the final stages of his adventures. He
supplied at first an intermittent link with the style and character they
had had to put off. Or, more accurately, which the King had had to
put off. Wilmot, like Charles I, hesitated to make himself ridiculous by
wearing disguise. 'I could never get my Lord Wilmot to put on any
disguise, he saying that he should look frightfully in it' Charles told
Pepys in 1680. His scruples did not end there. Throughout his travels
he was attended by his personal servant, Robert Swan, and he himself
did not share the King's experiences of life below stairs. He stayed
with old friends or at comfortable inns, in curious counterpoint to the
clandestine life of his master.

Wilmot apart, the only familiar figure to appear in the story was
Colonel Francis Wyndham, brother of the country squire whom
Charles had tried to make his first Secretary of State. It was in his
house at Trent on the borders of Somerset and Dorset that the King
passed the longest and perhaps the dullest part of his concealment.
The pursuit was no longer close. He was waiting for news of a channel
passage. Life at Trent was hardly more than suspended animation.
But the early days and the final stages of the escape were full of
movement and variety of contact in which Charles was on his own.
The society into which he was first led on the headlong flight from
Worcester, that of recusancy, with its underground arrangements for
sheltering priests and bringing up the young in beliefs and traditions
disapproved by the state, was far the most exciting. He was familiar
enough with Roman Catholicism as a mode of worship and as a
fashion. His mother despised all forms of Protestantism because they
were not à la mode. Her Catholicism was wholly French and
essentially Parisian. The staid, everyday Englishness of the Giffards of
Whiteladies and the Whitgreaves of Moseley perhaps opened a new
perspective. They had far too high a sense of honour to take advantage
of the King's situation by attempting to subvert his loyalty to the
Established Church. But Charles did find and read works of Catholic
instruction among the books at Moseley and discussed them with the
Benedictine priest, Father Huddlestone, who as Whitgreave's domestic chaplain and tutor was deep in the counsels of his escape. The
conversation with Catholicism was to be lifelong and Father Huddlestone was to have the last, as he had the first, word.

Charles's conduct was distinguished by good manners. To his
hostesses such as Mr Whitgreave's old mother or Mrs Hyde of Heale

House he was courteous and charming. To people accustomed to less formality such as the Penderels he was easy and affable, making the kind of jokes that they enjoyed and savoured over many retellings. His social touch astonished and delighted those charged with his preservation. Few Kings, few nobles come to that, would have survived so many encounters with blacksmiths and innkeepers, often inquisitive and sometimes provocative, without raising suspicion or antipathy. When at the very end of the last and successful journey to the coast the brother-in-law of the King's conductor arrived home drunk and quarrelsome accusing the King of being a Roundhead and intimating that he was by no means welcome in his house, Charles both accepted the rôle and soothed his host's asperity. On the next and last night he settled an ugly quarrel that had developed between the captain of the coal-brig that was to take him across to France and the faithful Royalist officer who had negotiated the terms of the charter. Next day when the vessel lay at anchor off Fécamp, within two miles of success, it was Charles's quick thinking that avoided an eleventh-hour disaster. Capture by a privateer could have lost the captain his ship and his passengers their hard-won freedom. A suspicious sail in the offing prompted the King to anticipate trouble. He asked to be put ashore in the ship's boat before the captain might come to the same conclusion as himself and perhaps run for it.

From the moment at Worcester, when he had privately decided to make for London if possible on his own, to the day he regained the safety of French soil Charles had shown a rapidity and soundness of judgment that must surely have nourished his self-confidence. It was galling that a story reflecting such credit on his conduct and policy should have to be kept secret for fear of harming those who had helped him, while the Scottish adventure, with which it had all begun, was open to everyone's censure. But the censure to which it was open was essentially moral and religious. If it had restored the King to his throne no doubt people would have been less ready to point this out, but it would not have been the less valid. To make solemn profession of beliefs he not only does not hold but actually detests, to leave friends who have risked their all to the merciless hatred of their bitterest enemies and to crown the proceedings by breaking bread with the murderers cannot leave a man with a clear conscience. When these actions are public knowledge it cannot leave him a clear reputation. It might be that Charles I's intrigues with the Irish Catholics that so distressed Sir Edward Hyde were, in principle, no less dishonest and disloyal: it might be that if they had come to anything their consequences could have been as shameful. But their ineffectiveness had made them no more than scraps of political wastepaper, to be seized on gratefully by pamphleteers and to be scrutinised by historians. Events had, as we have seen, offered Charles I a rôle in which doubts and criticisms were dazzled and blinded. 'I will either be a glorious King or a patient martyr' he had written in 1642. To fervent Royalists he had become both. It was against this light shining from eternity that his son would be seen.

7

Bad Debts

Like the Dunkirk evacuation in 1940, Charles II's escape could hardly be claimed as a victory but was felt to be a success. Low as Royalist fortunes had fallen, the ultimate in ignominy had been avoided. What humiliations might have been imposed, what bribes dangled, if the King had been taken prisoner by the Commonwealth, or whether he would have been exposed to a show trial and a public execution were questions that could now be dismissed with relief. On the positive side to have eluded capture for six weeks with a large price on a conspicuous head was an undeniable coup for the King. It offered at least presumptive evidence in favour of the belief that the country was still true to old loyalties and to the old ways. If that were so, a Restoration was only a matter of time.

Not that the two shifty-looking figures who presented themselves at the best inn in Rouen inspired any vision of a glorious future. The management was very reluctant to admit them and only agreed to do so when an English merchant to whom Charles sent for a credit reference guaranteed their bill. Even then, the King told Pepys in 1660, 'the people went into the rooms before he went away to see whether he had not stole something or other.' Dr Earle, the King's sub-tutor, happening to be in Rouen and hearing from his fellow Royalists of the King's arrival hurried round to the inn to congratulate his pupil. Meeting Charles he took him for a servant and asked where the King was to be found. News of his safe arrival was sent at once to Henrietta Maria in Paris. The King and Wilmot moved out of the smart hotel where they were made to feel such intruders to the house of another English resident. They bought clothes and hired a coach, setting out for Paris on the following day. After a night stop they were met several miles outside the city by Henrietta Maria, James, Duke of York, and a splendid delegation from the French Court headed by the Duke of Orleans. The Venetian ambassador who attended these ceremonies commented derisively on the meanness of the King's attire and the total absence of any retinue. In spite of their unworthy appearance the King and Wilmot were conducted in triumph to the Louvre. Charles made the most of being for once the centre of attention and regaled his listeners from the Venetian ambassador himself to Mademoiselle de Montpensier, with highly coloured and entirely fictitious accounts of his experience.

In spite of the enthusiasm displayed by the Court at his deliverance, in spite of his own uninhibited enjoyment of the pleasures of the beau monde, in spite of his well publicised reunion with his mother, Charles had moved much closer to the anti-French position so stoutly and consistently maintained by Hyde. Hyde, on his return from his fruitless embassy to Madrid, had paid his respects to Henrietta Maria in Paris and had then rejoined his wife and family in Antwerp. Charles's first act on reaching Paris was to summon his immediate attendance. Henrietta Maria tried to obstruct this by sending a message expressly forbidding any of the King's ministers rejoining him in Paris until further notice since his stay there was uncertain. Hyde disregarded this instruction. How right he was to do so was shown by the King's closeting himself with him in private audience for four or five days, recounting everything that had passed since they had parted over a year earlier. No clearer sign could have been given that Hyde had been restored to the place of chief adviser and that his opposition to the policies of the Queen had been entirely vindicated. From that moment he was in a class by himself.

Hyde was reinforced by the presence of Ormonde, who had landed in Brittany at the end of December. He too had tendered his duty to the Queen before settling down at Caen where his wife and children had been living during his long absence in Ireland. Ormonde was the paladin of Royalism, admired and respected by many of those he had fought against and commanding much wider support among the quarrelsome exiles of his party than anyone else. It says much for Hyde's vigour of mind and strength of personality that he, a man with no pretensions to aristocracy, was preferred to a great nobleman with every requisite qualification. Hyde himself points out in his *History* that he was the only surviving Privy Counsellor of Charles I among the exiles in Paris and that Ormonde's service had been, as was natural, confined to Ireland. The alliance of the two was the foundation on which the later Stuart monarchy was to rest. But the foundation is not, as a rule, that part of the building most easily perceived. The King wanted to have a confidential servant nearer in taste if not in age and summoned Wilmot to the Council. His mother's friends could not be left unrepresented since she was the main source of money and, as a senior member of the French Royal house, a guarantor of a status that all too easily invited scepticism. The miserable allowance that she obtained for her son was irregularly paid. Her own left nothing to spare. On the very night of his return, when he had been conducted to the Louvre in triumph, Charles was informed by his mother that he would have to go half-shares with her in the expenses of her table, beginning with the supper that he was about to eat. The embassies that had been despatched all over Europe to borrow money for the King had hardly covered their expenses except for that to the Czar who had responded with unexpected liberality. Unfortunately the money had been delivered to the Queen's favourite, Lord Jermyn, who had claimed the great part of it in satisfaction of debts allegedly contracted in the service of the Crown. Jermyn, unlike the King's ministers, kept a coach and lived sumptuously.

Charles II seems to have been unmoved by the dignity and uprightness with which Hyde and Ormonde accepted the discomforts and humiliation of poverty. Against their advice he threw himself at last into his mother's scheme for the Montpensier marriage. So vast a fortune would insulate him from the tedious importunities of followers and creditors. He now spoke fluent French and was every inch a man of the world. His suit might well have succeeded if Mademoiselle had not raised her sights to yet a higher cousinly target, Louis XIV himself, eleven years her junior and still only thirteen years old. Hyde and Ormonde opposed the project because it would repeat and exacerbate all the disadvantages of Charles I's marriage. But that did not prevent Charles II from embarking at once on the courtship of another French Catholic, less rich but more seductive. Fortunately for the Royalist party she was also mercenary. The time she took to calculate the chances of profit and loss gave time for ardour to cool. The pursuit of these ladies was expensive. Hunting and dancing require well-cut clothes as well as horses and coaches. The King was assiduous at such entertainments. But the impression he made on his own circle began to show traces of the melancholy, the cynicism and the coarseness that were to deepen with age. The brightness and promise of the young man who had enthused everyone who had to do with him in Jersey were evaporating early.

Jersey itself fell to the Commonwealth within a few months of the King's arrival in Paris. The run of the luck was all against him. France itself, even the Royal Family on whom so much depended, was divided by a civil war of little meaning but great danger. What was Charles to do if his cousin on the one side or his uncle on the other asked his good offices? Wisdom counselled non-involvement, but might he not miss an opportunity to make himself a figure of importance instead of a ubiquitous hanger-on? His brother James had obtained permission to join the French Army and took service under the great Turenne. He was exasperatingly successful. Brave, popular, straightforward and with a real military talent he rose to high rank and earned a much larger income than Charles could command. Like his father, Charles found himself outshone by a brother who was also much better looking. James's rising reputation attracted first one and then others of the Irish regiments serving in Spanish pay to transfer their allegiance. Mazarin was of course delighted and agreed to the condition that they should be released from French service in the event of any Royalist rising. In theory the exiled King now commanded a force of several thousand regular troops: in practice Mazarin redoubled his efforts to reach an understanding with Cromwell's government at the expense of Spain and Holland. Any such agreement would be bound to involve a more or less complete disavowal of the Stuart cause. Thus the real standing of the King sank lower while the successes of his brother made his own inactivity by contrast inglorious.

Yet inactivity was, in Hyde's view, his best and only policy. All he had to do was to sit still. King and minister were temperamentally incapable of understanding such a policy in an identical sense. For Hyde it meant the refusal of all temptation to take short cuts through declared principles and known loyalties: no more intriguing with Scotch Presbyterians or Irish Papists, no disguising of the ground on which Royalism stood. That was the negative side. The positive was to be the slow, industrious building up of a firm, consistent, moderate party in England to which those discontented with Cromwell's government would naturally adhere. This demanded a steady application to work that would have nothing to show for it. A vast correspondence would have to be maintained, a reputation for seriousness and sobriety cultivated, a strict eye kept on honours and rewards on the one hand and on marks of displeasure on the other. The King had so little to give and so much to ask that the most exact measurement of his favour could not be too fine. It was thus that he would establish his own *persona* and define his cause.

Patience, self-discipline and devotion were prerequisite to such a strategy. Such qualities, habitual to Hyde, were alien to the King. His servants from the days of his exile to the closing years of his reign are unanimous in their testimony to his brilliant abilities and to his disinclination to use them. From Hyde and Nicholas to Pepys and Halifax the story is the same. It was at this early stage too that his need for continuous and instant popularity in his own immediate circle was sadly remarked. At no time in his life, it seems, did he hold any conviction strongly enough to screw his courage to the sticking-place. It was not that he wanted courage: it was not that he had no convictions. On the contrary he had been convinced by events that Hyde and Nicholas and Ormonde were right and his mother and Jermyn were wrong. He defended his advisers against their fierce and sustained attacks without giving an inch. Yet when some courtier whom he had no reason to reward or distinguish solicited a place or an honour, he would grant it because it was less trouble than to say no, although he knew perfectly well that such tokens were all the currency he and his ministers had. 'When Kings keep not their words, even with their best and faithfullest servants for their own good, what can an honest man hope for?' wrote Nicholas to Hyde in despair at just such an act in April 1652.[1]

Two images were here in conflict and neither corresponded to reality. For Hyde and Nicholas regality of its nature implied awe and distance. A King could not be a jolly Santa Claus figure, showering gifts on his subjects with indiscriminate benevolence. Still less could he be a kindly uncle who would always reach into his pocket when approached. His gifts should be bestowed seldom and solemnly. The easy liberality commendable in a private gentleman was out of place in a monarch. For Charles this was too stiff, too statuesque, an idea of kingship. As Halifax remarked in his famous *Character of King Charles II*, 'Charles Stuart would be bribed against the King'. It may indeed be questioned whether he had any coherent view of his rôle as distinct from his rights. Did he really agree with his father's challenging assertion from the scaffold that a subject and a sovereign are clear different things? Could such a position be defended at all without first accepting the theological system on which it rested? That this meant little or nothing to him his public actions as well as his private life had already sufficiently shown. It was not that he had no religion: it was simply that it was too loose-jointed and too easy, too sugary and too superficial, to support the tight-knit, rigorous intensity of his father's hard-earned faith. He wished above all to appear a well-bred man, avoiding unpleasantness, smoothing and civilising the rough and the harsh. To make a fuss about taking bribes, to distress oneself because a scoundrel had won by his impudence what a trusted servant had scrupled to ask was to disturb the silent flow of life's river with vulgar splashing and shouting. His father might have reached the same conclusion by a different route. A King in Charles I's eyes ought not to concern himself with day-to-day reality and was not answerable to any criticism but that of his own conscience. Where they parted company was that the father was serious and thorough-going whereas the son was flippant and eclectic. Charles I did not seek to evade the unpleasant consequence of his beliefs. He did not abandon his conception of kingship when the going got rough. Charles II did not scruple to exchange the equableness of the man of the world for the claim to absolute obedience inherent in rule by divine right. What counted was what he wanted and how much he wanted it. The desire to escape hurting people's feelings by denying what it was in his power to give without inconvenience to himself was neither altruistic nor generous. It was simply a means to a pleasure, in this case social, and as such to be pursued with uninhibited appetite. He was not deterred from losing money at the gaming table or running up debts at his tailors by the bitter poverty of his loyal servants. His amusements took precedence of their needs. Men were sent into England at great personal risk to collect money from Royalist sympathisers that could keep him as a man of fashion. In the spring of 1653 Rupert at last returned to France after a cruise that had taken him to Africa and the West Indies. The King's only interest in this extraordinary adventure was in its cash yield. When it became apparent that even the guns from Rupert's ship would have to be sold to balance the books, a shrill and unkingly note entered their intercourse. When Rupert appeared in Paris he was received by his cousin but the issue led to a coolness between them. In 1654 the Prince removed himself and his friends from the exiled Court. Although he returned to England several months after the Restoration and received his fair share of honours and of naval commands it was notorious that Charles II neither liked nor trusted him. Pepys reports him as being of the opinion that Rupert was mad. It is ironic that the man who endowed the Stuart monarchy with so much of its glamour and romance should have been so deep in the bad books of both Kings.

Rupert's departure from Paris only preceded the King's by a month. Mazarin's policy of entente with Cromwell came to fruition in the autumn of 1654. The withdrawal of French countenance from the exiled Court was inevitable, although Henrietta Maria, as a daughter of France, could hardly be turned out of doors. James as a serving officer in the French Army could plausibly be retained without provocation. Henry, Duke of Gloucester, her youngest son aged fifteen, had been released by the English government in 1653 and sent to join his sister Mary in Holland. His mother's very natural desire to see a child she had last seen at the age of four could hardly be denied. That Cromwell regarded him as politically unimportant was sufficiently shown by his humanity in sending him abroad to rejoin his family. He therefore remained in Paris when Charles, having secured the secret continuation of his pension from Mazarin, set out for the Spanish Netherlands in July 1654.

This departure is generally reckoned the low-water mark of his fortunes. The Spanish possessions for which he was making were chilling in their reception. Cromwell had not yet shown his hand in the fiercely contested Franco-Spanish bidding for the English alliance. While there was anything to fear or hope in that quarter, civility to Charles II was a risk not worth taking. The Dutch, with whom Cromwell's government was actually at war, were even more insulting. Charles had offered to serve them at sea and to bring over part of the English fleet which he felt confident would adhere to him once his standard was hoisted. The offer had been refused and his sister had been warned that he would not be permitted to enter the territory of the United Provinces. The reversal of Orange fortunes that had followed the premature death of William II, his generous patron in the early years of exile, was partly the reason for this humiliating rejection. But partly it was the impression of idleness and frivolity that he had made on his hosts in 1648-9, an impression that up-to-date reports from Paris did nothing to efface. Only the diplomatically negligible free cities and electorates of the Holy Roman Empire offered sanctuary. In his own hereditary kingdoms the last remote flickering of revolt in Scotland and Ireland had fizzled out. His own political record was not one to inspire confidence and his personal life did nothing to improve matters. 'He is so damnably debauched he would undo us all.' Cromwell's reported response to a proposal that his constitutional difficulties could be overcome by marrying his daughter to the exiled King summed up what many were beginning to say. He was so poor that he had to leave Paris on horseback, harnessing his coach horses to a baggage cart. His court was riddled with corruption and treachery so that the bitterness of its divisions was well known to Cromwell's intelligence service.

To look for principle or honour or disinterested political intelligence in such a man in such a situation requires a faith of which few are capable. But to those who are prepared to settle on less exalted terms Charles II in 1654 had given proof of having acquired one characteristic of inestimable value in a political leader: he could admit that he was wrong. He had done this when he recalled Hyde and Ormonde to his service in 1651. He had given even more signal proof of it early in 1654 when Hyde's enemies in the Royalist party ranging from Scotch Presbyterians to English Roman Catholics like Sir Marmaduke Langdale, the commander of the Northern Horse during the Civil War, taking in such usually antagonistic figures as Henrietta Maria, Prince Rupert, Wilmot and Colepepper, combined to oust him. The spearhead of the attack, an attempt to prove him guilty of treason during the closing stages of the Civil War, was easily deflected. But in the course of the affair its instigator, desperately aware that his main charge wanted both evidence and credibility, adduced a much more recent conversation with Hyde in which the Chancellor had expressed himself with great freedom on his master's idleness, love of pleasure and disinclination to business. Challenged, Hyde refused to deny the words on oath though he claimed no recollection of them and would swear that he intended no malice or disaffection if he had spoken them. His crowing enemies crowded in for the kill but the King broke in to say that what had been alleged was nothing more, in fact much less, than his minister often said to his face and that the fault was his own for giving him grounds for saying so. He ended by declaring his entire confidence in his Chancellor and ordering that this expression he recorded in the minutes of the Council. It is improbable that the King was animated by a disinterested concern for justice or to any serious degree by loyalty to his ablest and most faithful servant. If the Queen and her improbable coalition had secured the dismissal of Hyde they would have foisted on him some other minister whose first loyalty would lie to his benefactors. Charles might not be interested in ruling himself but he certainly did not mean to be ruled by anyone else, above all not by his mother. Self-interest dictated the retention of Hyde and self-interest could command the service of an intelligence, an objectivity and a courage that were otherwise unemployed. If it is difficult to admire Charles II's motives it is impossible to deny his gifts.

The uprooting from Paris did not have the morally bracing effect that had been so devoutly hoped. The King was looking forward to seeing his sister Mary to whom and to whose husband and children he had become much attached during his stay with them four years earlier. Since he was *persona non grata* in the United Provinces she came to meet him at Spa, a few miles from Liège. The summer season was just opening there and the King threw himself into the festivities. There were balls every night and sometimes the dancing started in the afternoon. In spite of Hyde's careful estimates that would have enabled the King and Court to live within their frugal income Charles constantly expanded his retinue and spent freely. When the money ran out the debts ran up. This pattern of conduct remained constant through the years of exile. If habits of financial responsibility are not instilled by poverty they are unlikely to be formed by abundance. The history of Charles II's reign and the subsequent history of England might have been very different had he acquired them. Such at any rate is the conclusion of Professor C. D. Chandaman, the leading authority on the subject, in his book *The English Public Revenue 1660-1688*. Nothing gave his chief ministers more distress or wasted more of their time than the King's recidivist tendency to obtain credit under false pretences. It led, inevitably, to his involving himself in other shady activities that promised a quick supply of cash. In 1657 when he had removed to the Spanish Netherlands, by then at war with Cromwell, he tried to worm his way into the corrupt practices of Flemish officialdom, promising his good offices with the Spanish Viceroy in obtaining pardons or jobs in the Administration. The market however was too keen and the profits too small for an amateur operating on the fringe. To put so much at risk for so problematical a gain was not a good gamble.

Gambling was an important item of the King's expenditure. One of its by-products was the foundation of an important political family. Clarendon in his *History* speaks highly of the skill shown by the Clerk of the Royal Kitchen, Stephen Fox, in managing the housekeeping of this irregular establishment. So successful was he

> . . . that when his Majesty was once put to a Pinch by losing a sum of money to a Walloon Count, and in vain apply'd to him that had the care of his Privy-Purse to keep his Honour with that Nobleman, the King was agreeably surprised by the Tender of that, and as much more, by this frugal servant . . . whereupon the King was so sensibly touched . . . that being incapable of making a Pecuniary Reward he commanded Sir Edward Walker, then Garter King at Arms . . . to make him a Grant of Arms which was dated at Brussels October 30th 1658 . . . hereby to admit him into the number of the Gentility of his Kingdom who had exceeded even the Nobility by his Generous and Loyal Deportment to his distressed Sovereign.[2]

His son, Henry, the formidable henchman of Sir Robert Walpole, was to marry one of Charles II's granddaughters and the family fame was to reach its pinnacle in the person of their son, Charles James Fox. The strains of master and servant were united in a politician who possessed the Stuart touch in projecting a historical image and a gambler whose fortunes or skill brought him a good deal of success.

Part of Charles II's power of historical attraction derives from the consistency with which he put pleasure before virtue. In fiction, though not in life, the characters that delight everybody are those who live above their means and do not waste time worrying about the consequences to others or to themselves. From Falstaff through the stylish heroes of Restoration comedy, through Mr Jingle and Mr Sponge, to the creations of Evelyn Waugh the line runs true. During his exile the King exemplified the principle more clearly than during his reign. The enjoyments of Spa were brought to a premature end by an outbreak of plague. Careless of much else the King was prudent in the matter of health. He removed promptly to Aachen and shortly after settled in Cologne. In the autumn of 1655 he made a journey up the Rhine to the Frankfurt fair in great style. At Bonn he chartered a pleasure boat that was escorted by two other craft, a kitchen boat and a housekeeper's boat, so that the party travelled in luxury through country that had been ravaged by the Thirty Years War. Ormonde, who was attending the King, was saddened by sights that reminded him of what his own country had endured and might yet have to endure. Such reflections do not seem to have interrupted the general merriment. The only interlude of possible diplomatic significance was the meeting at Königstein between Charles, accompanied by his cousin Rupert, and Queen Christina of Sweden who had abdicated her throne and was on her way to Rome. As Queen she had been one of the first European monarchs to conclude a treaty with Cromwell and she had expressed herself with such freedom about the Stuarts in general and Charles I in particular that Rupert's mother, Elizabeth of Bohemia, had refused an invitation to meet her. Whether the King had any motive other than curiosity is not known, but nothing resulted.

In December when the King was back in Cologne he received the most extraordinary of all gifts for a man whose embarrassments were only too well-known, a pack of hounds sent over from England. For once Charles, though a great horseman, acted against his usual principles and attempted to return them or failing that to find them another home. The first proved too expensive and the second difficult so that the pack was eventually kennelled at Cologne. A couple of hunters were then obtained for the King. How all this was done when every post bewailed the poverty of the exiled Court is obscure. What is clear is the general tone of extravagance. 'We . . . pass our time as well as people can do that have no money, for we dance & play as if we had taken the plate fleet' wrote one of Cromwell's spies in the Royalist Court shortly before the expedition to Frankfurt. The King, unlike his principal advisers, would not confront the unpalatable fact of poverty. To live high by bilking, cadging, wheedling and dodging seemed to him preferable. Among the misfortunes of his situation was one which could be turned to account, namely that he, like the characters of fiction with whom an analogy has been drawn, was a rolling stone, never knowing how long he was going to be in one place and hoping always for a sudden and total change of scene. Impermanence grew to be the chief part of his experience, and evasiveness his first response. Professor Plumb has well written: 'Charles II's Court, after the Restoration, resembled in tone and manner his Court in exile. It lacked confidence, a sense of grandeur, all belief in its own inevitable destiny. The King and his courtiers were haunted by the thought that they might be back in Brussels, Cologne, Paris or Strasbourg.'[3] Yet Hyde and Ormonde who had shared these experiences clearly had no such apprehensions. Was it perhaps because they had accepted reality, instead of surrendering to shiftiness?

That Hyde was alive to the danger of the King's growing deviousness and at the same time unable to perceive that his master was hardly likely to imitate his own bulldog qualities is apparent from a letter he addressed to him in 1656:

> ... the eyes of all men are upon you; your oppression is known, your title is known, but your nature is not known; it is severally represented and it is that which men are most solicitous and inquisitive to understand, and upon the manifestation whereof most of your good or ill fortune will be founded. You have yet few servants in comparison of the number that must hereafter attend you ... And if you do not really and sensibly find more ease and quiet to yourself to flow from one day's clear and frank declaring your purposes and resolutions, both with reference to things and persons, than by all the reservation you can use, how dexterous soever, to leave people to believe that you intend what you do not intend, or that you like, or do not consider, that which you do absolutely dislike and abhor, I will gladly submit to any penalty you will impose.[4]

Charles II could be many things to many men. That he could appear to his chief minister, himself a shrewd observer, as likely to find relief of spirit in straightforwardness is evidence of his virtuosity.

8

Charles II's Religion

———————◆———————

Of all the questions on which Charles II has been suspected of duplicity, both in his lifetime and in history, the largest is his religion. It is well known that he died a Roman Catholic. There is abundant evidence to suggest that from very early days, certainly at the time he was on the run from the defeat at Worcester, he was markedly sympathetic to Catholicism. A number of people who knew him well were convinced that he had been secretly received into the Roman Communion while still in exile. Others thought that he was a sceptic whose supposed Catholic sympathies were either contrived to bamboozle Louis XIV into paying him large subsidies under the Secret Treaty of Dover or else expressed a genuine preference for a religious system that in seventeenth-century Europe favoured absolute monarchy against Republicanism and representative government. The issue was made the more sensitive by the circumstances of his family life. His mother was a militant Catholic: his father's championing of the Laudian party in the Church of England had identified him as perhaps a crypto-Catholic and at least a Catholic sympathiser. Charles himself in exile had tried to marry two French Catholics and after his restoration did in fact marry a devoutly Catholic Portuguese princess. Finally his brother James, long suspected of such tendencies, in 1669 formally adhered to the Church of Rome and remained constant to that profession even when it seemed likely to cost him the succession to the throne.

The most stringent injunctions that Charles I had left to his son were to maintain the rights of the Crown and the doctrines and order of the Church of England. It was on loyalty to this Church as a path between the absolutism of France or Spain, and the anarchy unintentionally let loose by Presbyterianism and encouraged by Independency that the Royalist party rested. When, in the struggles over James's right to succeed, the Whig and Tory parties were born the Tory toast was 'Church and King' not 'King and Church'. It was plain to Charles II from the first that though he might—and did—attempt to bring Cromwell's opponents of every religious and political hue into plots to overthrow the régime he would destroy the hopes of himself and his brothers if he were to be branded a Papist. Even his simulated flirtation with Presbyterianism—an infinitely less dangerous deviation—had brought his cause under intolerable strain. A genuine conversion to Rome would prove fatal.

It was therefore with the greatest alarm and anger that he heard of his mother's determined and unscrupulous attempt to convert his youngest brother Henry, Duke of Gloucester, who had been left behind in Paris. Henrietta Maria's tactics were designed for a swift coup. After Charles left in July the young Duke was allowed to run wild with noblemen's sons of his own age. His English tutor hardly saw anything of him and those that did were shocked by his spoilt and offensive behaviour. In October his mother packed him off to stay with an English convert, the Abbé Montagu, who was head of the rich abbey of St Martin at Pontoise. It seemed a sensible move but the English exiles remaining in Paris were horrified to hear rumours of strong pressure being brought to bear on the boy to change his religion and be educated by the Jesuits. The Abbé Montagu pressed the claims of Rome with every intellectual weapon and reinforced his attack with promises of wealth and security. A Cardinal's hat could easily be obtained for so illustrious a recruit. In the face of this Henry showed remarkable strength of mind. He boldly attempted to meet his adversary in argument and wrote at once to his brother, as did the young Duke's tutor. Unhappily for them Henrietta Maria had arranged that their letters should be stopped by the Post Office so that it was not until mid-November that news of all this reached Charles and Hyde at Cologne. The King wrote at once to Henry, to his mother, to his brother James and to his mother's secretary, Lord

Jermyn, in the strongest terms. 'If you herken to her', he wrote to Henry, 'or to any one else in that matter, you must never thinke to see Englande or me againe, and whatsoever mischiefe shall fall to me or my affairs upon this thing, I must lay all upon you as being the only cause of it.'

All these letters were wisely entrusted to Ormonde to present in person. No better choice of representative was possible. His age, his standing, his manners, his deep attachment to the memory of Charles I whose explicit instructions were being so openly defied would all have qualified him far beyond any alternative candidate. But he had in addition the special recommendation of being the only Protestant member of a great Catholic family and of living in perfect charity with his relations. Strenuous attempts had been made to convert him to Catholicism and he had neither been drawn from his allegiance nor driven into bigotry. As he himself wrote towards the end of his long life:

> . . . My father and mother lived & died papists: and only I, by God's merciful providence, was educated in the true protestant religion, from which I have never swerved towards either extreme, not when it was most dangerous to profess it & most advantageous to quit it. I reflect not upon any who have held another course, but will charitably hope that though their changes happened to be always to the prosperous side, yet they were made by the force of present conviction. My brothers and sisters . . . were very fruitful and very obstinate (they will call it constant) in their way . . . But . . . I am taught by nature, and also by instruction, that difference of opinion concerning matters of religion dissolves not the obligation of nature; and . . . I own, not only that I have done but that I will do, my relations of that or any other persuasion all the good I can.[1]

Ormonde had reached early in life, as a matter of principle, the religious toleration that with Charles II was a matter of preference. No doubt the King had been impelled towards this position by the odious bigotry of the Covenanters which had left such an ineffaceable impression. But the root of his tolerance was not to be found in experience or morality so much as in his lazy, easygoing nature. Early in his reign the balance of political forces turned his government towards a harsh treatment of Protestant Dissenters. From 1679 to 1681 the passions let loose by the Popish Plot forced him to countenance far more shameful and horrible acts against Roman Catholics.

His own Declarations of Indulgence were repudiated. There is no reason whatever to doubt the sincerity of his opinions but the evidence tells against their strength.

In its immediate objective Ormonde's mission was entirely successful. The Queen's plan was foiled, the young Duke travelled back with him to rejoin his brother in Cologne and an open breach in the family was avoided. But for all the energy of the King's reaction his motives, real and professed, were entirely political. He was not concerned, as his father would have been, to argue the truth or falsehood of the religious issue. As long as he was a refugee in a Catholic country he was open to the imputation of favouring Catholicism or at the least of unconscious exposure to its insidious influence. Hyde tells an illuminating story of the young King's reading through a collection of the English Penal Laws against Roman Catholics and asking incredulously if such statutes had really been in force. On being told that this was indeed the case the King asserted his intention of doing all he could to urge Parliament to repeal them. In conversation with his Catholic hosts he made no bones about his disapproval of the existing discrimination against their co-religionists in his own country. In 1656 his mother appears to have inspired reports of his conversion, which were reprinted in the Dutch newspapers. To counter this Hyde advised the recall of Dr Earle to the Court. The King had been far from punctilious in the observation of public worship, a fact that lent support to the rumours of secret Catholicism.

That the King had in fact been secretly received into the Catholic Church before his Restoration is asserted by Ormonde's biographer, Thomas Carte, on the evidence of Ormonde's papers. According to him Ormonde discovered this by chance when he walked into a church in Brussels very early one morning in 1659 and saw the King on his knees at mass. He kept his intelligence to himself until after the Restoration when he let Hyde as Lord Chancellor and Southampton as Lord Treasurer into the secret. They thereupon inserted a clause into the first Act of Parliament making it an offence to say that the King was a papist.[2] The difficulties of accepting any such story are legion. Why, if Charles was prepared to take so huge a risk purely through the intensity of his faith, did not that ardour reveal itself in other and less costly ways? Why should a succession of Popes have kept silent at the time and why should no documentary evidence exist in the Vatican archives of this notable feather in the Papal tiara? Why should the absolute rule forbidding Catholics to profess other ecclesiastical allegiance or to take the sacrament from schismatic or heretic priests be waived in his case? It was not in his brother's. That he may have been on his knees at mass in a Brussels church, that, left to himself, he would then and thereafter have sought reception into the Catholic church may easily be accepted. But that is not at all the same thing.

The documentary evidence for Charles's adherence to Catholicism before his well-known death-bed reception by Father Huddlestone, the very Benedictine who had been instrumental in his escape in 1651, consists of two papers rehearsing the well-worn arguments of Roman Catholic controversialists against the doctrine and orders of the Church of England written in the King's hand, with some crossings out and insertions possibly though not certainly in the hand of somebody else. These interesting exhibits were first shown by James II to Samuel Pepys, whose all but insatiable passion for the curiosities of history was for once fully slaked. Pepys was even allowed to borrow them and bursting with excitement, commanded the presence of his friend John Evelyn at Sunday dinner. 'I have something to show you I may not have another time' he wrote. Evelyn at once confirmed the King's hand, recognised the familiar arguments '. . . altogether weake, & have a thousand times ben Answerd irreplicably by our Divines' and observed that they were 'so well penn'd as to the discourse, as did by no means seeme to me to have ben put together by the late King'. The papers were subsequently published. Ormonde, who had also been given a private view of them by James II, formed much the same judgment of them as Evelyn had done. 'He did not think they were drawn up by the King who was too lazy to spend any time in that way, but having been composed by some Roman Catholic priest, his majesty by way of penance, or on some other occasion, copied them; for they were certainly in his handwriting . . .'[3]

In length of knowledge, if not in depth of intimacy, Ormonde was better qualified than any of Charles's courtiers to gauge his religion. His opinion is worthy of his opportunities:

Though the King showed but little concern for religion, Yet (the Duke thought) he did not want a sense of it. He often professed his belief of a Deity and of a Messiah, as foretold in the Old Testament & expected by the Jews; of a future state and other doctrines; but had very large notions of God's mercy, that he would not make his creatures for ever miserable on account of their personal failing. Upon this notion he indulged himself in his pleasures, but had frequently his hours of retirement for the exercise of his private devotions. He laid very little stress on the different systems of religion; and would frequently take delight to tease his brother, who was very serious and zealous in his way, with reflecting on the scandalous lives of some popes, and laughing at some particular tenents of the Roman Catholics . . .[4]

Religion like sex offers infinite scope for comedy but it by no means follows that those who joke on these subjects do not take them seriously. Charles's laziness and flippancy were too much a part of him not to be part of his religion. His father would have been scandalised, as Hyde was, darkly attributing the great part of the mischief to the buffooneries and mimicry of Buckingham. This opinion was endorsed by Bishop Burnet. No doubt they were right in emphasising the strange fascination that the Duke seems to have possessed for the King, so strongly reminiscent of that exerted by his father on the two previous generations of Stuarts. But it was an age of mockery and scepticism, cohabiting openly with religious faith and finding room for folklore and superstition. Even Cromwell and his major-generals had thought it a great joke to dress up in copes and mitres and to clown in them. Even Pepys, an early Fellow and President of the Royal Society, appears to have believed, half laughing at himself, that the possession of a hare's foot, particularly one that had the joint in it, was an effective remedy against flatulence. Both the King and Buckingham were creatures of their time, not independent-minded people who would go against the tide. Few men in any age have the vigour and intellectual capacity to think their position through to complete consistency. Charles may have had the second but he certainly lacked the first. The loose ends and mutual contradictions are well suggested in Ormonde's sketch.

The best-known and most brilliant portrayal of the King achieved by one of the ablest and most independent of his ministers is Halifax's *Character of King Charles II*. In the opening section concerned with his religion Halifax makes it clear that he believes that the King became a Roman Catholic during the years of exile which followed his escape from Worcester.

The Company he kept, the Men in his Pleasures, and the Arguments of State that he should not appear too much a Protestant, whilst he expected Assistance from a Popish Prince; all these, together with a habit encouraged by an Application to his Pleasures, did so loosen and untie him from his first Impressions, that I take it for granted after the first Year or two, he was no more a Protestant. If you ask me what he was, my answer must be, that he was of the Religion of a young Prince in his warm Blood, whose Enquiries were more applied to find Arguments against believing, than to lay any settled Foundation for acknowledging Providence, Mysteries, etc. A General Creed, and no very long one, may be presumed to be the utmost Religion of one, whose Age and Inclination could not well spare any thought that did not tend to his Pleasures.

In this kind of Indifference or Unthinkingness, which is too natural in the beginnings of Life to be heavily censured, I will suppose he might pass some considerable part of his Youth. I must presume too that no Occasions were lost, during that time, to intimate every thing to bend him towards Popery . . . When the critical Minute was, I'll not undertake to determine; but certainly the inward conviction doth generally precede the outward Declarations . . . I conclude that when he came into England he was as certainly a Roman Catholick, as that he was a Man of Pleasure; both very consistent by visible Experience.

All this, as Halifax himself makes plain, is pure speculation based on observation made at a much later period. Halifax never knew the exiled Court at first hand and was not on good terms with its stalwarts. Apart from the King himself, the Duke of York and the Duke of Buckingham, neither of them impartial sources, were for a time his political patrons and may have supplied him with reminiscence. So far as is known he met the King for the first time in 1660 and in spite of every advantage of wealth, connexion and ability only entered the government in 1672 and left it again in 1674. From 1679 to the end of the reign he was prominent as a courtier and a minister. As an authority on the last years of the King's life he is in the first rank.

Men that were earnest Protestants were under the sharpness of his Displeasure, expressed by Rallery, as well as by other ways. Men near him have made Discoveries from sudden breakings out in Discourse, etc which shewed there was a Root. It was not the least skilful part of his concealing himself, to make the World think he leaned towards an Indifference in Religion.

He had sicknesses before his Death, in which he did not trouble any Protestant Divines; those who saw him upon his death-bed, saw a great deal.

In Halifax's view dissimulation and love of ease were the two constants in the varying patterns of the King's behaviour. His judgment that Charles' apparent levity in matters of religion was a pretence is crucial to his interpretation of the King's character and motives. It is confirmed by a much less subtle and sceptical witness. Bishop Burnet records of a private conversation with the King:

> While we were talking of the ill state the church was in, I was struck to hear a prince of his course of life so much disgusted at the ambition, covetousness and scandals of the clergy. He said if the clergy had done their part, it had been an easy thing to have run down the nonconformists: but he added, they will do nothing and will have me do everything: and most of them do worse than if they did nothing.[5]

Of course it may be argued that this was a simple instance of the King's delight in deceiving; certainly Burnet's gullibility must have offered strong temptations to a man little enough disposed to resist them. Yet his record in appointments and promotions in the Church is no whit inferior to his father's. To the bench of bishops he sent such ornaments of the Great Tew circle as his old tutor John Earle and Robert Sanderson, his father's favourite preacher, leading lights of the Royal Society such as Seth Ward and John Wilkins, Cromwell's brother-in-law, scholars whose learning was matched by personal piety such as Isaac Barrow and John Pearson. His last episcopal appointment is perhaps his most famous, that of Thomas Ken, a Royal Chaplain and Canon of Winchester who had refused to accommodate Nell Gwyn in his house when the Court paid a visit in March 1683 in these words: 'A woman of ill-repute ought not to be endured in the house of a clergyman, least of all in that of the King's chaplain.' At the end of the following year the bishopric of Bath and Wells fell vacant. Charles, it is said, dismissed the various solicitations of his courtiers with an utterance that has the ring of authenticity: 'Odd's fish! Who shall have Bath and Wells but the little black fellow who would not give poor Nelly a lodging?'[6]

Ken's outspokenness appears to have raised him in the King's esteem. 'I must go and hear little Ken tell me of my faults,' he remarked when it was his turn to preach at Whitehall. Charles's acceptance of ecclesiastical reproof was unpredictable. Sheldon when Archbishop of Canterbury refused him the sacrament on the grounds of his scandalous life. The King never forgave him. On the other hand

Robert Frampton whose preaching Evelyn much admired and Pepys characterised as 'the most like an Apostle that ever I heard man' was more liberally treated. He preached two sermons before the Court in 1672, the first immediately after the battle of Solebay urging his congregation to show their gratitude to the killed and wounded by a generous provision for widows and orphans and the disabled, and the second attacking the growth of atheism and in particular its easy acceptance at Court. Both gave offence. The King however received Frampton in private audience and courteously explained that though the matter was well the manner was not,

> for, says he, Doctor, therein you made a direct speech to me which I cannot allow, for by that example some others, upon whose fidelity and modesty I cannot so well depend, will be taking the same liberty too, which may be of ill consequence, and therefore if you ever come there again, abridge yourself of that latitude.[7]

He then went on to question him about Turkish affairs—Frampton, the son of a Dorset yeoman, had made his way by a chaplaincy to the Levant Company—and next year made him Dean of Gloucester, promoting him to the bishopric eight years later.

Frampton and Ken were both men of unusual intelligence and articulacy whose conversation the King might enjoy. But that he could also discern and value sincerity and goodness when combined as they so often are with muddle and stupidity, is shown by the charming story recorded by Burnet.

> He [the King] told me he had a chaplain that was a very honest man, but a very great blockhead, to whom he had given a living in Suffolk, that was full of that sort of people: he had gone about among them from house to house, though he could not imagine what he could say to them, for, he said, he was a very silly fellow, but that he believed his nonsense suited their nonsense; yet he had brought them all to church: and, in reward of his diligence, he had given him a bishopric in Ireland.[8]

There were, of course, appointments of other kinds, as was inevitable when preferment in the Church formed an important part of the patronage by which political and public service was rewarded. Some of these were more or less unedifying. Isaac Vossius, a European scholar of vast erudition and uncouth behaviour, was lured to

England by the bait of a canonry at Windsor, although he made no attempt to disguise his own lack of Christian belief. According to the King who much enjoyed his conversation, Dr Vossius would believe any marvel as long as it was not to be found in the Bible. When Canon in Residence he used to take his Ovid with him into chapel.

What, then, did Charles II's religion amount to? Two themes emerge from the evidence with notable consistency. First, his real respect and value for true, unaffected Christianity, as exemplified by his tutors Duppa and Earle and distinguished by him in his own ecclesiastical promotions. Second, the belief, variously expressed, that 'God would not damn a man for a little irregular pleasure'. These two positions seem to derive from two different conceptions of the divine nature, one strong, the other weak. Two other themes, perhaps interlocked, are also conspicuous, tolerance and scepticism. It is these two that have shaped the image of the King as a modern-minded, witty, emancipated figure, deftly picking his way through the barbarities and absurdities of an age still not sobered from theological excess.

Such a representation has much to support it. We know that the King much enjoyed the conversation of learned sceptics such as Hobbes or Vossius and we know that he took pleasure in teasing his brother over the simple certainties of his faith. Whether in a man of Charles II's chameleonesque surface, quickness of wit and lightness of weight, any depth of sceptical conviction could be inferred may be doubted. To a man of his experience the pleasures of irreverence religious or political must have been hard to resist. The pressure of strong characters and reiterated certainties on an indolent and devious nature could only be rendered tolerable by laughter. Mockery became a mechanism of self-defence. In the same way the King's preference for religious toleration may be understood as a reaction to the gross, insufferable intrusions to which he had been subjected as a young man. He was not, as we shall see, by any means a champion of political toleration when he found himself re-established on his throne. The positive concern for justice, for fair play, for the rights of others on which the concept of tolerance rests was too strenuous for him.

It was also too serious. Charles II's wit, his sayings and his course of life, induced later generations to see in him a forerunner of Voltaire and the Enlightenment. But Voltaire's passion was left out of Charles II's make-up. Much more he was a forerunner of Louis XV without

Charles II with a lapdog and rattle. This, the earliest known portrait, was probably painted by an artist sent over by the French Royal family when the Prince was about a year old.

Charles II when Prince of Wales, by Dobson. Painted in Oxford, early in the
Civil War.

This engraving of a portrait of Charles II taken by Van den Hoecke in Brussels in 1649 suggests a personality in which watchfulness is well developed for a young man of nineteen.

Charles II c. 1651. Miniature by Des Granges. Versions of this portrait were rare and distinguished rewards for exceptional loyalty to the exiled King.

This Philippe de Champaigne portrait of Charles II painted at St. Germain in 1653 magnificently misrepresents the true facts of his situation. He had not been, as is suggested, victorious in war: the fleet in the background, whatever it is, is none of his. Even the armour and accoutrements were beyond his means. Yet perhaps of all pictures of the King it is the truest to his own aspirations, even to his conception of himself.

Portrait of Charles II by Luttichuys presented by the King to the Earl of Sandwich in gratitude for his part in restoring him to the throne.

Blooteling mezzotint from Lely portrait of Charles II. Asperities of character are mellowed by the softness of the medium.

Left. Red and black chalk drawing in profile of Charles II by Samuel Cooper taken soon after the Restoration. John Evelyn held the candle while the artist drew his sketch which was used for the head of the monarch on the early gold coinage of his reign. *Right.* Miniature of the King by Samuel Cooper signed and dated 1665.

Charles II in Garter robes by Lely, probably painted *c.* 1675 (*compare Blooteling mezzotint*).

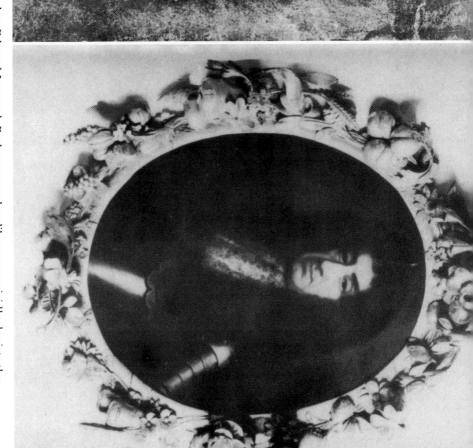

Left. Pastel portrait of Charles II in later life attributed to Edward Lutterel. Perhaps no other likeness so vividly depicts the ruthlessness that some of his contemporaries found in him. *Right.* Riley portrait of Charles II painted towards the end of the reign in its original frame.

the means to live as high. The pursuit of obvious pleasures and the cultivation of a certain elegance in the externals of life were, so far as those closest to him could see, his principal concerns. Scepticism and tolerance, like everything else, were subordinate, not ends or truths or principles that commanded assent. Tolerance for Protestant sects that might breed tiresome political beliefs was not to be valued at the same rate as for a Catholicism that in the seventeenth century upheld the authority of Kings and Princes and allowed them a broad licence in private morals. Scepticism was too deep and difficult and dangerous to have much attraction, fun though it was to assume a degree of it from time to time. In the end it seems probable that Charles II's religion was defensive and self-centred. He wanted to give as little as he must and get as much as he could. If this seems a strange spirit in which to embrace Christianity, it may only be the effect of living in an age when religious belief is very much a matter of contracting in rather than of contracting out. By far the greater part of educated Europeans in Charles II's time accepted a Christian explanation of the world and of their own experience of life, or at least appear to have thought that they did. It was the intellectual context in which they tried to make sense of things. It was forced on them by the very form and pressure of the time. Christianity was thus part of the furniture in the accommodation provided, not something that they had gone out and bought for themselves. It is therefore no argument against those, like Halifax, who maintain that Charles II's scepticism was a disguise, to assert that his course of life proves the contrary. It proves him lazy, self-indulgent, shallow, frivolous and shabby, qualities for which a great deal of evidence exists in other, some would say in all, departments of his life. But it tells in favour of Halifax's contention. He was anxious to obtain a form of Christianity that he could reconcile with his preferred mode of life. The death-bed reception into the Roman Catholic Church confirms such an interpretation. If the whole business were moonshine why bother? If it be argued that the decencies must be kept up that would hardly support the monarch's reception into a heavily proscribed communion, proscriptions to which the statutes of his own reign had substantially added.

The anatomy here attempted of Charles II's religion would seem at first sight to leave him nothing in common with his father. Their nature, temper, manners, style, upbringing, education and taste were so far apart that this is not surprising. Above all the seriousness and piety of Charles I were the direct antitheses of his son's flippancy. Yet in two respects there is a paradoxical resemblance. Charles I, identified by his public acts as an intolerant and persecuting churchman, was in religious disputation a notably charitable and understanding adversary. The death-bed tribute of Alexander Henderson, the chief of the Scotch Commissioners to Parliament during the Civil War, is more eloquent than any Royalist encomium:

> . . . in Matters of Religion, whether in relation to Kirk or State, I found him the most intelligent man that ever I spoke with: as far beyond my Expression as Expectation. I profess that I was oft-times astonished with the solidity & Quickness of his Reasons & Replies, wondered how he spending his time so much in sports & Recreations could have attained to so great a Knowledge; & must confess ingenuously that I was convinc'd in conscience & knew not how to give him any reasonable satisfaction. Yet the Sweetness of his Disposition is such that whatsoever I said was well taken . . . I never met with any Disputant of that mild & calm Temper.

If Charles I was perhaps closer than has sometimes been supposed to the tolerance and intellectual good manners of his son, Charles II was, as instances cited in this chapter have shown, ready to honour simplicity and goodness for all the cynicism of the face he turned to the world and for all the licence he allowed himself.

9

Remittance Man

———◆———

The firmness which the young King had shewn when confronted by his mother's attempt on his brother Henry's religion encouraged the hopes of his supporters. But it was not the prelude to action and initiative. His point gained, Charles relapsed into passivity. The plans for a general rising against Cromwell lacked thrust, co-ordination and leadership. The motives for such a venture were overwhelmingly negative: discontent with some measures of the government, dislike and fear of its military basis, alarm at its enormous cost. The central committee of the Royalist underground, the Sealed Knot, had been penetrated by Cromwell's intelligence. The squabbles and indiscretions of the exiled Court made it easy for the government in London to find out all it wanted to know about Royalist plans and to anticipate serious trouble. The rising of Penruddock and Grove in Wiltshire was the froth on what should have been a full tankard. It took only a few hours to deal with. That Cromwell should have been faced with no other disturbance, although his régime was passionately resented by a great part of the political nation, is eloquent of his extraordinary skill as a ruler. It says something too about Charles II. A comparison between his moody self-indulgence and the single-mindedness of his young nephew William of Orange in the two decades that followed is revealing. Charles behaved like a remittance man who believes that sooner or later the family will have a change of heart: William like a man who meant to win back a throne.

Apart from his success with his youngest brother, Charles's relations with his family became less and less happy. His mother was still opposed to the fundamentals of his policy and bitterly resentful at her exclusion from his affairs. His sister Mary who had been closest to him in affection had been won over to Henrietta Maria's side after a visit to Paris in 1656. His younger brother James had, as we have seen, loyally given up his career in the French Army in exchange for a command in Flanders now that Mazarin and Cromwell were open allies and the Spaniards actually at war with the Protectorate. But James did not conceal, indeed was all his life incapable of such a feat, that he had acted against his own strong preferences, both personal and professional, out of his sense of duty as his brother's heir and chief subject. The acceptance of this sacrifice was made the more galling from the courtesies and attentions paid by the Spanish authorities to the handsome, popular and successful young General. James's pay was still Charles's most reliable means of relief when the creditors grew obnoxious and the tradesmen refused supply.

In the affairs of his common-law family the King was also embarrassed. Lucy Walter, his long-discarded mistress, set herself up in London in the summer of 1656 with her two illegitimate children, the eldest of whom was Charles's son, the future Duke of Monmouth. She was arrested and sent to the Tower. Charles's warrant for her pension was found among her effects, a fact with which the government journalists made great play. She was soon afterwards deported and Charles attempted, unsuccessfully, to obtain custody of his son by force. This again led to undesirable publicity but a bargain was at last struck and the boy was sent to Paris to be brought up by Henrietta Maria. Since he was not in the line of succession his education as a Roman Catholic was a matter of indifference. However this expensive scandal still had life in it. The boy's tutors attempted to bribe an Anglican exile, the Dean of Peterborough, into forging a marriage certificate between the King and his ex-mistress. This the Dean indignantly refused but the story that Charles had secretly married Lucy Walter had been launched into the stream of history.

The Prince Charming of Royalist fairytale had become by the late 1650s a somewhat bedraggled figure. The shifts and turns to which he was ready to resort to raise money for his own comforts and pleasures, made self-respect impossible. The shady and the scandalous were

never far away. That this was no mere accident of poverty had
become clear to his most devoted servants. By January 1658 he had
become bored with the provincial society of Bruges and proposed
moving his household to Brussels, claiming that he would there be
better placed to exert pressure on the Spanish authorities.

'He must pardon me if I cannot believe it is that which disposes him
to the journey, or will be his employment there' wrote Ormonde to
Hyde.

> I must now freely confess to you that what you have written of the King's
> unreasonable impatience at his stay at Bruges is a greater danger to my
> hopes of his recovery than the strength of his enemies, or the weaknesses &
> backwardnesse of those that professe him friendship. Modesty, courage
> and many accidents may overcome those enemies, and unite and fix those
> friends, but I fear his immoderate delight in empty, effeminate and vulgar
> conversation is become an irresistible part of his nature, and will never
> suffer him to animate his own designs & others' actions with that spirit
> which is requisite for his quality and much more to his fortune.[1]

For nearly twenty years Hyde and Ormonde had laboured for the
Stuart case. They had forfeited possessions—in Ormonde's case very
great possessions—and careers. Their wives and children had shared
their exile and their penury. Ormonde himself was on the point of
leaving on a secret mission to England of great danger. While he was
in London he always slept in his clothes, changed his lodging every
day and made sure that it had more than one way out. The least he
could expect of the King was that he should take his situation seriously
and think more of his cause than of his amusements. Like Hyde he
conceived it to be part of his duty to tell the King of his faults and to
warn him of their political consequences. No doubt he did so with a
lighter touch and with less emphatic repetition. Charles always
appeared to take the reproofs of both men in good part, accepting the
disinterestedness of their motives, admitting the truth of what they
said, bearing them no ill will. But if he was easy to them he was still
easier to himself. No alteration was visible in his course of life. Even his
relations in the Royal Family of France and the House of Orange
came to look on him as disreputable.

No clearer evidence of this could be found than in the events that
followed the death of Cromwell in September 1658. This was the
deliverance on which hung every Royalist hope. Its circumstances

exceeded expectation. Cromwell had made no provision for a successor. His constitutional experiments had all failed. His abler son
Henry was in Ireland. Richard, who was hastily installed as Protector,
could hardly be taken seriously. Writs had gone out for a Parliament
to which a fair number of disguised Royalists should easily secure
election. The Army leaders were divided and ambitious, the soldiers
discontented by lengthening arrears of pay. A more favourable
conjunction for the Stuarts could hardly be imagined. Charles was at
that moment courting the young sister-in-law of his sister Mary,
Henrietta of Orange. On hearing of Cromwell's death his first act was
to send her mother a formal proposal for her hand. The Dowager
Princess seemed pleased at the prospect opening before her daughter
but within two months she had settled her marriage with a mere
German Prince. In the keenest market the King of England had not
fetched the very modest price of a younger daughter of a non-regnant
house. The reported censures of the priggish young Louis XIV were
far less damning.

The eighteen months that passed between the death of Cromwell
and the proclamation of Charles II by the Convention Parliament in
April 1660 form one of those rare periods where it seems possible to
perceive the secret and interior processes of history on the surface of
events. To many devout Royalists, though not, we may be sure, to
Charles II, it seemed in retrospect that God had lifted the veil from
the mystery of things, that he had taught his faithful people not to
expect a straightforward development of affairs simply because the
divine will was manifest and its outcome in human history certain, but
rather to drive home the point that whom the Lord loveth he
chasteneth. The chastening of Charles II might be, in Gibbon's
famous phrase, discernible only to the nicest theological eye, but the
zigzags, the changes and contrasts, the brilliant plotting of the course
of history could hardly escape the dullest observer.

To follow this complicated series of events from the elevation
afforded by three hundred years is not easy. To anticipate their likely
course from the ground level of day-to-day experience would seem
impossible. Clearly what the King did or did not do, what he
encouraged, what he played down, whom he openly favoured, whom
he secretly approached were themselves both initiatives and responses
in the historical process. Informing them all was the image or
impression that he made on his countrymen. He had not only to act in
the executive sense but also in the theatrical. The great questions that

had been with him from the moment of his succession in 1649 insisted themselves on him with the force of a final demand: should he leap or should he sit still? Should he secure foreign assistance, far more likely to be offered now that Cromwell was dead, or should he stick to Hyde's policy of letting England find her own way back to her old institutions? The pressure for immediate action was very strong. The new régime was unsteady and uncertain, the most vigorous of the secret Royalist conspirators were keen to strike before a more formidable military government had established itself, there were the incalculable gains to be won from boldness and decision. Besides, the King himself was much too realistic and intelligent not to know how poor a figure he had cut over the last interminable years of exile. On the other side were ranged the advisers on whom the King had come to rely. Hyde, Colepepper, Ormonde, Nicholas, all counselled patience. In the thieves' quarrels that were bound to follow, honest men would come by their own. Indeed a little judicious stirring of the pot might help to bring this about. Similarly it would be most unwise to take premature advantage of the brightening diplomatic prospects. Much better wait, and let the situation develop.

On the whole Charles accepted this advice. But it was embarrassing for him to meet the arguments and pleas of his supporters in England who were actively planning a general rising with any response that smacked of the faint-hearted. The Royalist underground was under no central control. The body known as the Sealed Knot that had the best claim to such a position was thought by the more vigorous and enterprising agents to suffer from an excess of seniority and from the habits and attitudes of men who have been long in command without fighting, let alone winning, a battle. No one suspected that one of its leading members, Sir Richard Willys, a distinguished cavalry officer and protégé of Prince Rupert, had been in the pay of Cromwell's Secret Service for the last three years. This, however, was made plain to the King by one of the cryptographers, recruited then as now from among peacetime dons, who thought it politic to insure his own future against a Stuart restoration. Samuel Morland, who had been Pepys's tutor at Magdalene, obtained a promise (not honoured) of the Garter in exchange for this revelation. Naturally he was not at first believed. What was the word of this treacherous pipsqueak against the honourable record and honest poverty of an old Cavalier? Morland sent over letters written to Thurloe, Cromwell's head of intelligence, in Willys's own hand. Even then some of Willys's closest associates refused to believe the evidence. At this most crucial moment the Royalist secret organisation, such as it was, was crippled by a bitter and protracted controversy. Security, never its strong point, was at a minimum. Co-ordination of local insurrection became impossible. The argument for lying low had become overwhelming by the late summer of 1659 when it had originally been planned that the rising should break out. The authorities had ample information and most of the possible leaders were already in prison. The King seems to have been genuinely anxious to avoid throwing away lives and readily accepted that the moment was not propitious. But unfortunately he shared with his father an inability to say no in terms that admitted of no misinterpretation. Under pressure from Mordaunt, the most daring of the younger Royalist *maquisards*, he vacillated. The confusion that followed might have been much more costly than it was. Edward Mountagu, the Cromwellian General at Sea who had been in secret touch with a Royalist agent in Copenhagen brought the fleet back from the Sound, where he had been sent to counteract Dutch influence, to support the projected rising. When he arrived in home waters he found that nothing had happened. Or almost nothing. Sir George Booth, a very rich Presbyterian whose liaison with the exiled Court was poor, had not heard that the plan had been called off. He had risen with considerable support in Cheshire and Lancashire but his staff work was abysmal and his courage not of the kind that leads men to victory against odds. As in Cromwell's lifetime the forces of insurgent Royalism were dispersed with hardly a shot fired. Mountagu adroitly explained the return of the fleet by claiming that it had not been re-victualled as it should, laid down his commission and retired to Hinchingbrooke. The misfiring of the plan had barely grazed the conspirators.

It was at this decisive moment in his career that Charles II's powers of decision were conspicuous by their absence. From the death of Cromwell change and motion had become the chief characteristic of English politics. Forces long dormant or restrained were beginning to stir. Now more than ever was the opportunity for the young King so long obscured to stamp his image on the course of events. This did not mean that he had to take rash initiatives or attempt by hurried stoking of the oven to transform the half-baked into the successful. But it did mean that whether he chose action or inaction he must be seen to have made a choice, to have checked or spurred. In the events of that summer the feebleness of Sir George Booth was of more value to the Royalist cause than the leadership of the King. Had his collapse not been so abject and instantaneous Mountagu might well have committed the fleet to the reinforcement of failure. Even more alarmingly Turenne had offered, and James, unable to make contact with his brother, had accepted, the assistance of his own regiment, fully armed and equipped, together with the shipping needed to take it across the channel. How far this enterprise would have gone, since the offer was made without the knowledge and in opposition to the policy of the French government, is impossible to guess. But that it would have gone far enough to do severe, perhaps irreparable, damage to the prospects of a Stuart restoration seems highly possible. The troops, and James himself, were actually about to embark when news reached them that the revolt was over and that Booth was a prisoner. Everything that Hyde had stood for was to have been put at risk without any likelihood of worthwhile advantage. The New Model Army was a formidable military opponent. To meet it on its home ground with foreign troops, themselves without any motive beyond obedience to orders and conscious of inferiority in numbers and quality, was to invite disaster. If foreign intervention were to be worth having it must at least have the full backing of the government concerned. Charles had sounded Mazarin and had obtained nothing beyond expressions of goodwill. He knew that France and Spain were on the point of ending their long war and may well have judged that neither power would be likely to embark on new adventures until negotiations had been concluded. He was ready to leave for England at a moment's notice if there were a change of heart and French support were forthcoming. But high-spirited and hopeful as were the letters he wrote from the channel ports they are essentially passive. His state of mind is cheerful, even optimistic but there is nothing of the will, the force of mind, the resolution that imposes itself on events or at least convinces others of a serious intention to do so.

If all had gone well a general rising all over England would have been supported by the English regiments in the Spanish service transported from Flanders, while Charles himself would sail from a French port, confident that he could draw on the armies and resources of France if they were needed. But from the start it had been clear that there was not the remotest possibility of this conjunction. The Spaniards, as hitherto, promised what was asked and performed nothing. The Royalists in England were, as we have seen, in disarray. The French government did not share the chivalry of Turenne.

Charles drifted westward along the channel coast, hawking and
hunting when occasion offered. He did not look like a man who meant
business. Indeed he looked uncommonly like the man who had drifted
about the Rhineland and the Low Countries for the past six or seven
years, taking his pleasures where he could find them and waiting for
the times to alter. He was travelling westward partly because he had
left one brother, Henry, in Flanders and another, James, at Calais
who could act in the increasingly improbable event of a rising in
south-eastern England. He himself would be available if anything
happened in the south west. But a scarcely less important consideration was that it brought him steadily nearer the Pyrenees where
the Franco-Spanish treaty was to be signed at a conference of the
heads of government. The two super-powers of seventeenth-century
Europe had both expressed their strong wish to see him restored to his
rights and the principles of monarchy once more asserted. They would
never have such a chance of making good their professions as at this
rare moment of international harmony.

Charles was at St Malo when he heard of Booth's defeat and
capture. He determined to leave at once for Fuenterrabia, where
Velazquez was designing a setting worthy of the great peace conference. Sir Henry Bennett, his envoy at Madrid, had long been
pressing him to come and had added to his solicitations the confidential encouragement of the Spanish government. The rapidity of
Charles's decision was not matched by any urgency of execution. On
the contrary he seized the opportunity of an agreeable excursion at the
pleasantest time of year. He happened to have with him companions
ideally suited to such an expedition: Ormonde, whose presence
supplied the dignity and authority that would be so sorely needed at so
grand a meeting, Bristol, whose knowledge of France and Spain was
probably more extensive than that of any other servant of the Crown,
and O'Neil whose experience as agent and courier ensured the best
possible travelling arrangements. It was early September when the
little party left St Malo. For more than a fortnight they disappeared
from view. On September 22nd Charles wrote from La Rochelle to
ask for some clean clothes. A week later he told his despairing
Chancellor that he was tired of waiting for a ship and would pursue his
journey by land. It was during this period that Turenne had made his
offer of help, about which it had not been possible to consult the King.
Worse still, while he was dawdling agreeably through the Dordogne—
he had disdained the direct route through Bordeaux—the Treaty of

the Pyrenees had come and gone. Ormonde hurried to Toulouse to intercept Mazarin on his homeward journey. The King, alert at last to the danger of a missed opportunity, raced into Spain to catch Don Luis on the road to Madrid. Even in this he was unfortunate. The Spanish minister had decided to stay on at San Sebastian to await his arrival. He was disconcerted and suspicious at hearing that his guest was now between him and his capital. A cordial meeting at which Charles exerted all his powers of pleasing redressed matters. But what had been achieved? Nothing. Whether anything could have been must remain doubtful. Mazarin was not going to take any risks on Charles's behalf and it is difficult to see what the Spaniards could have done to induce him to change his mind. What had been thrown into humiliating prominence was the irresponsible behaviour of the King of England.

In his *History* Clarendon (as Hyde had then become) makes the King return to Brussels on hearing of Booth's defeat. He was writing in his second and final exile, without access to his own papers and with no companions by whose recollections he could check his own. No wonder if details, especially details of chronology, are often wrong. Yet easy and obvious as such an explanation is, would not the King's chief minister remember in all its acuteness the anxiety and exasperation he must himself have experienced at this example of self-indulgence and frivolity? The author of the *History* was writing for publication, not confiding private thoughts and memories to trusted friends. Whatever freedom he may have allowed himself in speaking to his master, whatever candour in writing to Ormonde or Nicholas, he had a high sense of what was due to the cause he served. Both as an artist and as an autobiographer he was preparing for the climax of his life's work, the restoration of the old, loved forms in Church and State amid scenes of universal rejoicing. Was this the moment at which to exhibit the central character in so futile an aspect? The monarchy that Hyde wished to restore drew its strength from its image, not from its troops or its Treasury.

The friendliness of Don Luis's reception issued in no political advantage but it did produce a welcome relief in the shape of hard cash. When weighed at the bank the coin turned out to be worth a great deal less than its face value, but for the King and for those of his followers who had found excuses to join him on the Spanish border it was magic. Charles was in no hurry to return to the familiar embarrassments of his northern exile. He attempted a last marriage negotiation, this time for the hand of Mazarin's niece, one of the great beauties as well as one of the great fortunes of the age. The Cardinal was no more prepared to stake his own money than his master's on the Stuart chances. The project had been supported by Henrietta Maria's favourite, Lord Jermyn, who had travelled down to Toulouse to represent her influence at the French Court. Charles took this opportunity of repairing the worst of the family breaches. When at last he turned north he took in Paris on his way, staying with one of his mother's courtiers among whom he distributed honours and places. The reconciliation was complete. Indeed it was enriched by the strong mutual attraction that sprang up between the King and his youngest sister, Henriette, now in all the freshness and grace of her 'teens, whom he had last seen as a child of ten. Her premature death ten years later was to be one of the few griefs to touch his heart.

Refreshed by his holiday and by the rare pleasure of family harmony Charles returned to Brussels at the end of December. The extreme volatility of English politics made his presence imperative. Indeed many thought that had he appeared in England in the late autumn he would have been restored forthwith. Lambert's defeat of Sir George Booth had turned out to be no more than a military incident. The government had grown weaker and had itself been ejected by the Army leaders, who in their turn had failed to consolidate a régime and had had to recall the men they had displaced. Public opinion was veering strongly towards a Restoration as offering the only convincing prospect of stability and continuity. A deal between the King and one of the more powerful generals seemed to offer excellent possibilities. Fleetwood, Cromwell's son-in-law, was the man who generally presided over the deliberations of the senior officers but he was very much a political general. The two generals in active commands who might well adhere to the King were Lambert in England and Monck in Scotland. Monck had actually been a Royalist officer in the Civil War and had only taken service under Cromwell at its end after two years as prisoner of war. Lambert had been a Parliament man from the beginning but in every other way was more suitable. He was a well-to-do Yorkshire country gentleman of cultivated tastes and his elder daughter was said to be both charming and beautiful. Monck came of an ancient family of undistinguished Devon gentry and had married a vulgar and assertive wife. The independence of Monck's command and the well-found, well-disciplined force he had under him made him the chief object of Royalist overtures. Monck however was playing his cards very close to his chest. He would give no undertaking of any kind, not even to his brother, a Royalist clergyman. Lambert on the other hand was thought to be much more approachable. Negotiations for the hand of his daughter were suggested first to the Duke of York and then to the King himself. But it is not clear that Lambert himself had authorised them. The King showed no anxiety to prosecute the matter and the Duke of York, unknown both to his brother and to her father, the Chancellor, had secretly engaged himself to Anne Hyde.

It was something that this disastrous commitment was as yet concealed from the King and his minister. Their troubles at the beginning of the year 1660 were serious enough. The Royalist party in England was once again breaking into fiercely quarrelling factions and in Flanders the opposition to Hyde became the more venomous as the great prize of the kingdom seemed to be so tantalisingly close and yet still to elude the grasp. Had the golden opportunity come and gone? On the face of things it seemed so. Early in January the Rump, surprised to find itself again in apparent possession and anxious to mend its fences, voted the imposition of a new oath abjuring the House of Stuart. At the same time Monck who had declared for a free Parliament against the Army coup crossed the border at Coldstream and began his march south. No one knew what he had in mind. Even the Parliament to whose rescue he was supposedly marching was deeply apprehensive, in spite of his irreproachable professions.

Charles II and Hyde were overwhelmed with contradictory reports from their supporters in England. 'I believe,' wrote Hyde to Sir Henry Bennett in Spain, 'if you did at this instant receive twenty letters from London . . . you would receive so many several opinions of the state of affairs there, according to the constitution of the persons who write, and it was never harder for me to make a judgement of the state there than now.' His colleague Ormonde writing on the same day to Jermyn in Paris analyses and forecasts with a percipience that perhaps owes something to his having been in London so recently. He divines that Monck means more than simple loyalty to the Rump, but that what that more amounts to may be contingent on events: 'But what his further intentions are, or for whom, I will not so much as guess, supposing it possible that they are but conditionally formed by himself, to be pursued, or laid aside, as he shall find his power capable of accomplishing them upon the place.' He sees no evidence to justify optimism on the surface of events but admits the hope of 'a general inclination towards the King, grounded on as general a despair of a settlement without him'. It is on what underlies what is happening that he bases his confidence:

> Though the submission to the parliament seems universal and hearty in all those that have any military or civil authority in the three kingdoms; and though I conceive the appearance of its being so, and the drawing of the Army towards London, reason enough to stop the King if he were ready to embark with a force that a month since in the judgment of all men would have done his work; yet you may take it for a certain truth, that many of those who pretended to secure places for the parliament, and possessed themselves accordingly of them, did it with a purpose of making use of them in the end to the King's advantage, if the contest had been kept up a little longer. Of this we have good evidence, besides the known inclination of many of the persons that acted.

The oaths and abjurations by which the Rump set such store are also in his view unreliable indications of loyalty 'since all in any sort of power there have long learned and often practised the absolving themselves in such cases'. Critical and cautious in considering the evidence open to him Ormonde is clear and confident in his conclusions. As a forecast of how matters were likely to develop it turned out astonishingly accurate. That it was made when so many well-informed people were beginning to despair of the King's prospects is the higher tribute.

Charles II was well served by the judgment of these steadfast servants of his father. The defects of his own qualities enabled him to make the better use of theirs. Suddenly the divisions of those who had been his enemies produced a pattern of forces that made his restoration so effortless as to seem inevitable. Not a shot was fired: no foreign soldier set foot on English soil. After long years the inertia of the son regained what the father's instability had seemed to render irretrievable. Hyde's long-term strategy, Ormonde's tactical analysis had both been allowed to prove themselves right. 'He that cannot say no and he that cannot sit still is not fit for business.' Judged by this maxim of one of his most capable ministers, Sir William Coventry, Charles II must be commended on the second count as much as he is open to censure on the first.

The moment of transition has been caught and fixed by the most universally observant witness in our history, Samuel Pepys. One day in early February Monck marched into the City on the Parliament's orders to destroy the gates and chains that were the outward expression of its independence of Westminster and Whitehall. Two days later he marched back there again on his own initiative and sent the Speaker a letter demanding fresh elections. The Rump's day was done. Everyone knew that a free Parliament would bring in the King. Why Monck changed his allegiance at this point and not earlier, whether indeed he did change it or had been secretly aiming at a Restoration from the first, will always be open to question. It is clear that even so well-informed and close-range a student of affairs as Pepys did not at first realise the direction and speed in which they were moving. He had seen that, in the twinkling of an eye, everything had been transformed: '. . . and it was very strange how the countenance of men in the Hall was all changed with joy in half an hour's time'. But at his first confidential discussion with his cousin and patron Edward Mountagu a good three weeks later, a Stuart Restoration was rated no more than the most likely of three possibilities, the other two being a return to Richard Cromwell's Protectorate or the usurpation by Monck of complete political power. Mountagu told Pepys that he did not believe Richard would last long if he were brought in again 'no, nor the King neither (though he seems to think that he will come in), unless he carry himself very soberly and well'.

This the King showed every sign of doing. He met every approach and every visitor in an affable and conciliatory spirit. He made no awkward stipulations. He pressed for no reprisals. Everything was to be settled with a free Parliament and the only pardon he would refuse would be to those who signed his father's death-warrant. And even here he was flexible and evidently much more inclined to mercy than were most of his supporters. 'The King seems to be a very sober man.' Pepy's first impression of his future employer recorded in his Diary entry for May 17th 1660 is but one instance of many. Except in the strict sense of not being addicted to the national vice of drunkenness—and in this context the word hardly bears that sense—the epithet is not perhaps the first that would have occurred to those who had shared his exile. Yet given the change in his circumstances it is consistent with his character. His activities in Scotland and his subsequent adventures in England in the years 1650-1 had revealed his natural powers as an actor. Without a part an actor cannot realise himself. Charles was now embarking on the rôle of a monarch ruling by law and precedent, not by arbitrary power or military force, that Hyde had written for him and for his father. The disreputable young man who had obtained credit under false pretences was another part in a different play. There might be some elements in common, there might be a style of interpretation that the regular playgoer could recognise. Prince Hal and Henry V in Shakespeare's recreation are not mutually incompatible. Indeed the parts were presumably written to be performed by the same actor.

The triumphant reception of Hyde's masterpiece astonished even its principals. Charles II's remark that he must have only himself to blame for having been so long abroad when everyone was so anxious to have him at home is more than an admirable witticism. Twenty years of civil war and barren experiment in constitution-building overlay the memory of Charles I's personal rule—an incomparably inferior performance to Cromwell's. To find the old traditions, the sure, known ways, embodied in a graceful and agreeable young man was as intoxicating as the conduits that ran with wine when the King re-entered London. In suddenness and violence of emotion the Restoration was like a runaway marriage. But in spite of appearances it was not Charles II's person so much as the marriage settlement that really inspired these transports. That, surely, was what he was saying with his delicate mockery.

10

The Restored King and his Old Servants

———◆———

After the celebrations were over there was time for second thoughts. Had the surviving leaders of the old Parliamentary and Cromwellian parties given too much? Had the King asked too little? Had Hyde succeeded in fixing the powers of the monarchy at the exact point that he and his friends desired, namely in the constitutional position of 1641 with the prerogative courts, Star Chamber and High Commission, trodden underfoot or had they miscalculated? If so, was Charles II in reality stronger or weaker than his father had been at his accession? Where did he and his subjects stand in the bitterly contested matter of Church government and religious uniformity? Would the grants of public revenue that had been made to him for life render him less dependent on Parliamentary taxation than his predecessors had been? Answers to these questions differed widely at the time as they have differed since. Whether such questions are answerable except in the development of subsequent events is itself debatable. But what concerns us here is what Charles II thought about such matters and how the conclusions that he drew affected his character and conduct, including in that term his establishment of a public style and personality.

The wild enthusiasm with which he had been received made him for the first time know himself a power in his own right. It was not

Hyde or the bishops who were greeted with such fervour. On the contrary the raptures of the populace were easily restrained when these venerable survivors were paraded before them. It was certainly not his mother, who did not even visit England until several months after her son had been restored; it was not Prince Rupert, the personification of Stuart glamour and good looks, the Cavalier *par excellence*, who, like his aunt, was a late arrival at the Restoration Court. Charles II had had to wait long for a favourable wind, but when it blew he found himself the master of the vessel.

Such a transformation must work on even the deepest and most disciplined character. What is surprising is the restraint shewn by a man who was neither. Perhaps the coolness of his head helped him to avoid its being turned too easily. His treatment of the men immediately responsible for his change of fortune, Monck, Mountagu and the rest, was everything that they could wish. He deferred to them, he consulted them, he showered them with honours and rewards. But in doing so he did not abandon his old friends, Ormonde, Southampton and Hyde. Hyde's faithful service and wise counsel were rewarded by lands and titles (he was raised in the Coronation Honours to the earldom of Clarendon by which name he has stamped his personality on the history of England) and, much more importantly, by being entrusted with the Great Seal. He was not Prime Minister, a title and a concept that were hateful to him as violating the old mysterious harmonies of government, but he was the nearest thing to it that his ideas would allow. He held the principal political and legal office under the King as head of the Executive and presided over the Upper House of Parliament as the responsible minister of the King's government. He was thus, as he had been in exile, the target for the virulent jealousy of courtiers whose reason for existence was the obtaining of office, influence, patronage and place. He was the target of the unpopularity and resentment incident to government by its very nature. He was fat, gouty, short-tempered, sharp-tongued, fearless, honest, brilliant, dictatorial and self-satisfied. He had been the King's most successful, most trusted counsellor for sixteen years (except for two early and disastrous interruptions). When their relationship had begun Charles II had been fourteen, Clarendon in his middle thirties. It was scarcely to be expected that it could escape some violent strain.

The most obvious cause of tension lay in the Chancellor's overbearing manners. His loyal friend and colleague Sir Edward Nicholas had complained of these during their days of disappointment and affliction. Now that every prophecy had been fulfilled, every hope transcended, humility was not to be looked for. The Council notes that passed between the King and his ministers, preserved in the Clarendon MSS in the Bodleian, show a tiresomely schoolmasterish tone in the older man sometimes provoking the younger to a mild obstructiveness. Charles II rarely showed his feelings in public but there is ample testimony to his delight in the malice and mockery of which Clarendon was the frequent object in more intimate surroundings. The King's first and most dominant mistress, Lady Castlemaine (the first, that is, of the post-Restoration series) was his bitter enemy and the young courtiers whose company Clarendon thought unfit for his master, Buckingham, the Berkeleys and the rest, lost no opportunity of wearing down Charles's loyalty to his old servant.

All this might in the end have broken the tie. But a far more dangerous twist was given to their mutual relation when it became known in September 1660 that Clarendon's daughter Anne had been secretly married to James, Duke of York. Every circumstance conspired to ensure disaster to the minister. The King was still unmarried so that it was perfectly possible that Anne Hyde might find herself Queen of England. The wedding had taken place at dead of night in the Chancellor's own house, though of course without his knowledge. The Queen Dowager, Henrietta Maria, loathed him above all men and seized with passion on what seemed the final exposure of his ambitious intrigues. The bride was already pregnant when the marriage took place—a matter sufficiently disgraceful in itself but made more scandalous by immediate and circumstantial claims by various courtiers to paternity.

In this nightmare Charles not only stood by his old servant but treated him with imaginative and even affectionate consideration. The evidence for this is Clarendon's own, written down years later in his second exile when experience of a very different kind must have been fresh in his consciousness. His account of the transaction is of the first importance both for the understanding of the King's character and of Clarendon's apprehension of it. Throughout he credits him with generosity and chivalry. When the Duke broke the news

the King was much troubled with it . . . His majesty was very much perplexed to resolve what to do: he knew the chancellor so well that he concluded he was not privy to it, nor would ever approve it; and yet that it might draw much prejudice upon him by the jealousy of those who were not well acquainted with his nature.

He accordingly sent for Ormonde and Southampton, Clarendon's two closest friends and political associates, to break the news at a private meeting in Whitehall to which he himself would come as soon as the worst of the shock and distress were over. He knew that Anne was the apple of her father's eye and how gross was the offence to his standards of public and private morals. Clarendon, when he heard, was thunderstruck. He would turn her out of his house as a whore. If it were true that she had made a clandestine marriage with the heir to the throne he would have her sent to the Tower and himself move for the cutting off of her head. As he raved and wept the King came in. Southampton told him that there was no point in talking to him.

> Whereupon his majesty, looking upon him with a wonderful benignity, said 'Chancellor, I knew this business would trouble you, and therefore I appointed your two friends to confer first with you upon it, before I would speak with you myself: but you must now lay aside all passion that disturbs you, and consider that this business will not do itself; that it will quickly take air; and therefore it is fit that I first resolve what to do before other men uncalled presume to give their counsel: tell me therefore what you would have me do and I will follow your advice.'

It is an affecting scene and needs to be remembered when the miserable ending of this relationship provokes disgust. Charles II had every reason to be annoyed. He had gained nothing and lost a great deal by his brother's action. An important diplomatic card had been thrown away. A vast figure had suddenly and unthinkingly been thrust into the delicate calculations of the balance of domestic politics. His mother had been infuriated. The standing of his family both at home and abroad was disparaged by such an alliance. The Hydes were not nobles. They were not even aristocrats. They were good, sound minor gentry with strong professional connexions. No wonder Henrietta Maria made offensive remarks about her daughter-in-law smelling of her father's old green bag. A daughter of France expected her children to do better for themselves than to marry into the Wiltshire squirearchy. No doubt Clarendon was only too well aware of this, no doubt he had known nothing of his daughter's intrigue and would have stopped it if he had. But from the King's point of view this did not lessen the damage that he had suffered directly through his connexion with the Chancellor and his family. It says a lot for his charity that his first concern was with the older man's feelings. He calmed him down. He stood by him against his attackers. He sustained him when the allegations of his daughter's promiscuity were so categorical that even the bridegroom wavered. When these were at last admitted to be nothing more than malicious invention the King imposed a general reconciliation on his family, his minister and the courtiers who had defamed the bride's honour. Clarendon had every reason for gratitude.

Yet this affair in the end, at least in Clarendon's opinion, was the main cause of the final breach. Another marriage, the King's, was to inflame their relations. The Restoration had put this in the forefront of politics and diplomacy. Those who like Clarendon were deeply concerned to head the King off from Catholic Frenchwomen had urged the advantages of the Protestant ruling houses of Germany, only to be met with Charles's objection that their women were 'all foggy and I cannot like any one of them for a wife'. The House of Orange was already closely allied to the Stuarts and in the early 1660s rather a liability than an asset to the strengthening of relations with the Dutch Republic. That virtually eliminated the Protestant powers. If the King were to follow his father in marrying a Catholic there was much to be said for Portugal. The kingdom itself was small and struggling to maintain the independence it had recently retrieved from Spain. Overseas it had an empire far too big for its military and commercial base. The marriage of interests with the nascent imperial power of England was obvious. Sentiment, for once, could reinforce policy. The House of Braganza had suffered severely for the help and hospitality it had shewn Prince Rupert's squadron in the winter of 1649-50. In Princess Catherine it had a candidate of marriageable age and charm of character. Negotiations had been opened even before the Restoration and; after some hard bargaining on the part of the more powerful country, were brought to a successful conclusion early in 1661.

This marriage led to the first serious trouble between Clarendon and the King. Its failure provided the minister's enemies with abundant ammunition. For failure it was all along the line; a failure in the most ordinary sense that the partners appear to have derived no pleasure or comfort from their association, a failure from the financial and imperial points of view. The huge unpaid dowry was a constant cause of governmental nagging and the colony of Tangier that was to have given England the command of the Straits swallowed a huge proportion of public expenditure before it was finally abandoned at the end of the reign.

Above all it failed in the elementary purpose of producing an heir. It was soon and repeatedly asserted that Clarendon had known that Princess Catherine was barren and had thus cleverly secured the succession of his own descendants through his son-in-law James.

Whether Charles II ultimately brought himself to believe this we can only guess. It is far from clear that Clarendon was a champion, still less the initiator, of the Portuguese alliance. According to two sources who knew Ormonde well he told them that the King's resolution was taken without his knowledge or that of Clarendon. They were simply informed of the decision and, as principal ministers, charged with its execution.[1] Clarendon, in this account, is said to have raised difficulties and counselled caution. If this is true, and if Clarendon's own record of the circumstances of his daughter's marriage be accepted, the King must have known the imputations against his Chancellor to be false. But it is easy to allow a convenient fiction, especially if repeated by congenial company about someone whom one has come to find tiresome, to acquire the status of received truth. Perhaps he did come to believe it or at least to persuade himself that he did. But the origins of his resentment against his minister can be explained much more simply. The refusal of Clarendon to countenance or Lady Castlemaine to abate her claims for public recognition of her private power over the King was bound to issue in quarrels, tantrums, scenes, unpleasantnesses that were to Charles II to be avoided at all costs. His marriage, had it been successful, might have disposed of this difficulty. In fact it intensified it.

Clarendon's detestation of Lady Castlemaine grew from his own relation to the two Kings he served. It was, like that relationship, both public and private, personal and moral, religious and political. In his autobiography he makes no attempt to disguise the reality of her power and influence but he refused her the historical recognition of naming her. Just as he had, in his capacity as Chancellor, treated her requests as beneath his notice, just as he had forbidden his wife to receive her or even to speak to her at Court, so he denies her so much as an entry in his index. She remains throughout 'the lady' though it is clear that in its modern connotation that is the last description he would have chosen for her. Her father had been his close friend and had died fighting for Charles I. Clarendon saw the manners and morals of the educated world into which he had been born as being the real object of the Restoration. Church and King were only the emblems of the ideals they embodied. What he and the King had to do was to turn back the tide of licence and set an example of order and decency. Morals, politics and religion were not, to his way of thinking, separable. God had chastened his people by the trials of civil war and had blessed them by bringing them back into the right way. 'God, who had wrought such miracles for him,' he told Charles II, 'expected some proportionable return.' In Lady Castlemaine, the daughter of his old friend, he recognised the enemy of all that he and her father had stood for.

How bitter and extreme an enemy only became plain after the arrival of Queen Catherine. The King had often parried the Chancellor's reproaches by saying that continence was hardly to be expected of a healthy man in the vigour of his youth but that marriage would put an end to such irregularities. What happened in the event was that Lady Castlemaine demanded approval of her status in the form of a place as one of the Ladies of the Queen's Bedchamber. The Queen was outraged. The King spurred by Lady Castlemaine's fury and flattered by his younger courtiers' comparing him to his famous grandfather Henri IV turned first stubborn and then bullying. Her Portuguese attendants were sent home, except for a few for whose retention she was forced to beg. She was humiliated, isolated, driven to despair. Clarendon remonstrated with his master and reminded him how he himself had censured his cousin Louis XIV for forcing his Queen to receive his mistress at Court as 'such a piece of ill-nature, that he could never be guilty of'. He went on to remind him of his saying that he would never have mistresses after he was married. His memory, indeed, was inconveniently long. He recalled telling the young King of his father's deploring *his* father's, James I's, choice of tutors and guardians, and Charles II's eager agreement that character and principle are largely formed by imitation and example of one's immediate circle. All this the King with mounting irritation admitted to be true. But as Humpty Dumpty would no doubt have divined in Clarendon's place the point was who was to be master. That both Clarendon and the much more easygoing Ormonde thought his conduct cruel and unworthy provoked a vehemence strongly suggestive of a guilty conscience:

You know how true a friend I have been to you. If you will oblige me eternally make this business as easy as you can, of what opinion soever you are of, for I am resolved to go through with this matter, let what will come on it; which again I solemnly swear before Almighty God. Therefore, if you desire to have the continuance of my friendship, meddle no more with this business, except it be to beat down all false and scandalous reports, and to facilitate what I am sure my honour is so much concerned in. And whosoever I find to be my Lady Castlemaine's enemy in this matter, I do promise upon my word to be his enemy as long as I live. You may show this letter to my Lord Lieutenant [Ormonde]; and if you both have a mind to oblige me, carry yourselves like friends to me in this matter.

The King's honour was indeed deeply concerned. He invokes it here to justify himself by his promise given to his mistress. His despicable treatment of his wife was wholly successful. She broke down completely, even fawning on Lady Castlemaine. But Clarendon's obstructiveness was neither forgotten nor forgiven. Gradually it formed a possible basis for a new interpretation of his character. No longer the wise father-figure who had guided the King back to a bloodless recovery of his inheritance he began to take shape as a mischievous, moralising old bore who had been playing his own game from the start. It was freely asserted that he had blocked a move to endow the King on his Restoration with a perpetual revenue large enough to exempt him from the necessity of Parliamentary grants. True or not, it was certainly consistent. Clarendon wanted no part in the notions of Laud and Strafford or in the centralised autocracy of Louis XIV. Charles II did not share his minister's Parliamentary enthusiasm. As Bishop Burnet recalled:

> The King said once to the earl of Essex, as he told me, that he did not wish to be like a Grand Signior, with some mutes about him, and bags of bowstrings to strangle men as he has a mind to it: but he did not think he was a King, as long as a company of fellows were looking into all his actions, and examining his ministers as well as his accounts. [2]

This outburst is most likely to have been provoked by events in the later part of the reign but there is no reason to doubt that it expressed the King's settled opinion. The contempt and dislike with which his father and mother habitually spoke of the institution must have been

more vivid and comprehensible than the traditionalism of his minister. It was Clarendon's argument through his years of office that if the
King would but apply himself to his business as he did to his pleasures
he would find his Parliament responsive. Either way the issue was a
cause of friction, which could easily be represented as the skilful
manipulation of the older hand to promote his own policies and
frustrate the desires of his master. Much more plausibly it could be
argued that the Parliamentary settlement of religion by the Act of
Uniformity, and its reinforcement by the harsh laws against dissent
collectively known as the Clarendon Code, constituted a conscious
defiance of the King's known preference for toleration. The Archbishop rather than the Chancellor was certainly the moving spirit, but
was not the Archbishop one of the Chancellor's old friends, a fellow-
member of that circle cherished in his memory that had frequented
Lord Falkland's house at Great Tew?

Clarendon's enemies and rivals made sure that none of this was lost
on the King. For his part the minister grew more and more
exasperated by the King's refusal to take his duties seriously and by
the slipperiness and evasion, the inevitable result of his indiscriminate
indulgence to cadgers, that confused administration and policy. The
mismanagement of the Dutch War, culminating in the disaster of the
Medway, when the English flagship was towed out of the fleet base by
the jeering enemy, shook the government out of its foundations and
brought Parliament baying for blood. Popular opinion fixed on
Clarendon and the King accepted the chance with alacrity. Both men
had opposed the war policy and Clarendon could hardly be saddled
with responsibility for its misconduct but his eminence and his
magnificent style of life made him the obvious target. Probably the
King could not have saved him had he wished to. Clarendon, serene in
consciousness of virtue and in confidence of his knowledge of the
constitution, dismissed any notion of danger. The 'formidable power
of the Parliament', he told the King, 'was more or less or nothing as he
chose to make it: that it was yet in his own power to govern them; but
if they found it was in theirs to govern him, nobody knew what the end
would be.' Warming to his theme he instanced the misfortunes of
Richard II, which gave him an opportunity to remind the King yet
again of the disrespect to which his relations with Lady Castlemaine
exposed him. After two hours of this 'the King rose without saying
anything but appeared not well pleased with all that had been said'. It
was the end of their long association.

The scene that followed is described by Clarendon with his characteristic restraint:

> The garden [at Whitehall], that used to be private, had now many in it to observe the countenance of the King when he came out of the room: and when the chancellor returned, the lady, the Lord Arlington and Mr May, looked together out of her open window with great gaiety and triumph, which all people observed.

So it appeared to the principal actor. But Pepys, though not himself an eye-witness has caught the scene imperishably from one who was:

> This day Mr Pierce the surgeon was with me; and tells me how this business of my Lord Chancellors was certainly designed in my Lady Castlemaine's chamber, and that when he went from the King on Monday morning, she was in bed (though about 12 a-clock) and ran out in her smock into her Aviary looking into White-hall-garden, and thither her woman brought her her nightgown, and stood joying herself at the old man's going away.

Charles II had put up with a great deal from Clarendon. He had sustained him under constant and powerful attack during all their long connexion. But as Charles had said himself at the beginning of his last audience 'he did believe that never King had a better servant'. If the old man had become personally intolerable in the freedom he allowed himself and politically a liability through his obstinate attachment to the ideas and methods of a bygone age it was a vile thing to humiliate him at the end of such a career of service in front of such odious parasites. It was the more cruel to a man suffering the shock of bereavement. The happy marriage of more than thirty years had recently ended by sudden death. Whatever the power of Lady Castlemaine's sexuality, whatever the beauties of her person, she was a deeply repulsive character, coarse, vindictive, greedy and querulous. The letter she wrote to the King in 1678 when she discovered that her then lover was also having an affair with her daughter is one of the nastiest in the language.

But beneath the long-smouldering resentment over Lady Castlemaine lay a fiercer fire. Frances Stuart, la belle Stuart, the court beauty to end all court beauties, roused a more violent desire in Charles II than any of her rivals or successors. Her personal attractions cut a wide swathe. Louis XIV made strenuous efforts to keep her in France, where she had been brought up, as a member of his Court. Pepys, an enthusiastic amateur of such matters, was provoked to transports of cerebral lust. Courtiers and artists besieged her with declarations of passion. Perfection of face and figure enhanced by a Parisian flair for dress and style were combined with apparently innocent emptiness of head. Within a few months of her arrival in England the King was besotted with her. When the Queen was thought to be dying it was widely reported that la belle Stuart would succeed her. In spite of her ingenuousness and frivolity she shewed great determination in refusing to allow the King to make her his mistress. The Queen recovered but la belle Stuart stood firm. Exasperated and inflamed the King began to investigate, as a last resort, the possibility of divorce. Early in 1667 his cousin the Duke of Richmond lost his wife and within a fortnight proposed himself as Frances Stuart's suitor. The King, playing for time, ordered Clarendon to investigate and report on the Duke's personal estate, ostensibly so that a suitable marriage settlement could be arranged but really, so it was thought, to put himself in a position to obstruct the affair while secretly inquiring into his chances of ending his own marriage. But the Duke persuaded Frances Stuart into an immediate and private wedding. The King's fury when he heard about it was uncontrollable. In his rage he accused Clarendon, not to his face, of having advised the lady to close with so advantageous an offer for his own ulterior purpose of securing the throne for his grandchildren. The idea was of course eagerly suggested by the fallen Chancellor's old enemies. Anne Hyde's marriage had brought down her father at last.

The King had not received him since the interview so abruptly ended and so callously staged. In a final letter, pathetic in its context but not at all abject in its tone, the ex-minister protested his entire innocence of any concern in the Richmond marriage and his readiness to go once again into exile. He does however ask that he may be told in what he has offended:

I should die in peace (and truly I do heartily wish that God Almighty would free you from further trouble, by taking me to himself) if I could know or guess at the grounds of your displeasure, which I am sure must proceed from your believing that I have said or done somewhat I have neither said [nor] done.

Charles read the letter through and then burned it in a candle that was on the table. He made no reply beyond saying that there was something in it he did not understand and that he wondered why the Chancellor did not withdraw himself.

This Clarendon promptly did, leaving behind the noble collection of portraits, documents and books from which the history of the great events he had played such a part in was to have been written. Nothing was done by his former employer to ease the harshness of his exile. On the contrary he was subjected to the annoyances and frustrations that governments know so well how to inflict. Old, ill and lonely he was harried by the French authorities and on one occasion at least beaten up by a party of English seamen. It would have cost Charles II no trouble to see that his greatest servant was properly treated in exile. The Stuarts are commonly charged with ingratitude. The King's conduct here deserves a harsher description.

For a time it seemed that Ormonde's known friendship for Clarendon and the support that he had lent him over the business of the Queen would expose him to the same vindictiveness. The King raised no objection to the project of impeaching him but at the last moment chose instead to dismiss him from his Lord Lieutenancy. Changing his tune, he even 'declared how well satisfied he was with the duke of Ormond's thirty years service to his father and himself; that the change he now made was not out of distrust or displeasure'.[3]

There are many points of similarity, indeed in some respects of sympathy, between the King and Ormonde. Both were regarded as patterns of courtesy and good breeding. Both took great care of their health and attached great importance to regular exercise. At an advanced age Ormonde still began his day by going out riding for two or three hours. The King's strenuousness both as a horseman and as a walker was often contrasted with his laziness as a monarch. Both paid scrupulous attention to formality in dress:

The Duke of Ormond always wore his hat (as the King did) just as it came from the block, stiff, without a button and uncocked; and imitated him constantly in his habit as well as behaviour. His dress was plain, but very elegant and neat: nobody wore his clothes better, but he still suited them to the weather. For this end, in our uncertain clime, he had ten different sorts of waistcoats and drawers, satin, silk, plain and quilted, cloth, etc. His first question in the morning was, which way the wind sat; and he called for his waistcoat and drawers accordingly. No severity of weather or condition of health served him for a reason for not observing that decorum of dress which he thought a point of respect to persons and places. In winter-time people were allowed to come to Court with double-breasted coats, a sort of undress. The Duke would never take advantage of that indulgence; but let it be never so cold, he always came in his proper habit; and indeed the King himself, the best judge of manners of his time, always did the same, though too many neglected his example to make use of the liberty he was pleased to allow.

The cheerfulness of his temper, the liveliness of his conversation, the ready flow and pleasant turn of his wit, and the care he always took to adapt himself to the King's manner and humour, rendered him very agreeable to that prince who ever loved him.[4]

Thus his biographer, summing up at the close of four fat volumes. Perhaps the approaching end of so vast a labour has relaxed his usual severity of judgment. The concluding clause is difficult to reconcile with much that has gone before. Charles II liked people to be easy and Ormonde both by temperament and manners was one of the easiest men of his time. He liked men of the world and Ormonde was certainly that. But to say that he 'ever loved him' is to credit him with a steadiness of affection of which by middle life he was hardly capable. His treatment of this loyal and distinguished servant was capricious and ungrateful. No doubt he liked him as one likes a good fire or a comfortable chair, but if he thought about him at all it was simply to wonder for a moment why he put up with the treatment he received:

'Yonder comes Ormond; I have done all I can to disoblige that man, and to make him as discontented as others; but he will not be out of humour with me; he will be loyal in spite of my teeth; I must even take him in again, and he is the fittest person to govern Ireland.'

The King's words to those standing near him when, in 1677, he decided to make him Lord Lieutenant for the third time, have the ring of truth. He had had Ormonde to supper the night before after not so much as speaking to him during his regular attendance at Court for the whole of the preceding year. Most damning of all was his pardoning of the well-named Colonel Blood who had confessed, besides other violent crimes, to being the ringleader in an attempt to murder Ormonde by dragging him out of his coach one night as he came up St James's and stringing him up at Tyburn. Only Ormonde's fitness and horsemanship had saved him. He got his foot under the boot of the man to whom he had been tied and tipped him out of the saddle. Help arrived while they were struggling on the ground.

Ormonde was sixty at the time and very lucky to survive. It was outrageous that the author of such an attempt on one who had done the Crown such service should not only go unpunished but actually receive the King's favour. Clearly some scandalous figure with the power and the will to dominate Charles was lurking in the background. Lady Castlemaine, now promoted Duchess of Cleveland, and the Duke of Buckingham, 'that vile man' as Ormonde justly called him, were the favourites of contemporary opinion. Ormonde himself made no protest or remonstration. When the King sent one of his ministers to explain his reasons Ormonde replied that the King's pleasure was reason enough for him and he required no others. But Ormonde's son, Ossory, took a less respectful view. Coming to Court one day he found Buckingham standing by the King. There was no shorthand writer present but one of the Royal chaplains who was there recalled the gist of his words as follows:

> My lord, I know well that you are at the bottom of this late attempt of Blood's upon my father; and therefore I give you fair warning; if my father comes to a violent end by sword or pistol, if he dies by the hand of a ruffian, or by the more secret way of poison, I shall not be at a loss to know the first author of it; I shall consider you as the assassin; I shall treat you as such; and wherever I meet you I shall pistol you, though you stood behind the King's chair; and I tell it you in his majesty's presence, that you may be sure I shall keep my word.

Buckingham's cowardice was well known. In the preceding two years he had engineered a duel with a man whose physical disabilities offered him a contemptible victory and had evaded a challenge from a more formidable figure by betraying it to the King. The public humiliation to which Ossory's words exposed him was great, but the disgrace to the King implied by the manner, timing and matter of the speech was the more cutting. His connivance was assumed and his authority scorned. Charles I had once faced open defiance in his own Court at Newark in the closing year of the First Civil War. Sir Richard Willys, the same man who was later to betray the plots of the Royalist underground to Cromwell's secret service, egged on by Prince Rupert, had burst in on him at dinner with a refusal to accept his supersession as Governor of the town. Unable to speak for anger the King had refused to listen and rose at once from the table. Such a reaction was not possible to his son because it could only spring from sincerity, from a simple, unquestioning belief in the honesty of a man's motives and conduct. This the father for all his deviousness never for an instant lacked. It was this that had carried him through the unforgettable scenes of the trial and execution. It was this that in the memory of his old servants who linked the two reigns, Clarendon, Ormonde, Sir Philip Warwick, gave beauty to a character in many ways so stunted and inept. The son had all the advantages the father lacked. He was easy, self-confident, affable and witty. His great height and his splendid bearing were made to express kingship. The physical and intellectual equipment was superb. The comparison with Ormonde is as revealing as that with Charles I. It was only the spirit that was wanting.

I I

Good King Charles's Golden Days

———◆———

There are few clean breaks in history. When Clarendon fell his old friends such as Ormonde and his more recent supporters such as Sandwich, Pepys's original patron, passed into eclipse. But in political terms they lived to fight another day. Sandwich was appointed Admiral of the Blue in the Third Dutch War that broke out in 1672. Ormonde, as we have seen, was reappointed to the Lord Lieutenancy of Ireland in 1677, to display once again his steadiness of temper and integrity of judgment in the dangers and hysteria of the Popish plot. When he was at last dismissed in the closing weeks of the reign, once again ungraciously, it was to make way for one of Clarendon's sons, who had survived their father's disgrace. Thus the men and the traditions that Charles II had inherited from his father could be said to have stayed the course of his reign even if they were not always up with the leaders in the race.

Yet Charles's dismissal of Clarendon, the tone and the manner of it, the cold denial of so much as a private reconciling word or the inconspicuous relaxation of the harsh terms imposed by a soon forgotten popular clamour, marks a turning point in the way in which the King saw himself and in which he was seen. When Bab May clasped his knees and congratulated him on at last emancipating himself from his leading strings, he no doubt divined with the flair of the successful sycophant exactly what his master wanted to hear. Self-examination was not Charles II's preferred method of forming his opinion of himself. He aspired to be a man of the world, a man of fashion: and where would such a figure be without a looking-glass? What he saw reflected helped to shape what there was to reflect. The presenting of a surface to the world, always next to his pleasures his chief preoccupation, became, it seems, his only serious concern. At the same time the points of view from which it is possible to see him also change. The anxious clucking of the hen looking after her chickens, that note so often to be caught in the exchanges of the older generation that survived from the Court of Charles I, gives way to the more detached, more amused, perhaps more cynical observation of Charles II's own contemporaries. Pepys and Evelyn, Halifax and Burnet, Sheffield, Duke of Buckingham, Sir William Temple, Roger North, Dryden, Marvell, Rochester, differ from each other (or some of them do) in their estimate of the King but resemble each other in their approach. Partly this is the natural change of idiom from one generation to another, partly the mere fact of contemporaneity. Those who belonged to the same generation as Winston Churchill for example saw him in a different way from the battle-worn chieftains of the Liberal and the Tory parties in the first decade of this century or from those whose political consciousness dates only from the Second World War. In every man's life necessarily there is a time when most of the observations of him will be made from above, then from alongside and lastly from below. But what especially distinguishes the view of the younger men from that of their seniors is the degree to which it reflects the King's own style. Those who attack, attack with his own weapons of wit, levity, scepticism, risqué jokes and downright coarseness. Those who defend, defend with an injured rationality or an amused tolerance. The magic and the mystery with which monarchy had from early times surrounded itself and to which Charles I had so powerfully contributed could not survive the solid fact of Charles II. 'I do perceive the King is a man like other men.' Pepys's simple recognition sums up as so often the perception of his age.

In every age some people had discerned the equality of men before the facts of existence. 'If you prick us, do we not bleed?' But as in the priesthood a man had not been held to lose the element of common humanity by assuming functions and powers that go beyond it, so a King had been to men like Clarendon, a man certainly but a special kind of man. Such an instance may suggest that the appearance of transcending the ordinary and the commonplace is part of the distinction. No doubt priest or King cut a more convincing figure if such an impression is conveyed as it manifestly was by Charles I. Incompetence to the business of kingship is not fatal to the illusion. Sauntering is. The *vieux boulevardier* may command affection, gratitude and loyalty as Edward VII certainly did but he can hardly command reverence. 'There's a divinity doth hedge a King' asserts no claim that his subjects will find him sympathetic. Rather by stressing his apartness it implies the reverse.

In the end Charles's seeming openness came to be regarded by his contemporaries as itself a more subtle device for distancing people from what he really thought or intended than the stiff formality with which Charles I stares down opposition or even inquiry in the great Van Dyck portraits. Deception was his method. Louis XIV, the leaders of the Dutch Republic, his nephew William III, all had good reason to know that he was totally untrustworthy. His relationship with foreign powers had at least the merit of predictability. With his English ministers the element of caprice made rational assessment of his probable behaviour much more difficult. He was capable of loyalty to a faithful servant under fierce attack when loyalty required courage. But he might go as far or further to protect a crony or a favourite from the consequences of incompetence or even crime. He could promote merit, as at the very end of his reign he did with Pepys, creating a new post for him that gave full scope to his genius as a naval administrator and paying him the rate for the job. He could reward past service as he did to Pepys's old colleague, Sir William Penn, whose son had disabled himself for honours or public office by turning Quaker. The peerage that the King was anxious to confer on the dying veteran of the first two Dutch wars was converted into a hereditary grant of the American colony of Sylvania to which the family name was to be prefixed in perpetuity. He could keep his word to a man who had beggared himself for the Stuarts as we have seen in the case of Sir George Carteret.

On the other hand his prodigality towards mistresses, bastards and boon companions dwarfed the recognition accorded to honest service. Many cavaliers who had sacrificed their estates for the Royalist cause were embittered by the callous dismissal of their petitions for relief. So far as can be seen Charles II did not allow principle much weight in the regular conduct of life. It was not that he did not appreciate, perhaps even admire, its application by other people or see that such a perception was relevant to himself. His relations with Duppa, Earle and Ken are instances already cited to the contrary. Bishop Burnet provides others, both entertaining and convincing, from his own first hand experience. When he first met him in 1673 the King was sufficiently taken with him to make him a Royal Chaplain and to grant him 'a long private audience, that lasted about an hour, in which I took all the freedoms with him that I thought became my profession'. Readers of the *History of My Own Time* will know that Burnet's view of his pastoral obligations was not inhibited by shyness or by tact. 'I went through some other things, with relation to his course of life, and entered into many particulars with much freedom. He bore it all very well; and thanked me for it.' Five years later when the flames of the Popish plot, raging out of all control, seemed to be being fanned towards the Queen, Burnet was summoned to another tête-à-tête, this time conducted to the royal presence by Will Chiffinch, the page of the back stairs.

> The King spoke much to me concerning Oates's accusing the queen, with the whole progress of it. He said she was a weak woman and had some disagreeable humours; but was not capable of a wicked thing; and considering his faultiness towards her in other things, he thought it a horrid thing to abandon her. He said he looked on falsehood and cruelty as the greatest of crimes in the sight of God. He knew he had led a bad life, of which he spoke with some sense, but he was breaking himself of all his faults, and he would never do a base and a wicked thing.

Three years later Burnet was attending the death-bed of a woman who had been one of the King's mistresses.

> I saw her often for some weeks, and among other things I desired her to write a letter to the King, expressing the sense she had of her past life: and at her desire I drew such a letter as might be fit for her to write: but she never had strength enough to write it. So upon that I resolved to write a very plain letter to the King. I set before him his past ill life, and the effects it had had on the nation, with the judgments of God that lay on him: and that was but a small part of the punishment that he might look for. I pressed him upon that earnestly to change the whole course of his life. I carried this letter to Chiffinch on the twenty-ninth of January; and told the King in the letter, that I hoped the reflections on what had befallen his

father on the thirtieth of January, might move him to consider these things more carefully.

This allusion to his father's execution set in the context of his own disreputable course of life might have been expected to offend a much milder character than Charles II. He was understandably infuriated and made his displeasure known. Burnet was therefore by no means his usual confident self when he was next taken to see the King some ten months later by Halifax. The tables had been turned with a vengeance since the occasion of his last interview when even the Queen was thought to be in danger. The plot had burned itself out and the King had moved over to a ferocious counter-offensive. The Earl of Shaftesbury, whom Charles had from the beginning identified—wrongly in Burnet's view—as the real author of the plot, was in the Tower awaiting trial. Burnet was very much in the confidence of the other Whig leaders and Charles, anxious to tap so valuable a source, exerted all his powers of pleasing. He roundly accused Shaftesbury of the improper judicial practices with which he himself had been charged and to the delight of his guest 'used upon that a Scotch proverb very pleasantly, "At doomsday we shall see whose arse is blackest."' Resisting these blandishments Burnet survived to write one of the most vigorous and unflattering characterisations of the King which will be considered in its place. His evidence here quoted of the King's moral opinions is the more convincing for coming from a man who summed up against him.

If the fall of Clarendon be taken as confirming the emancipation, in his own eyes and those of his contemporaries, of the King from the ideas and standards of an earlier generation something may be learned of what the new style was to be by considering the men who displaced him. To a great extent they had indeed already done so. The old tree was not felled by a few flashing strokes of the axe. Buckingham was so much a courtier and a member of the King's most intimate circle, a boyhood friend and the son of Charles I's great favourite, that his relationship and influence reached back to the earlier part of the King's life and have therefore been discussed there. Ashley, later Earl of Shaftesbury, was much more politician than courtier, owed least of all to the King's favour and ultimately became, as we have seen, by far his most formidable adversary in the culmination of the Popish plot, the great duel to exclude James, Duke of York, from the succession. A power in his own right, a Cromwellian

Royalist, the type that had underpinned the Restoration, he was to inaugurate the organisation of party and thus to point the way to a transformation of Parliamentary functions. Such a man had ideas beyond supplanting Clarendon as the King's Chief Minister. The two men who had already risen high in the Government and who perhaps saw themselves as great servants of the Crown in the old tradition adapted to the requirements of a new age were Arlington and Sir William Coventry.

Both, unlike Shaftesbury or Sandwich or the now ailing Monck, were True Blue Royalists, untarnished by any Parliamentary or Cromwellian connexion. Both indeed had fought in the Civil War, a fact that Arlington was thought to exaggerate in the conspicuous patch he wore on his nose which had been slightly scarred in a minor skirmish. As Sir Henry Bennet he had been a member of Charles II's Court in exile and had latterly represented him as his agent in Madrid. Of all Charles II's intimate circle he was much the most cultivated, as Evelyn, the best qualified judge, makes plain: 'he never plays, but reades much, having both the Latine, French & Spanish tongues in perfection: has traveled much, & is absolutely the best bred & Courtly person his Majestie has about him.'[1] His manners and his intelligence had carried him far. But for the accident of the Civil War he had been destined for the parsonage of Harlington (of which his title was a mis-spelling). His fastidiousness as a scholar and connoisseur did not extend to morals and politics. He was as ready to assist at his master's pleasures as Clarendon had been to disapprove them. He was not to be inhibited in policy or manoeuvre by any intrusion of conscience. He was, in short, as easy and as much a man of the world as the King could wish. The marriage of his only daughter, at the age of five, to the Duke of Grafton, one of the King's sons by Lady Castlemaine, set the seal on his position. The ambition that had driven him was not altogether satisfied: he confided to a friend that he thought Ormonde took too little notice of his elevation. 'That lord', said Ormonde, 'expects to be treated as if he had been born with a blue ribbon, and forgets Harry Bennet that was but a very little gentleman.'[2]

Clarendon, so similar in his origins, a clever, University-bred scion of a minor gentry family with legal connexions, was his opposite in everything else. It was not to his new earldom but to his high and ancient office that he had expected deference. Indeed much as he disapproved of Arlington it was his other junior colleague Sir William

Coventry who aroused his anger precisely because at Council meetings he showed so little respect to the great officers of state. Coventry came from a much less obscure background. His father had been Charles I's Lord Keeper so that the world of the Court and the aristocracy had been familiar to him in childhood. Although of impeccably Royalist antecedents he had lived peacefully in England under the Commonwealth and Protectorate so that the eyes with which he saw politics and society were very different from Clarendon's, misted as they were with the vision of things gone beyond recall. There was not only a generation but a revolution and an exile between them. In any case their cast of mind was wholly different, Clarendon's religious, philosophical and conservative, Coventry's quick, executive and radical. Pepys, who knew the older man slightly and the younger intimately, admired them both. But there is no question which of the two he would have picked for a colleague in the transaction of business. The golden opinions of Coventry that stud the *Diary* are the more striking because the two men were in fact colleagues and Coventry was the senior. Pepys, an egotist of awe-inspiring proportions and an administrator of genius, cannot have been a critic that those privileged to work with him would have willingly chosen. Lord Brouncker, the first President of the Royal Society, Sir William Penn, the victorious admiral of the two Dutch wars, Sir William Batten, perhaps the most experienced sea-officer of his day, all these highly distinguished figures are by turns pitied, despised or simply abused by their exacting colleague at the Navy Board. But Coventry is 'the best Minister of State the King hath'. 'The ability and integrity of Sir W. Coventry in all the King's concernments I do and must admire.'

Clarendon, of course, thought differently. It was not only Coventry's irreverence in contradicting and interrupting the grave senators of the Privy Council. It was not only his irritating conceit of himself. He had proved himself incompetent and corrupt in his administration of the Navy and had lowered the efficiency of the service by promoting ex-Cromwellian officers in preference to much more experienced Royalists. How and where these Royalists had obtained these useful qualifications Clarendon does not pause to explain. Pepys from first to last laments the scarcity and poor quality of Royalist captains. But he laments even more the incompetent and unprofessional officers foisted on the service by the favour of the King and the Duke of York. The Cromwellians were promoted by both

Pepys and Coventry because the size and quality of the officer corps inherited at the Restoration were assets it would have been mad to throw away. Early in the reign Coventry did indeed have qualms about the political danger of having so few senior officers with a past record of commitment to the Stuarts. But in all the crises of the régime there was no failure of loyalty on the part of the sea-officers. Even when James II was overthrown in 1688 it was the Army, commanded by a general of Royalist antecedents and connected to the Stuarts by strong family ties, which deserted to the other side.

Coventry was not only a naval administrator whom Pepys delighted to praise. He was a Parliamentary orator and debater of the first quality acknowledged as such by Andrew Marvell with whom he did not often see eye to eye. Witty, astringent, never uncertain of his own opinion or at a loss for words in which to express it, convivial and combative he had everything that the aging Clarendon lacked as a pilot of government policy through the treacherous waters of Restoration politics. Yet within two years of the old man's dismissal the young one had been expelled from the Council and sent to the Tower. Arlington and Buckingham, bitter rivals though they were, joined forces to eliminate a potential leader. The King was easily brought to agree. Coventry was not a sycophant or a trifler.

> He tells me that he doth foresee very great wants and great disorders by reason thereof—insomuch as he is represented to the King by his enemies as a melancholy man, and one that is still prophesying ill events, so as the King called him *Visionaire* . . . whereas, others that would please the King do make him believe that all is safe.

Pepys shared his friend's pessimism, so amply justified by the subsequent course of events. Like Coventry, he had seen at first hand the frivolity and recklessness of Charles II's attitude towards his responsibilities. 'The serving a Prince that minds not his business is most unhappy for them that serve him well.'

It was the more exasperating because of the King's evident capacity. He could be tireless in his attendance at Council, masterly in his command of business, exemplary in disentangling what mattered from what did not. He was a shrewd judge of men. Pepys never had cause to complain that the King undervalued his abilities. Alone of his Council the King saw through Titus Oates from the start. It is scarcely conceivable that a man of such high intelligence did not see what a servant he had in Coventry. The only hypothesis that seems to offer a consistent explanation of his conduct is that he simply did not care. He would, as Coventry himself saw, rather be amused and pleased. Pepys was as fond of being amused and pleased as any man but even he could not understand Charles II's mentality. Reflecting on his behaviour in the leisure of retirement he wrote:

> No King ever did so unaccountable a thing to oblige his people by, as to dissolve a commission of the Admiralty then in his own hand, who best understands the business of the sea of any prince the world ever had, and things never better done, and put it into hands which he knew were wholly ignorant thereof, sporting himself with their ignorance .

Pepys had no difficulty in sympathising with his master's laziness or lechery. He could be tart or censorious about such conduct in others but he understood it only too well. What defeated him was the disorientating lack of priority or proportion in a man occupying such a commanding position and endowed with such superior talents. Pepys did not exaggerate, at least as far as English history is concerned, in the claims he made for the King's knowledge of and interest in everything to do with the sea. He loved handling ships and sailing his own yachts. He was keenly interested in warship design. He liked visiting dockyards and bases. Except for his brother who had actually commanded the fleet in battle no occupant of the throne has been so highly qualified for the post of Lord High Admiral. Yet, as Pepys says, in 1679 he appointed a Commission to discharge this function which he knew would let everything go to rack and ruin, in particular the thirty new ships for which Parliament had been coaxed into voting, a naval building programme more ambitious than anything his father could have achieved by Ship Money. And to rack and ruin they went without the King lifting a finger. Yet five years later the same man appoints Pepys to put everything in order again. Small wonder that even that indefatigable student of human nature should confess himself baffled.

The vacuum at the core of the King's nature, if such a reading of him be right, has not only perplexed and frustrated those anxious to serve him in life and to extol him to posterity. It has also been a gift to the opposition. The obvious explanation of want of consistency, of uprightness, of candour, is villainy. In that age of plots what supposition more natural than that the King himself was the arch-plotter, aiming at an absolute monarchy secured in its power by a standing Army and sanctioned by that traditional sanctifier of everything arbitrary and tyrannical, the Roman Catholic Church? There was a great deal of evidence on the surface to support such a hypothesis. The King's Catholic sympathies were well known, even if they could not be publicly acknowledged. His troubled relations with the House of Commons, his efforts to keep some military force in being, his complicity in finding posts for Catholic officers in the Tangier garrison all pointed the same way. The case would have been clinched if the terms of the Secret Treaty of Dover had become known. By these Charles accepted a subsidy from Louis XIV in return for joining him in destroying the power of the Dutch Republic and for declaring himself a Roman Catholic and pledging his readiness to force that creed on his countrymen with the assistance of French arms. Whether Charles had any serious intention of doing anything of the kind is more than doubtful, but the fact of his assent to an expression of policy justifying the darkest suspicions of contemporaries is incontestable. The obverse of the popular image of the witty, worldly, endearingly disreputable monarch as a sinister and unscrupulous tyrant bears at least as much resemblance to the sitter as the sunnier representation on the face. What both agree on is his untrustworthiness.

This is seized on in a satirical poem, usually attributed to Marvell, published on the occasion of the King's receiving the freedom of the City in 1674. In the trade and commerce of seventeenth-century London apprenticeship was a fundamental institution. Brilliant play is made with the idea of kingship as a craft.

> He ne'er knew, not he
> How to serve or be free,
> Though he's passed through so many adventures;
> But e'er since he was bound
> ('Tis the same to be crowned)
> Has ev'ry day broke his indentures.
>
> He spends all his days
> In running to plays
> When in his shop he should be poring;
> And wastes all his nights
> In his constant delights

Of revelling, drinking and whoring.

His word nor his oath
Cannot bind him to troth
He values not credit nor history;
And though he has served now
Two 'prenticeships through
He knows not his trade nor mystery.

Flippancy brings its own revenges.

The King has been criticised by his ministers and civil servants for his frivolity, by his opponents for his leanings towards Catholicism and autocracy à la Louis XIV, and by historians in general for the low tone of public morals under his régime. But what earned him as much obloquy and resentment from contemporaries of nearly every persuasion was what historians have either grudgingly or enthusiastically approved—his efforts to establish religious toleration. Here if anywhere can be found a political principle to which he was consistent in his attachment. What he had said to Clarendon in the early days of his exile he tried on his return to put into practice. Outmanoeuvred by the Cavalier party in Parliament, determined to get some of their own back on their opponents who had turned clergymen out of their livings and forbidden the Book of Common Prayer, the King had found little support elsewhere. The Protestant Dissenters only wanted toleration for themselves and were outraged at the thought of admitting Papists to an equal liberty. Charles therefore had to rely on his own powers as sovereign and on his ingenuity in interpreting them. He hit on the expedient of suspending the penalties against dissent, a right that might plausibly be held to inhere in the Crown, partly because it was the recipient of the proceeds in the form of fines and partly because the prerogative of mercy was one of the oldest and most acceptable attributes of kingship. The Declaration of Indulgence however provoked a furore. The anti-Catholic mania was approaching its crisis. A great part of the political nation was firmly convinced that the Catholics had started the Fire of London, a conviction to which the Monument still gives expression. As the Popish plot was soon to show the political passions of the country were as violent and indecent as the behaviour of the Court favourites.

The contrast between the King and his subjects on this issue puts him in a favourable light. But when the Popish plot and the Exclusion

Crisis that followed hard on its heels had been met and mastered, thanks to the King's steadiness of nerve and adroitness in switching French support from his opponents to himself, did he show in victory the justice, the magnanimity, the mercy, that should have adorned the champion of toleration? It cannot be said that he did. The trial and execution of Russell and of Sidney were long to feature in the sacred books of Whig martyrology. Indeed after Russell's execution in Lincoln's Inn Field the crowd pressed forward to dip handkerchiefs in his blood, an echo of that never-to-be-forgotten scene outside the Banqueting House at Whitehall. The evidence brought against them did not begin to support the charge of high treason: the conduct of the trials was as disgraceful as anything done in the first flush of the Popish plot. As everyone knew the victims suffered because they were members of prominent and powerful Whig families with a personal record of hostility to the Court. Arthur Capel, Earl of Essex, another of the Opposition leaders, died in the Tower by his own hand. His character and record make it in the highest degree unlikely that he had conspired to assassinate the King and the Duke of York. He was clearly in a depressed and confused state of mind at the time of his arrest, anxious for the well-being of his family and troubled in conscience that he might have brought others into jeopardy. His melancholy was darkened by recollections of his last meeting with his father, the Royalist hero of the Second Civil War, who had been imprisoned in the Tower before his execution, in the very room, it appears, in which his son now found himself. Charles's reported remark 'My lord Essex should have tried my mercy. I owe that family a life' may, if it be authentic, suggest that he was consciously setting limits to a clearly conceived policy of vengeance.

The truth seems to be that Charles II was merciful and vindictive by the ebb and flow of his inclinations. As in so much else he did not ride to an anchor of principle, or if he did it was on a very long cable. At the beginning of his reign he certainly restrained the passions of his supporters. In the most intimate and unselfconscious records that have survived, the notes which passed at meetings of the Privy Council between the King and Clarendon, he declares that he is weary of hanging and suggests that the Regicide Bill be let sleep. There is no reason to doubt that the easiness of his temper inclined him towards letting people alone so long as they gave no trouble. Every other Stuart sovereign except his two nieces Mary and Anne has been accused by their contemporaries of enjoying cruelty. This charge seems to be one of the few that no one has brought against Charles II. On the other hand, for all his temperamental preference for clemency, he was ready to connive at cruelty and injustice when it suited him. He had promised in his Declaration from Breda that no one should be put out of his mercy except those who had had a hand in the death of his father. Sir Henry Vane was prominent among the Republicans who had done their best to prevent a Stuart Restoration. But he had also been prominent amongst the Parliamentarians and close associates of Cromwell who had refused to countenance the trial of Charles I. If any opponent of the Stuarts had a right to consider himself guaranteed by the King's specific pledge he had. Yet Charles was so annoyed by his refusal to disavow his past actions and opinions that he wrote a letter to Clarendon containing the damning words '. . . certaynly he is too dangerous a man to lett live, if we can honestly put him out of the way'. The use of 'honestly' in that context is instructive. Vane, as a result, was executed.

If the history of England under Charles II yields by the standards of the age an impression of comparative mildness, that of Scotland as David Ogg has most clearly pointed out does not. Judicial torture and ruthless persecution were common form. Charles himself did not revisit his northern kingdom but he knew very well what was going on and what he was doing when he sent his brother James there to take charge of it. An element of terror disfigures nearly all government in the seventeenth century. Even Cromwell, in general a tolerant and humane ruler, understood the uses of random ferocity. The execution of Dr Hewitt and of Sir Henry Slingsby are examples, as is the selling of Royalist prisoners into slavery in Barbados. And if Charles broke his word over Vane, Cromwell's refusal of mercy to Penruddock who had accepted quarter was equally dishonourable. Few civil governors or military commanders maintained the unblemished standards of Ormonde who not only exemplified a merciful humanity but reproved his son for taking part in the attack on the Dutch Smyrna convoy in 1672 before war had been officially declared.

Charles II as the instigator of this shameful and, as it happened, unsuccessful action certainly cannot stand comparison with his old servant, in matters of honour. But he surely justifies Evelyn's temperate praise: 'A prince of many Virtues & many great Imperfections, Debonaire, Easy of accesse, not bloudy or Cruel.' As a young man in exile he had shewn markedly little enthusiasm for the plots to assassinate Cromwell that were mooted from time to time. Hyde and

Ormonde had had no misgivings about such projects. By bringing about the death of the King Cromwell had put himself outside the laws of peace or of war. Charles no doubt agreed with them. Certainly he would not have discouraged such attempts or been backward in taking advantage of success. But he remained cool towards them. It is possible that he feared reprisal. He must have suspected that his Court had been penetrated by the Protector's agents though it is doubtful if he or any of his advisers were aware of how thoroughly this had been done. It is also possible that the idea of assassination was simply distasteful to him.

'Not bloudy or Cruel.' The judgment stands the firmer for being cast in the negative. While not himself taking pleasure in inflicting pain he seems not to have been troubled by conscience or compassion if he were responsible for the suffering of others. Easiness to himself is the surest clue to follow. No doubt he was sincere when he scribbled in Council that he was weary of hanging. Even at the end of his reign when his moods were blacker and his authority more formidable he could react in the same way. 'Pooh, pooh. Leave a hunted partridge.' His reported answer to the offer to betray Argyll, hiding in London from the torture and imprisonment that James was eager to inflict on him in Edinburgh, has the ring of truth. Perhaps he was influenced by a distant recollection of the family's civility in that dreadful period of humiliation that made the very thought of Scotland odious to him. But such magnanimity to a defeated opponent was certainly not to be counted on. The regicides who had fled abroad were pursued with a persistence that is obscured by its lack of success. The three who escaped to New England eluded all the government's efforts to arrest them, and Switzerland maintained its tradition of political asylum. But three who had escaped to Germany were lured over the Dutch border where the masterful and unscrupulous English ambassador, Sir George Downing, had prepared a trap. They were hurriedly bundled aboard an English ship and, two years after the Restoration, suffered the public vivisection prescribed for High Treason. As late as 1670 Downing's successor Sir William Temple made great efforts to secure the extradition of Cornet Joyce who had carried off Charles I from Holmby House in 1647. Temple was not the man for Downing's strong-arm methods. Although De Witt made conciliatory noises, he had to respect the legal independence of the municipal authorities. The burghers of Rotterdam showed an obstinate attachment to the rule of law. Joyce could not be arrested for opinions or even for threats. Temple tried bribing the police but Joyce was forewarned. Rotterdam had beaten Whitehall.

Charles I, by nature shy and reserved, became more open and articulate in the closing stages of his life. With his son the opposite is true. The cool wariness that had always formed so large an element in his character became more pronounced. Like an animal, he had lived most intensely in his appetites. Women and food lost none of their importance as age approached. A courtier visiting him at Windsor in the autumn of 1679 after a severe attack of fever predicted that 'the King . . . will soon recover his strength as well as his health, having exchanged water-gruels and potions for mutton and partridges, on which he feeds frequently and heartily'. His attentions to his mistresses showed no diminution. On the contrary the freedom he had always allowed himself in conversation extended to behaviour. According to Burnet '. . . his fondness to lady Portsmouth increased much, and broke out in very indecent instances . . . the King caressed and kissed her in the view of all the people; which he had never done on any occasion or to any person formerly'. He continued to spend much time in the open air, walking, fishing, riding. Watchful, voracious, ready to spring, Charles II in maturity showed a tigerishness that warned his ministers against a too easy presumption of royal support. Whether or not Clarendon had been right in thinking his nature originally generous and affectionate there is no questioning the verdict of Halifax, who served him so well in the later part of his reign:

> He lived with his Ministers as he did with his Mistresses; he used them, but he was not in love with them. He shewed his judgment in this, that he cannot properly be said ever to have had a *Favourite*, though some might look so at a distance.

This was the great lesson he had learned from his father's precept and from his disastrous failure to practise what he preached. It had been reinforced by the shifts and humiliations in which he had grown to manhood. He had learned to live without trusting and without being trusted. Nothing, except the objects of desire, was what it seemed. He was as sceptical about the transactions of the Royal Society as he was about the contents of the sermons to which he was so frequently required to listen. Only the naïve expect things and people to be genuine. The man of the world knows better.

His own court was as good an example as any. Antony Wood had the opportunity of observing its quality when it removed to Oxford in the autumn of 1665 to avoid the plague. 'They, though they were neat and gay in their apparell, yet they were very nasty and beastly, leaving at their departure their excrements in every corner, in chimneys, studies, colehouses, cellars. Rude, rough, whoremongers; vaine, empty, carelesse.' Wood was known in his own university as a crabbed recluse of preternatural acidity. But his severity is confirmed by the judgment of John Evelyn who was none of these things. He attributes these disgusting habits to the example of the King:

> He tooke delight to have a number of little spaniels follow him, & lie in his bed-Chamber, where often times he suffered the bitches to puppy and give suck, which rendered it very offensive, & indeede made the whole Court nasty and stinking.

We know from the intimate recollections of even so neat and orderly a person as Pepys that the standards of personal hygiene in the seventeenth century were not exacting. Yet even contemporaries found the court revolting. Antony Wood's description suggests to the modern reader the more lurid accounts of occupation by a commune of drop-outs. To the old, solid England of great houses, universities, parsonages and manors, to the Verneys, the Hydes, and innumerable others, similar feelings of shock and repugnance towards Charles II and the tone he set were not the less real for being politically unavowable. The last thing they wanted to do was to get rid of him. Yet the feeling colours the age. The names Court and Country, given to the first groupings in Parliament that preceded regular parties, express it, as does the treatment of the comedy of manners on the Restoration stage. For all their uncouthness the booby squires stand for honour and fair dealing, while the politeness of fashionable society conventionally covers a cold heart and a mean spirit.

To maintaining appearances Charles II had brought the practice of a lifetime. He paid, as we have seen, great attention to his clothes and to the way he wore them. Friends and enemies agree on his extraordinary control over his temper. His public behaviour to his mistresses had, until the last few years of his life, not been indecorous. Although he lived in a drunken age, although many of his cronies were notable tipplers, he very rarely drank too much and despised sottishness in others. In the face of death and in great pain he preserved his own high standards of courtesy and correctness, of style and wit. He asked his wife's pardon for his treatment of her but did not forget his mistresses, he accepted the ministrations of the bishops of the Church of England but was privately received into the Roman Catholic Church, he expressed his affection for his brother and died, it appeared, in charity with all men.

'Those who saw him on his death-bed', says Halifax darkly, à propos of his secret Catholicism, 'saw a great deal.' But those who were not so privileged soon heard of the courage and good nature the King had shewn in his last fight and were ready to embalm him in the national memory with these best of all preservatives.

12

Early Notices

———◆———

The King's death had been sudden. In those days of slow and irregular communication many of his subjects knew that he was dead before they had heard that he was ill. The shock enhanced the sense of public loss. 'Everybody is in a great damp since they have hard the doolfall news' wrote Sir Ralph Verney's housekeeper from Middle Claydon and no doubt she spoke for England. Her betters, feeling that the occasion called for more exalted language, easily betrayed themselves into hyperbole. 'The King's death is a great trouble to all his good subjects in the Country . . . I believe never a better prince or man lived in the world or will be more missed than he . . .' Thus Sir Ralph's cousin and neighbour. And thus from a hundred pulpits the even more absurd grandiloquence of the full-bottomed *oraison funèbre*.

The timing of Charles II's death was fortunate for his reputation. The scandals and failures and mismanagement of his reign were forgotten. Fresh in people's minds was his recent weathering of the storm that had driven the country close to the rocks they thought they had left behind them. 'Forty-one is come again' was a terrible sentence.

> The sober part of *Israel*, free from stain,
> Well knew the value of a peaceful Reign;

And, looking backward with a wise Affright,
Saw seams of wounds, dishonest to the sight:
In contemplation of whose ugly Scars,
They curst the memory of Civil Wars.

Moving forwards, his memory had hardly had time to fade before his brother had steered the nation into a collision from which it was lucky to escape with nothing broken in the Revolution of 1688. It might be that Charles himself if he had lived would have moved in the general direction taken by James, though it is inconceivable that he would have been either as maladroit or as transparent. There were signs that he might be about to embark on his father's policy of ruling without Parliament (and this in clear breach of the Triennial Act passed in his own reign), bringing his government more and more into dependence on French subsidies. There were signs too that he was preparing to go much further than he had hitherto dared in his consistent policy of Catholic emancipation. Certainly it is difficult to see where else he was likely to go. But like Cromwell he died at a moment when the wind had fallen and the tide was slack. Both men, so dissimilar in personal character, were great opportunists, skilful tacticians and adept at disguising their intentions. In both cases historical projection would be more than usually unsafe.

James's brief reign illuminated his brother's qualities and threw his defects into shadow. Charm, humour, tact and courtesy are not qualities that his most fervent defenders would claim for him, yet every witness however hostile allows them to Charles II. They may not be the highest virtues but they are the surest emollients. James's candour and straightforwardness made it difficult for him to disguise anger and resentment. To disagree with him was to be met by rudeness and aggressiveness. The family talent for public relations was never more conspicuous by its absence. By contrast Charles's urbanity was remembered, his deviousness palliated.

Halifax, the author of the acknowledged masterpiece in the literature of this subject *The Character of King Charles II*, had served both brothers as a minister and Privy Counsellor. His celebrated portrait resounds with a silent comparison of the two men, swelling to its crescendo in the conclusion. Here he somewhat unctuously varnishes over, but does not paint out, the sharp and striking picture he has drawn:

After all this, when some rough strokes of the pencil have made several parts of the picture look a little hard, it is justice that would be due to every man, much more to a Prince, to make some amends, and to reconcile men as much as may be to it by the last finishing.

...It is but justice therefore to this Prince to give all due softenings to the less shining parts of his life, to offer flowers and leaves to hide, instead of using aggravations to expose them.

One can imagine the sardonic gleam in the eye of the sitter if in some Elysian library he were ever permitted to read these graceful insincerities. Himself a connoisseur of hypocrisy he might even recognise the perhaps unconscious tribute of imitation. But we cannot doubt that he would at once take the allusion to his brother in the crucial passage:

That yieldingness, whatever foundations it might lay to the disadvantage of posterity, was a specific to preserve us in peace for his own time. If he loved too much to lie upon his own down bed of ease, his subjects had the pleasure during his reign of lolling and stretching upon theirs. As a sword is sooner broken upon a feather bed than upon a table, so his pliantness broke the blow of a present mischief much better than a more immediate resistance would perhaps have done.

Ruin saw this, and therefore removed him first to make way for further overturnings.

If he dissembled, let us remember first, that he was a King, and that dissimulation is a jewel of the crown . . .

The essence of Halifax's rendering of the King is the contrast between the richness of its particulars and the emptiness of the whole. We are given an impression of immense vitality and quickness of apprehension but left to find the key in an inertia of spirit that medieval theologians would have identified as accidie. For example the section entitled 'His Amours, Mistresses, etc.' opens energetically: 'It may be said that his Inclinations to Love were the Effects of Health, and a good Constitution, with as little mixture of the Seraphick part as ever Man had: And though from that Foundation Men often raise their Passions; I am apt to think his stayed as much as any Men's ever did in the *lower Region*. This made him like easy Mistresses . . .'

Thus already the physical exuberance is being skilfully counterpointed to an emotional poverty. This prepares the reader for a deeper insight. Charles took his mistresses, Halifax asserts, either at second hand—'they were generally resigned to him while he was abroad [i.e. before the Restoration] with an implied Bargain' or on advice—'After he was restored, Mistresses were recommended to him.' Even in so deeply personal a matter he was not enough of a person to care or to bother. The point is clinched by the end of the second paragraph:

> It was resolved generally by others whom he should have in his arms, as well as whom he should have in his Councils. Of a man who was so capable of choosing, he chose as seldom as any Man that ever lived.

Other writers, Dryden for example, have used the freely admitted fact of Charles's sexual promiscuity to suggest a geniality and warmth of nature. Halifax, without the least degree of censoriousness, with, indeed, a weary man-of-the-worldliness that Charles himself might have envied, uses it to show him as a cold fish.

Before reaching his Conclusion, which is not so much a drawing together of what has been said as an excusing or even an unsaying of it, Halifax examines his character under six different heads. The order itself is instructive. First comes Religion, followed, not inappropriately some might think, by Dissimulation; then his Amours and Mistresses lead by a natural transition of the argument to his conduct to his ministers. His Wit and Conversation are rightly given precedence of the general survey of his Talents, Temper, Habits etc that forms the sixth and last division of the subject. Common to all of the last three is the emphasis on the King's powers of memory:

> He had at least as good a Memory for the Faults of his Ministers as for their services; and whenever they fell, the whole Inventory came out; there was not a slip omitted.

This observation is made without rancour, following immediately upon and balancing a grateful recollection of the ease of doing business with him: 'He was free of access to them, which was a very gaining Quality.'

But in the following two sections it is argued that the excellence of his memory was the enemy of other talents and above all of his judgment:

> His Chain of Memory was longer than his Chain of Thought; the first

could bear any Burden, the other was tired by being carried on too long; it
was fit to ride a Heat, but it had not Wind enough for a long course.

A very great Memory often forgetteth how much time is lost by repeating
things of no Use. It was one Reason of his talking so much; since a great
Memory will always have something to say, and will be discharg-
ing itself, whether in or out of season, if a good Judgment doth not go along
with it, to make it stop and turn . . . Sometimes he would make shrewd
Applications, etc, at others he would bring things out of it that never deserved
to be laid in it.

Combined with his fondness, so often remarked, for telling stories,
his memory dominated his conventional style, itself acquired in the
unsuitable company he had kept in exile:

> By his being abroad, he contracted a Habit of conversing familiarly,
> which added to his natural Genius, made him very apt to talk; perhaps
> more than a very nice judgment would approve.

But no account of his conversation could begin without addressing
itself to his wit. Halifax opens his discussion by defining it:

> His Wit consisted chiefly in the Quickness of his Apprehension. His
> Apprehension made him find Faults, and that led him to short sayings
> upon them, not always equal, but often very good.

This is a cool assessment of a King whose wit has passed into legend. It
is difficult not to conclude that Halifax's valuation of the quality has
been depressed by his opinion of its propriety in a Head of State:

> The Thing called Wit, a Prince may taste, but it is dangerous for him to take
> too much of it; it hath Allurements which by refining his Thoughts, take off
> from their dignity in applying them less to the governing part. There is a
> Charm in Wit, which a Prince must resist: and that to him was no easy
> matter; it was contesting with Nature upon Terms of Disadvantage.

He returns to the point in connexion with Charles's concern to appear
the man of the world:

> His fine Gentlemanship did him no Good, encouraged in it by being too
> much applauded.

His Wit was better suited to his Condition before he was restored than afterwards. The Wit of a Gentleman, and that of a crowned Head, ought to be different things. As there is a Crown Law, there is a Crown Wit too. To use it with Reserve is very good and very rare. There is a Dignity in doing things seldom,   even   without   any   other   Circumstance.   Where Wit will run continually, the Spring is apt to fail; so that it groweth vulgar . . .

Halifax's criticism is in effect threefold. First, that wit itself is essentially unkingly. Second that Charles II's wit was malicious or at least censorious, with consequent ill effects on his own character:

He was so good at finding out other Mens weak sides, that it made him less intent to cure his own . . . Men love to see themselves in the false Looking-glass of other Mens Failings. It maketh a Man think well of himself at the time, and by sending his thoughts abroad to get Food for Laughing, they are less at leisure to see Faults at home.

And thirdly that *qua* wit it was not of the finest quality: it was not enriched by cultivation or reflection:

His Wit was not acquired by Reading; that which he had above his original Stock by Nature, was from Company, in which he was very capable to observe. He could not so properly be said to have a Wit very much raised, as a plain, gaining, well-bred, recommending kind of Wit.

It must be remembered that Halifax himself was one of the wittiest men of his time and that his mind was well stored and active. Clearly he found Charles II's delight in the commonplace and the superficial all but incomprehensible: 'But of all Men that ever liked those who had Wit, he could the best endure those who had none.' Ormonde and Hyde had earlier been dismayed by the same phenomenon. Love of ease, he insists, was the beginning and the end of everything with Charles II:

When once the Aversion to bear Uneasiness taketh place in a Man's mind, it doth so check all the Passions, that they are dampt into a kind of Indifference; they grow faint and languishing, and come to be subordinate to that fundamental Maxim of not purchasing any thing at the price of a Difficulty. This made that he had as little Eagerness to oblige as he had to hurt Men; the Motive of his giving Bounties was rather to make Men less uneasy to him, than more easy to themselves; and yet no ill-nature all this while. He would slide from an asking face and could guess very well . . .

It was love of ease that imposed such discipline and order as the King admitted to the conduct of his life:

He grew by Age into a pretty exact Distribution of his Hours, both for his Business, Pleasures and the Exercise for his Health, of which he took as much care as could possibly consist with some Liberties he was resolved to indulge in himself. He walked by his Watch, and when he pulled it out to look upon it, skilful Men would make haste with what they had to say to him.

Halifax's *Character* though written within a few years of the King's death (he himself died in 1695) was not published until 1750. His most recent editor, Professor J. P. Kenyon, points out that it seems to have excited little comment and that it remained unreprinted until Miss Foxcroft's massive re-establishment of the author's reputation as recently as 1898.[1] Thus while it is by common consent the most brilliant and the most suggestive of all portrayals of the King it has had little or no influence in forming the popular image of him. In this century as it has become more widely known it has probably been the most powerful solvent of the traditional view, at least among historians.

The other much more famous likeness attempted by a contemporary is that to be found in Bishop Burnet's *History of My Own Time*. Burnet, as we have seen, was a friend of Halifax's and they certainly discussed the King's character on at least one occasion.[2] There is thus a good deal of common ground between them and it is probable that each was influenced by the insights of the other, though neither had the opportunity of reading the other man's work. Burnet began to write his history in 1683, having already established a reputation as a historian and a biographer of what we should now call a scientific kind. He made heroic efforts to master original materials and to cite authorities in an age which had just begun to appreciate the importance of archives but had not had the time or technique to put them in order. He fully recognised that writing the history of his own violent and factious period in so candid a spirit was a very dangerous undertaking. Indeed he says so at the outset. 'I must begin with a character of the King and Duke [Charles II and James II], but I must give them at present very imperfect, otherwise what I write may happen to be seized upon, and I know not what may be made of that; but I will venture a good deal now, and if ever I outlive them I will say the rest when it may be more safe.' Fortunately he did outlive them. He finished his first version in 1686. He rewrote it entirely, and brought it up to date in 1703. He revised it again in 1711. The work was finally published in two volumes, the first in 1724, the second in 1734, long after his own death in 1715.

His picture of the King was thus several times reworked or, to turn the metaphor to engraving, exists in several states. His full length may be found in two substantially different versions, the earlier of which did not appear in his *History*. And besides these two considered portraits there is a careful sketch of the King as he was at the time of his restoration. None of them approach the artistry of Halifax but the two earliest have a vigour and a life that convince the reader of the author's direct observation and of his honesty in recording his impressions. The last and longest is a set piece of vituperation so elaborate and remorseless as to defeat its own ends. Much use is made of the earlier likenesses but these are heightened by various accusations not previously brought or here substantiated, such as cowardice after the battle of Worcester or incest with his favourite sister Henriette. He is compared to the Emperor Tiberius as he appears in the pages of Suetonius, the personification of vice, tyranny and double-dealing, and the resemblance is enhanced for Burnet by the recollection of a statue he had seen in Rome portraying the Emperor in his last days. This, he and its owners agreed, would have been the very image of the King except for the fact that the aging Tiberius had lost all his teeth while Charles had kept his. If the reasoning is weak, the language is robust; the tone that of a man who means to drive home his message. Its opening phrase is heavy with the wrath to come:

> Thus lived and died King Charles the second. He was the greatest instance in history of the various revolutions of which any one man seemed capable. He was bred up the first twelve years of his life with the splendour that became the heir of so great a crown. After that he passed eighteen years in great inequalities, unhappy in the war, in the loss of his father, and of the crown of England. Scotland did not only receive him, though upon terms hard of digestion, but made an attempt upon England for him, though a feeble one. He lost the battle of Worcester with too much

indifference: and then he showed more care of his person than became one who had so much at stake. He wandered about England for ten weeks after that, hid from place to place: but, under all the apprehensions that he had then upon him, he shewed a temper so careless, and so much turned to levity, that he was then diverting himself with little household sports in as unconcerned a manner as if he had made no loss, and had been in no danger at all. He got at last out of England: but he had been obliged to so many, who had been faithful to him, and careful of him, that he seemed afterwards to resolve to make an equal return to them all, and finding it not so easy to reward them as they deserved, he forgot them all alike. Most princes seem to have this pretty deep in them, and think that they ought never to remember past services, but that their acceptance of them is a full reward. He, of all in our age, exerted this piece of prerogative in the amplest manner, for he never seemed to charge his memory, or to trouble his thoughts, with the sense of any of the services that had been done him.

Pas trop de zèle! Is the King to be blamed for taking too much or too little care of his own safety when he was on the run? To charge him with both raises doubts about the motives of the prosecution. And to select his treatment of those who had helped and protected him as the prime instance of his ingratitude is to bungle a case that could hardly otherwise be lost. Pensions, jewels, places, were liberally bestowed on the men and women who had acted a part in this favourite passage of royal reminiscence. Burnet himself had written a brief biographical sketch, later to be immortalised by Johnson's praise, of the poet Rochester, whose father had been made an Earl simply for sharing the King's adventures. At least this seems to be the only possible explanation of that honour. And he must have known very well that his own predecessor at Salisbury, Dr Humphrey Henchman, had been rewarded with that see on the Restoration at least partly for the energy and courage he had shewn through a long and crucial passage of the escape. Examples of the King's punctiliousness in this instance would be as easy to multiply as those of his dereliction in almost every other. But with the bit between his teeth and the turf under his hooves Burnet is not easy to stop:

While he was abroad at Paris, Cologne or Brussels, he never seemed to lay anything to heart. He pursued all his diversions and irregular pleasures in a free career; and seemed to be as serene under the loss of a crown as the greatest philosopher could have been. Nor did he willingly hearken to any of those projects with which he often complained that his chancellor persecuted him. That in which he seemed most concerned was to find money for supporting his expense. So that it was often said that if Cromwell would have compounded the matter, and had given him a good round pension, that he might have been induced to resign his title to him. During his exile he delivered himself so entirely to his pleasures, that he became incapable of application. He spent little of his time in reading or study, and yet less in thinking: and in the state his affairs were then in, he accustomed himself to say to every person, and upon all occasions, that which he thought would please them. So that words or promises went very easily from him, and he had so ill an opinion of mankind, that he thought the great art of living and of governing was to manage all things and all persons with a depth of craft and dissimulation . . . He had great vices, but scarce any virtues to correct them. He had in him some vices that were less hurtful, which corrected his more hurtful ones. He was during the active part of his life given up to sloth and lewdness, to such a degree that he hated business, and could not bear the engaging in anything that gave him much trouble, or put him under any constraint; and though he desired to become absolute, and to overturn both our religion and our laws, yet he would neither run the risk nor give himself the trouble, which so great a design required. He had an appearance of gentleness in his outward deportment: but he seemed to have no bowels nor tenderness in his nature: and in the end of his life he became cruel. He was apt to forgive all crimes, even blood itself, yet he never forgave any thing that was done against himself, after his first and general act of indemnity, which was to be reckoned as done rather upon maxims of state than inclinations of mercy . . .

There is still much here for which no evidence is known to exist, such as the suggestion that Charles would have accepted an offer from Cromwell to buy him out of his inheritance. But there is a skilful confusion of the fair and the unfair, an adroit evocation of subconscious echoes as in the phrase 'even blood itself', recalling the scandalous pardoning of the Colonel of that name, that carries more conviction. The most important element is the introduction of the theme of Charles's conscious villainy as opposed to his lazy drifting into bad ways and worse counsels. This is taken up again almost immediately:

When he saw young men of quality that had more than ordinary in them, he drew them about him and set himself to corrupt them both in

religion and morality; in which he proved so unhappily successful that he
left England much changed at his death from what he had found it at his
restoration . . .

Burnet is now well embarked on the conspiracy theory of history,
the conspiracy 'to overturn both our religion and our laws', which he
had earlier considered to have been true enough of the King's
sympathies and inclinations but irreconcilable with his laziness and
love of pleasure. It is at this point that he introduces his comparison
with Tiberius in the last and more lurid stage of his career. Burnet has
still some difficulties to negotiate in demonstrating the consistency and
tenacity of a man whom he has earlier shewn to be conspicuously
lacking in those qualities but he is within sight of home:

> His ill conduct in the first Dutch war, and those terrible calamities of the
> plague and fire of London, with that loss and reproach he suffered by the
> insult at Chatham, made all people conclude there was a curse upon his
> government. His throwing the public hatred at that time upon Lord
> Clarendon was both unjust and ingrateful. And when his people had
> brought him out of all his difficulties upon his entering into the triple alliance
> [with Holland and Sweden to counter French aggrandisement], his selling
> that to France, and his entering on the second Dutch war with as little colour
> as he had for the first, his beginning it with the attempt on the Dutch Smyrna
> fleet, the shutting up the exchequer, and his declaration for toleration, which
> was a step for the introduction of popery, was such a chain of black actions,
> flowing from blacker designs, that it amazed those who had known all this, to
> see with what impudent strains of flattery addresses were penned during his
> life, and yet more grossly after his death . . .

His diplomacy, tortuous and dishonourable as it might appear, was,
it is here argued, simply directed to the building up of France and the
destruction of the Protestant powers. His secret Catholicism, not his
love of ease or need for money, is the key that unlocks everything.

> No part of his character looked wickeder as well as meaner than that he
> was, all the while that he was professing to be of the church of England,
> expressing both zeal and affection to it, yet secretly reconciled to the
> church of Rome: thus mocking God, and deceiving the world with so gross
> a prevarication. And his not having the honesty or courage to own it at the
> last, and not shewing any sign of the least remorse for his ill led life, or any

tenderness either for his subjects in general or for the queen and his servants, and his recommending only his whores and bastards to his brother's care, would have been strange conclusion to any other life, but was well enough suited to all the other parts of his . . .

Burnet wrote this after the Revolution of 1688, in which he himself had played so notable a part, had brought England about on the opposite tack. For the last twenty-five years of his life the country was engaged in fighting the two great wars against Louis XIV. Both as an active politician and as a writer of history Burnet was committed to Whig principles. Thornhill's painting of the apotheosis of William III, the centrepiece of his great ceiling at Greenwich, shows the King trampling '. . . Tyranny under his feet, which is expressed as a French personage with his leaden crown fallen off, his chains, yoke and iron sword broken to pieces: cardinal's cap, triple crowned mitres, etc tumbling down. Just beneath is Time bringing Truth to light . . .' No better summary could be found of the principles that throughout a long life animated Burnet. Fair-minded as he generally was he could hardly, as he looked back, over fifty years in politics, see Charles II as anything but the most formidable enemy of everything he had stood for. In so doing he was certainly unjust in one particular: they had both been consistent in advocating religious toleration and, so far as circumstances allowed, true to their principles in practising it.

The portrait that he drew from life in 1683 is much more sympathetic. It is, so to speak, the original document to which the *History* itself stands in the relation of a secondary authority. Ranke thought so highly of it that he printed it as an appendix to his great *History of England principally in the Seventeenth Century*.

The King is certainly the best bred man in the world, for the Queen mother observed often the great defects of the late King's breeding and the stiff roughness that was in him, by which he disobliged very many and did often prejudice his affairs very much; so she gave strict orders that the young princes should be bred to a wonderfull civility. The King is civil rather to an excess and has a softeness and gentleness with him, both in his air and expressions that has a charm in it. The Duke would also pass for an extraordinary civil and sweet tempered man, if the King were not much above him in it, who is more naturally and universally civil than the Duke. The King has a vast deal of wit, indeed no man has more, and a great deal of judgement, when he thinks fitt to employ it; he has strange command of himselfe, he can pass from business to pleasure and from pleasure to business in so easy a manner that all things seem alike to him; he has the greatest art of concealing himselfe of any man alive, so that those about him cannot tell, when he is ill or well pleased, and in private discourse he will hear all sorts of things in such a manner, that a man cannot know, whether he hears them or not, or whether he is well or ill pleased with them. He is very affable not only in publick but in private, only he talks too much and runns out too long and too farr; he has a very ill opinion both of men and women, and so is infinitely distrustfull, he thinks the world is governed wholly by interests, and indeed he has known so much of the baseness of mankind, that no wonder if he has hard thoughts of them; but when he is satisfied, that his interests become likewise the interests of his Ministers, then he delivers himself up to them in all their humours and revenges: for excusing this he has often said, that he must oblige his ministers and support their credit as necessary for his service, yet he has often kept up differences amongst his ministers and has ballanced his favours pretty equally among them, which considering his tempers must be uneasy to them, except it be that there is art necessary, and he naturally inclines for refineings and loves an intrigue. His love of pleasure and his vast expence with his women together with the great influence they have had in all his affaires both at home and abroad is the chief load that will lay on him; for not only the women themselves have great power, but his court is full of pimps and bauds, and all matters, in which one desires to succeed, must be put in their hands. He has very mercyfull inclinations, when one submitts wholly to him, but is severe enough to those that oppose him and speeks of all people with a sharpness, that is not suitable to the greatness of a Prince. He is apt to believe what is told him, so that the first impression goes deepest, for he thinks all apologies are lies; he has knowledge in many things chiefly in all navy affaires, even in the architecture of shipps he judges as critically as any of the trade can do and knows the smallest things belonging to it, he understands much natural philosophy and is a good chymist, he knows many mechanical things and the inferiour parts of the mathematicks, but not the demonstrative. He is very little conversant in books, and young and old he could never apply himself to literature: he is very kind to those he loves, but never thinks of doeing any thing for them, so that, if they can find things for themselves, he will easily enough grant them, but he never setts himself to find out any thing for them, and I never heard of above three or four instances of any places, that he gave of his own motion, so that those, who have received most of his bounty, think, they owe the thanks more to his instruments than to himself; he never enters upon business with any himself, but if his ministers can once draw him into business, they may hold him at it as long as they will. He loves his ease so much, that the great secret of all his ministers is to find out his temper exactly and to be easy to him. He has many odd opinions about religion and morality, he thinks an implicitness in Religion is necessary for the safety of Government and he looks upon all inquisitiveness into those things as mischievious to the State; he thinks all appetites are free and that God will never damn a man for allowing himselfe a little pleasure, and on this has so fixed his thoughts, that no disorders of any kind have ever been seen to give him any trouble when they were over, and in sickness, except his ague in 79, he seemed to have no concern on his mind and yet I believe he is no Atheist, but that rather he has formed an odd idea of the Goodness of God in his mind; he thinks, to be wicked and to design mischief, is the only thing that God hates, and has said to me often, that he was sure, he was not guilty of that. I think I have gone pretty far and scarce know how I should scape under the present Chief Justice, if this should happen to be seased on.

Among the many interesting features of this sketch is its historical and comparative approach. Charles II's excellent manners result from the recognition of his father's shortcomings in this respect and are themselves favourably contrasted with his brother's. Burnet is a historian and sees that people must be set in their contexts if we are ever to understand them. The version of the portrait with which he introduces Charles II to his readers on the Restoration in 1660 is substantially the one drawn from life twenty-three years later, but some of the inferences drawn from its features and some of the moral judgments are more hostile. Although we have his own statement that he revised the whole text at a time when his final denunciation of the King had already been written it is still however very far removed from those bitter certainties as to his real nature.

Almost every detail discernible in the first and second states of Burnet's portrait can be confirmed from other sources by no means wholly or even largely of his way of thinking. Pepys, Evelyn, Halifax, even Clarendon and Ormonde could all be so invoked. They would, however, largely be found to dissent from the final summary with which Burnet dismisses him from his story. It is here that the Whig interpretation of the King's place in history is fixed. Burnet's verdict on Charles II is the verdict of Whig historians in its most extreme form. Even Macaulay follows him only as far as the second state of the portrait in which idleness and dissipation are allowed to have the upper hand over any inclination to subvert the constitution and betray the country to Louis XIV. It is to the image of the Stuarts in the eighteenth century, the period of the Whig ascendancy, that we must now turn.

13

The Stuarts under
the Georges

———◆———

The triumph of Whig principles in 1688 and their consolidation in the
Hanoverian succession in 1714 necessarily involved an official party
view of recent history. The Stuarts were identified with tyranny,
popery and subservience to France. Sir James Thornhill who gave
such exuberant expression to the blessings of Whig rule on the walls
and ceilings of the Painted Hall at Greenwich was professionally
described as 'a history Painter'. A proper view of the past was very
much the concern of the present. It was a profession of political faith.

However unfair or downright unhistorical it might be to lump
Charles I's passionate Anglicanism and Charles II's apparent scep-
ticism and preference for religious toleration with the headlong
Catholic zeal of James II, the Revolution made such an identification
inescapable. James had abandoned his throne to his daughter and
son-in-law but he had not abdicated his claims. He set up his Court in
Exile, as his mother had done, at St Germain, where his son, a cradle
Catholic, succeeded him. The Stuarts were, after 1688, palpably
Catholics and pensioners of France. Doubtless if restored to the throne
they would prove to be absolutists as well. To draw a distinction
between them and their immediate forebears was difficult and
intellectually embarrassing. It was much simpler to be either for them
or against them. If one was for them it was advisable to disguise the

fact except in certain strongholds of Jacobitism such as the University of Oxford or the Northumbrian border country. The Jacobite risings of 1715 and 1745 were serious affairs.

Since the Whigs were so clearly identified with the Revolution and the House of Hanover it seemed to follow that the Tories must be the party of the Stuarts. If parties were the outcome of strict logical argument this would have been the case. In practice it was very far from true. There were Jacobite Tories and anti-Jacobite Tories. There were even a large number of Roman Catholics, in Professor Plumb's view the majority, who were not at all anxious for a second Stuart Restoration. The situation was further complicated by the Non-jurors, the clergy who had not been able to reconcile their consciences to swearing an oath of allegiance to William and Mary while James, to whom they were already so bound, was alive. Here again it certainly did not follow that such men were Jacobites, although a number were; still less, that they represented a crypto-Catholic party in the Church of England. The leaders of the Non-jurors had been prominent in the opposition to James's Catholicising policy. But whatever they were, the one thing none of these people could be was Whig. They were, in fact, trapped in the ideological dead-end of a too explicit political theory. If they believed in divine right and in the unlawfulness of resistance to the sovereign, logically they had nowhere else to go but Jacobitism. The fact that they didn't want to go there was their misfortune.

The Whigs naturally exploited their advantage to the full. History could only be Whig history: the Stuart past must be shewn to lead to the Stuart present. Toryism was to be broken in pieces like a potter's vessel. So complete was the disarray of their opponents that no crude propagandist distortion was necessary. Even the materials of Tory history could be used. Thus White Kennet—whose *Complete History of England*, published in 1706, is the most scholarly and considerable achievement in this field—makes a large use of Clarendon's *History of the Rebellion* that had just issued from the press. He reprints his character of King Charles I and of many other leading figures on either side in the Civil War. He is charitable to Archbishop Laud, giving him credit for his intentions while censuring his judgment. He has no use for Cromwell. But like his friend and patron Burnet he is uninhibited by doubts or reservations in his portrayal of Charles II as politically sinister, though he is a great deal more polite. The root of all evil was his supposed love of France, '. . . a Fatal Friendship that

was Incompatible with the Interest of England'. Nonetheless he was 'a
Prince endowed with all the Qualities that might justly have rendered
him the Delight of Mankind, and entitled him to the Character of one
of the greatest Genius's that ever sate upon a Throne'. Kennet
contradicts Burnet in finding him merciful and good-natured, and is
kinder to him in his private capacities: 'A respectful, civil Husband, a
fond Father, a kind Brother, an easy Enemy but none of the firmest
or most grateful of Friends . . . When he had a mind to lay aside the
King . . . there were a thousand irresistible charms in his Conversation.'

Kennet stressed his powers as an actor, 'No Age produced a greater
Master in the Art of Dissimulation . . .' 'Never Prince loved ceremony
less, or despised the Pageantry of a Crown more: yet he was Master of
something in his Person and Aspect, that commanded both Love and
Veneration at once.' He concludes his portrait by borrowing Burnet's
as yet unpublished comparison of the King with Tiberius (the
attendant circumstances of the comparison make this unquestionable)
but is careful to remove most of the venom that the Bishop of Salisbury
intended:

And as there was a Great Likeness between these two Princes in their
Faces, there was likewise some in their maxims of Government, the time of
their Age in which they came to govern, the length of their Reigns and the
Suspicions about the manner of their Death. And, indeed, excepting
Tiberius's Temper, his Cruelty, Jealousy and Unnatural Lusts anyone
that's acquainted with both their Stories will easily find something of a
Parallel betwixt them. Nor is this any Reflection upon the Memory of
King Charles, for, except in what I have named, Tiberius may be
reckoned among the wisest and the bravest of those that wore the Imperial
Purple.

White Kennet was born in the year of the Restoration. As a young
man at Oxford at the time of the Popish Plot and the Exclusion Crisis
he had thrown himself into the thick of Tory politics, which he
combined like so many of the most original scholars of his day with a
deep and scientific historical curiosity. It was James II's attack on the
Church of England that drove him into alliance with the Whigs and to
a wholehearted acceptance of Revolution principles. Yet in writing
his history, for which to the fury of his Tory critics he claimed
impartiality, he carefully avoided drawing on his own experience and

recollection, relying instead on contemporary material which in that age was necessarily what he could find in print: Acts of Parliament, pamphlets, speeches, sermons, reports of trials and the like. To support the detached and scientific spirit in which he claimed to write he withheld his name from the title-page though the fact of his authorship was widely known from the first.

This combination of sweet reason and self-effacement in a writer who had changed to the winning side enraged his Tory readers. The rector of Whitechapel had him painted as Judas Iscariot in an altarpiece which the Bishop of London eventually ordered to be removed. Roger North, the brother and biographer of Charles II's Lord Keeper, compiled a critique of the work in a spirit robustly expressed on his title-page:

> *Examen: or, an Enquiry into the Credit and Veracity of a Pretended Complete History; shewing the perverse and wicked design of it, and the many falsities and abuses of truth contained in it. Together with some Memoirs occasionally inserted. All tending to vindicate the Honour of the late King Charles the Second, and his Happy Reign, from the intended Aspersions of that Foul Pen.*

Although it was not published until 1740 when both North and Kennet were dead it exemplifies the extreme and untenable championship of Charles II into which the Tories were goaded by frenzy and frustration. The fact of the King's receipt of a subsidy from Louis XIV is denied. His Catholicism is denied. The story of his death-bed reception into the Roman Catholic Church, even the publication of the papers in his own hand setting out the standard Roman Catholic objections to the Church of England are, it is argued, simply the propaganda tricks of his brother, James II. The author is carried away into asserting Charles II's devout adherence to the national church. 'For no Man in the world kept more Decorum in his Expressions and Behaviour, with Respect to Things sacred, than the King did; and scarce ever failed the Service and Sermon, with the Sacraments at the stated Times; Healings, and Washing of the Feet of the Poor, as the Order of his Chapel required'.[1] Summing up his case (he had had a highly successful career at the bar until he had been forced to give it up as a Non-juror) he goes so far as to argue that 'he might (comparatively) pass for a Saint'.[2] One wonders what comparisons he had in mind.

Roger North had lived in and about the Court. He was con-

scientious, honourable, learned and industrious. When he describes
Charles II as 'a King, in his Time, of all Europe the best'[3] or that
'bating his being addicted to his Pleasures, chiefly of Women, and the
Consequences, he had as many virtues and as few Faults as may
readily be found in any one Man'[4] he shows what can be done for the
character of the King when a man is really put to it. In his life of his
brother, the Lord Keeper, where his purpose is not so consciously
controversial, he allows the King faults that were only made good by
his superior abilities. 'Such supine Errors and Neglects had he been
guilty of; and without a singular Penetration, and good Judgment of
Men & Things . . . he had been as his Father was, lost.'[5] The
comparison prompts the author into speculating how Charles II
would have fared in his father's situation but he recoils into the safer
conclusion that the son certainly profited from the father's experience.
North and his generation had no room for manoeuvre. The Stuarts
whom they had supported had let their opponents occupy all the
commanding heights. Sir Richard Bulstrode, the long-lived survivor
of a yet earlier generation who had himself fought for Charles I from
the first battles of the Civil War, strikes the same note in his *Memoirs
and Reflections upon the Reign and Government of King Charles I and King
Charles II* (1721):

> Fear of Popery, Arbitrary Government and evil Counsellors, in my
> Memory, since the year 1641, have made our *English* Nation run mad, cost
> an Infinite Treasure, with the Lives of some Thousand English; and, in
> conclusion, instead of Religion, setting up Enthusiasm; instead of Liberty,
> the Nation was enslaved to a military Power; instead of Property, Plunder,
> Sacrilege & Sequestration; and they were just playing the same Game over
> again in this King's Time, if by little less than a miracle they had not been
> prevented . . . [6]

Bulstrode, unlike North, had adhered to James II in exile (he had
earlier been converted to Roman Catholicism while living in Bruges to
escape his creditors). But there is the same sense of outrage that the
King who had saved his country from a recrudescence of civil war
should be written down by the party that had been playing with fire.
Not content with asserting Charles II's uncontested and incontestable
qualities of easiness, affability and courtesy they claim for him virtues
both as man and as King from which even Tory historians were soon
to recede.

The links of the earliest Tories were to the Cavaliers. Charles I and Charles II were to be defended as parts of the same system of political ideas. The fact that the Whigs were prepared to treat Charles I with some respect while throwing the full weight of their attack on Charles II dictated the tactics of their opponents. But as the century wore on the temper of English politics changed from excitements, conflicts and alarms to a smooth, successful complacency. Even such sudden and violent storms as the 'fifteen and the 'forty-five were weathered without straining the timbers. The Non-jurors died off or were re-absorbed into the national church. One of Roger North's own sons became a clergyman and survived to accept a canonry at Windsor from George III. The bandwagon had moved on.

As a consequence the Tory writers of the succeeding generation no longer felt it necessary to uphold Charles I and Charles II as the pillars on which their lintel rested. It was open to them, as it had not been to their fathers, to abandon Charles II, or at least not to rally to his defence, and to throw the spotlight on the more stirring, more appealing figure of Charles I. This tendency may be clearly observed in so learned a historian and so extreme a Tory as Thomas Carte, whose Jacobitism forced him to flee the country under an assumed name in 1715 and landed him in prison in 1745. His partisanship was such that in spite of his unrivalled knowledge of the documents he attempted to deny the fact of Charles I's double-dealing in conducting negotiations with the Irish Catholics behind the back of Ormonde, his own viceroy. In his *Life of Ormonde* Carte heaps praise on the character of Charles I, contrasting it bitterly and opprobriously with that of his father. On the other hand Charles II receives much more matter-of-fact treatment. Carte accuses him, in particular, of 'foul ingratitude' and hypocrisy in taking the Covenant in 1650. Although he does not use quite such strong language in describing the King's conduct towards the subject of his biography he certainly leaves the reader to infer that it would not be out of place. The inconsistency is interesting. At the beginning of his very long book Carte quotes Sir Robert Southwell's fine judgment of Ormonde: 'I think his whole life was a straight line, if ever a man in the world's were so.' He goes on to make it good. That life, as we have seen, was spent in loyalty and service to the two Kings, both of whom at one time or another played him false. Why should the first escape censure?

Surely the most compelling answer is that Charles I was naturally endowed and tragically drawn to become a figure of myth and of cult.

His son was of the earth earthy. The early Tory historians, Sir Richard Bulstrode, Carte himself and others, tell with slight variations a story of Bernini's bust (now destroyed). According to Carte's version, on its arrival it was unpacked and set on a table in the garden of the King's house in Chelsea for the Court to view. 'As they were viewing it, an hawk flew over their heads with a partridge in his claws, which he had wounded to death. Some of the partridge's blood fell on the neck of the statue, where it always remained without being wiped off, and was seen by hundreds of people as long as the bust was in being.'[7] Sir Richard Bulstrode more dramatically transfers the scene to the King's last visit to Greenwich after he had seen off Henrietta Maria at Dover on the very eve of the Civil War: 'The King commanded his Statue to be carried from the Greenwich Garden into the Magazine: In the carriage of it, the Face being upwards, a Swallow, or some other Bird, flying over it, dunged in the Face of the King's Statue, which was wiped off immediately by those that carried it: but notwithstanding all Endeavours, it could not be gotten off, but turned into Blood.'[8] If a similar misfortune were recorded of any statue of Charles II, ribald anecdote rather than pious credulity would have been more likely to preserve it for posterity. Ribaldry may flesh out the personal image but it is fatal to political mythology.

Bernini's bust, destroyed in the Whitehall fire of 1698, was a work of art so extraordinary in its quality and its origins that legend naturally gathered round it. The English sculptor Nicholas Stone visiting Rome in October 1638 went to call on Bernini and found him confined to his bed but in very good humour. Bernini at once asked his visitor whether he had seen the head of the King and what was said of it. Stone told him that it was admired by all who had seen it 'not only for the exquisiteness of the work but the likenesse and nere resemblance itt had to the King's countenance. He sayd that divers had tolde him so much but he could nott belive itt.' He asked anxiously how it had survived the journey and how it was kept. Stone reassured him on both points, perhaps not entirely to his satisfaction on the second. 'I toke (sayth he) as much care for the packing as studye in the making of itt.'

He had been so exercised by the impossibility of his task that he had accepted a portrait commission from a visiting Englishman partly so as to show the difference between working from the life and working from a painting. This came to the ears of the Pope, his patron, who at once sent Cardinal Barberini to forbid him 'for the Pope would have

no other picture sent into England from his hand but his Majesty'.
Bernini defaced his model and told his client that there had been an
accident in the studio. The Pope, not content with this exercise of
proprietorship,

> . . . would have him doe another picture in marble after a painting for
> some other prince. I told the Pope (says he) that if thaire were the best
> picture done by the hand of Raphyell yett he would not undertake to doe
> itt (sayes he) I told his Hollinesse that itt was impossible that a picture in
> marble could have the resemblance of a living man . . . for doe not wee see
> that when a man is affrighted, thare comes a pallnesse on a sudden?
> Presently wee say he likes not [does not look] the same man. How can itt
> then possible be that a marble picture can resemble the nature when itt is
> all one colour, where, to the contrary, a man has on[e] colour in his face,
> another in his haire, a third in his lipps, and his eyes yett different from all
> the rest?[9]

Berniri did not apparently confide in Nicholas Stone his apprehensions of the King's tragic destiny but John Evelyn, who paid two long
visits to Rome a few years later, had evidently heard the story.

It was said at the beginning of this book that the distinguishing
characteristic of the Stuart's power of self-projection was that it could
evade the foreclosures of time. Again and again after a long period of
dormancy there is a second blossoming yet more profuse than the first.
As Charles II's genial, loose-living, corrupt and amusing *persona*
passed for a time out of favour with the political and literary
champions of his house, so his father's rose with the calm serenity of a
full moon on a clear night. The image that Van Dyck had scattered
through the great houses of England was the favourite inspiration of
eighteenth-century engravers who heightened the dignity the painter
had conveyed and softened the hardness and obstinacy with the
pathos of a tragic victim. From the safe distance of the Whig
supremacy it was easier to idealise Charles I. His age was worlds away.
That of his son, by contrast, bore a distinct family resemblance to the
contemporary scene. If one wanted rulers who were genial, loose-
living, corrupt and amusing need one look far? What of the Foxes,
father and son, themselves the by-product of Charles II's Court? What
of the Whig Dukes, whose vast landed interest upheld the whole
system? Were not some of them his direct if illegitimate descendants
and were not others connected by family relationships? The tone of

polite society, sceptical, worldly, self-indulgent, was one in which he would surely have been at home. More refined in language and personal habits, the aristocracy of Georgian England was much closer to the spirit of Charles II's Court than some Tories would have been ready to admit.

Dr Johnson, Boswell tells us, 'arraigned the modern politicks of this country, as entirely devoid of all principle of whatever kind. "Politicks (said he) are now nothing more than means of rising in the world. With this sole view do men engage in politicks, and their whole conduct proceeds upon it. How different in that respect is the state of the nation now from what it was in the time of Charles the First, during the Usurpation, and after the Restoration in the time of Charles the Second."' Johnson's Toryism was of a seventeenth, not an eighteenth-century vintage. He accepted divine right and looked on the Revolution of 1688 with horror. The political conflicts that he here claimed to regret took on in his mind the aspect of demonology. Charles II by being on the side of the angels was easily identified as one of them. Boswell says that he was a 'Prince, for whom he had an extraordinary partiality'. But his indictment of the politics of his own time foreshadows the Romantic revival that was to nourish both the Republican and the reborn Tory traditions in the age of the French Revolution. Men who found eighteenth-century politics insufficiently ideological would find more to their mind in the age of Laud and Strafford, of Pym and Falkland, of Hyde and Selden than in that of Arlington and Danby. Charles I was not only a more promising symbol of high-mindedness and purity than his son. He had also enunciated political and constitutional principles in memorable language. His conduct of his own defence and his speech from the scaffold, penetrating in analysis and noble in expression, incontestably his own, amply justify the admiration of contemporaries for his mastery of argument and style. But besides these there was the series of manifestoes drafted for him by Hyde in the propaganda war that preceded the outbreak of hostilities in 1642. Lastly there was the book that rightly or wrongly was attributed to him, the *Eikon Basilike*. Charles I, like his father, was a published author.

It is on this account that he earns his highest praise from David Hume, the Scottish philosopher, who in the middle of the eighteenth century challenged the traditional Whig version with his own *History of England*.[10] The Toryism of Hume was only Tory in the sense that it was implacably anti-Whig. The Stuarts and all that they stood for were repulsive to his sceptical, rationalist, pragmatical turn of mind, but the Stuarts were not the reigning orthodoxy that he aimed to destroy. They thus required delicate handling if they were not to impede or deflect the main thrust of his attack. With his impish pleasure in paradox Hume selects Charles I for commendation (though even that is not very warm) and Charles II, in tone and temper the monarch most congenial to him, for unsparing political criticism. James I, the true source of High Tory doctrines, is treated with a dismissive scorn that no Whig historian had surpassed. Even his publications are ingeniously used, against Hume's main argument, to lower him in historical esteem:

> It may safely be affirmed that the mediocrity of James's talents in literature . . . is one cause of that contempt under which his memory labours . . . Of the first twenty Roman emperors, counting from Caesar to Severus, above the half were authors; and though few of them seem to have been eminent in that profession, it is always remarked to their praise that by their example they encouraged literature.[11]

Charles I's literary accomplishment is perhaps overpraised as his honesty certainly is: '. . . The *Eikon* . . . must be acknowledged the best prose composition which at the time of its publication was to be found in the English language.'[12] 'Some historians have rashly questioned the good faith of this prince: But, for this reproach, the most malignant scouting of his conduct which in every circumstance is now thoroughly known, affords not any reasonable foundation . . .'[13] In spite of this summing up in favour of the defendant the verdict on the King is cautious. Attention is distracted from its measured terms by a characteristic piece of Whig-baiting:

> The character of this prince, as that of most men, if not of all men, was mixed . . . He deserves the epithet of a good, rather than of a great man . . . Had he been born an absolute prince, his humanity and good sense had rendered his reign happy and his memory precious . . .[14]

It may be thought that Hume's itch to tease sometimes gets the better of his candour. Neither humanity nor good sense are virtues for which Charles I was principally admired. His critics would roundly deny him both: there are many accusations against him of callousness and want of pity: even his fervent admirers like Sir Philip Warwick admit a certain coldness and lack of generosity in him. And as for good sense, it is a claim that would seem to require some qualification.

Hume's view of Charles II is, by contrast, curiously close to the conventional Whig interpretation:

> When we consider him as a sovereign his character though not altogether destitute of virtue, was in the main dangerous to his people, and dishonourable to himself. Negligent of the interests of the nation, careless of its glory, averse to its religion, jealous of its liberty, lavish of its treasure, sparing only of its blood; he exposed it by his measures, though he appeared ever but in sport, to the danger of a furious civil war, and even to the ruin and ignominy of a foreign conquest.

Burnet and White Kennet could hardly have found a word to quarrel with. To make up, perhaps, for the severe if just judgment of the King's public character Hume enthusiastically accepts the most favourable estimate of the private man.

> When considered as a companion he appears the most amiable and engaging of men: and indeed in this view his deportment must be allowed altogether unexceptionable . . . This indeed is the most shining part of the King's character . . .
>
> In the duties of private life, his conduct, though not free from exception, was, in the main, laudable. He was an easy, generous lover, a civil, obliging husband, a friendly brother, an indulgent father, and a good natured master . . .[15]

Thus there are certain strange congruities in the perspective offered by Thomas Carte the Jacobite archivist and David Hume the philosopher of the Enlightenment. Both have a low opinion of James I, both insist (against plenty of evidence available to them) that Charles I was incapable of bad faith, and both, either largely or wholly, abandon any systematic defence of Charles II's kingship. Clearly James I was too grotesquely repulsive a figure to be anything but a liability to a Stuart revivalist like Carte. Hume who had no such interest is anxious to discredit James I as a political thinker. The last thing he wanted was to see a faded, peeling Whiggism replaced by a political creed that claimed divine sanction and would certainly attempt to revive the declining influence of religion. As for the Stuarts themselves he was not concerned to advance their personal or historical reputation.

The first English historian to offer a cool, fair, and scholarly account of the Stuarts is the first Roman Catholic to publish a full scale *History of England.* John Lingard's sixth volume covering the reigns of James I and Charles I appeared in 1825. In the full flood of the Romantic Revival the temptation to let the colour and excitement of the story unbalance criticism must have been strong, not least to a member of a church still under civil and political disabilities that both Charles I and Charles II had tried to lighten. Lingard indeed gives credit to Charles I for his lenity towards Roman Catholics, clerical and lay. But that does not prevent him from drawing his readers' attention to Charles's mercilessness towards other religious dissenters. The atrocious cruelties inflicted on Alexander Leighton who had written a fanatical pamphlet against episcopacy are described in full. Charles is reported to have had some qualms[16] about the whipping, the branding, the nostril-slitting, the ear-cropping with which Archbishop Laud was happy to defend his beliefs but these brutalities were in fact inflicted.

> Neither [writes Lingard] was his punishment yet terminated. Marked, degraded, mutilated as he was, he returned to prison to be immured there for life, unless the King should at any subsequent period think him a fit object for mercy. But from Charles he found no mercy: and it was only at the end of ten years that he obtained his liberty from the parliament, then in arms against the King.[17]

With the same unflinching honesty Lingard pinpoints 'that habit of duplicity which had ever marked his conduct since his first entrance into public life'.[18] The negotiations with the Irish Catholics behind Ormonde's back are fully set out and Hume's treatment of evidence is sternly reproved.[19]

Charles II presents stiffer obstacles which are nonetheless cleared with the same triumphant straightforwardness. It is in the King's total lack of this very quality that Lingard finds the solution to the historical problems presented by his life and conduct. He accepts the evidence of Charles's persistent inclinations towards the Church of Rome but rejects any assertion of his reconciliation until he was on his deathbed. He accepts James's account of the King's tearful protestations of his desire to announce his own conversion but coolly concludes 'that his real object was to deceive both his brother and the King of France'.[20] Of his private character Lingard paints an attractive picture: 'He was kind, familiar, communicative. He delighted in social converse, narrated with infinite humour; and as he was the first to seize and expose what might be ridiculous in others, so he never refused to join in the laugh when it was raised at his own expense.' He emphasises his immense popularity and shrewdly related it to the boom in England's trade:

> In conclusion it may be proper to remark that during his reign the arts improved, trade met with encouragement, and the wealth and comforts of the people increased. To this flourishing state of the nation we must attribute the acknowledged fact, that, whatever were the personal failings or vices of the King, he never forfeited the love of his subjects. Men are always ready to idolize the sovereign under whose sway they feel themselves happy.[21]

The conclusion perhaps assumes an optimistic view of the rationality and the gratitude of human beings. But if men often do not know when they are well off they are generally aware of whether things are getting better or worse. Lingard is surely right to identify this growing sense of solid prosperity after the social and economic dislocation of civil war and military rule as the brightest jewel in Charles II's Crown. 'Good King Charles's Golden Days' may well give romantic expression to the popular recognition that there was more money about.

14

Romantic Revivals

———————◆———————

Lingard himself in his young days as a Catholic seminarist had been forced to fly for his life from the first violent eruptions of the French Revolution. This experience does not seem to have coloured his historical approach. In tone, temper and understanding he belongs to the eighteenth century, calm, clear, rational and precise. Yet even as he wrote, the first of the great transforming forces of the new age had begun to bring Regency England closer to the passions and struggles of the seventeenth century. The novels of Sir Walter Scott in the words of C. S. Lewis 'almost created that historical sense which we now all take for granted'.[1] Or as Leslie Stephen had written much earlier: 'Scott understood and nobody has better illustrated by example, the true mode of connecting past and present.'[2] Their opinion has been widely shared by historians. 'Walter Scott', wrote G. M. Trevelyan, 'did more than any professed historian to alter mankind's vision of its past. Not only did he invent the historical novel, but he revolutionised the study and the scope of history itself . . . The difference between Gibbon and Macaulay is a measure of the influence of Scott.'[3]

Briefly the argument of these authorities is that Scott combined his extraordinary knowledge of the sources, written and traditional, of Scottish history with his creative energy as a novelist to establish once and for all one simple fact: the fact of change. To the eighteenth-century eye men always and everywhere were essentially rational and identical. Their differences were simply to be explained to the degrees of ignorance and barbarism under which they laboured. To quote again Trevelyan's essay already cited: 'Gibbon did not perceive the extent to which the habits and thoughts of men, no less than the forms of society, differ from country to country and from age to age. The men of the Fifteenth century are in his handling much the same as the men of the Fifth.'[4] What Gibbon would have made of the Stuarts may easily be inferred from his famous judgment of Antoninus Pius: 'His reign is marked by the rare advantage of furnishing very few materials for history; which is, indeed, little more than the register of the crimes, follies and misfortunes of mankind.' No one could say that of Charles I or Charles II.

Scott's great insight is that we are all men of our time, and not only of our time, but of our particular circumstances and of our individual and collective loyalties which may often be in conflict; that we act upon our environment and upon each other and are ourselves changed in the process. This destroys for ever the static conception of the past. It is not a register but a moving film. The characters have different ideas and preoccupations from our own but if we attend to what they are saying and doing we may come, to some extent at least, to understand them. The fact that Scott's own sympathies were Royalist and Tory is of little importance in estimating his contribution to the revival of the Stuart image in all its glamour and its pathos. He was in any case a man of such largeness of mind that he could sympathise imaginatively with persons and points of view that his reason and his judgment disapproved. Still less did it mean that he exempted members of the House of Stuart from the criticism of his sceptical political intelligence or of his acute moral sense. For him they, like their opponents, were people, and therefore to be understood. And imaginative sympathy was the *sine qua non* of understanding.

Scott's own historical consciousness extended backwards to the generation that remembered the 'forty-five. As a young man he met and talked to men who had been out in the rebellion, men who had opposed it as destructive to Scotland's rising prosperity and men who had, perhaps shamefacedly, stood neutral. Even in his time over the great part of the Highlands the language and traditions and religion of the people were insulated by lack of communications. He caught and retained the accents and the ways of thought of an age before his own.

By reading he could even extend this command a generation or two further back yet. The novels in which Scott brought back the Scotland of the days before his yesterday, from the late seventeenth century to the 'forty-five are works of historical genius. From the point of view of the present inquiry their importance though indirect is profound. In the first place they opened up a new and inexhaustibly enriching historical method. In the second they gave imaginative flesh and blood to the bones of the old seventeenth-century conflicts of which the Jacobite rebellions were the bequest.

In Scott's manhood Jacobitism was no more than a haunting memory. He himself was on the best of terms with the Prince Regent. In 1822 he was the moving spirit in the junketings that celebrated the first visit of a Hanoverian sovereign to Edinburgh. The tendency of his novels, as of his life, was always towards acceptance of existing institutions and against political escapades. But, like the stability which he upheld, his own position had not been reached without a struggle and was not maintained without a certain inner tension. Shortly before his death he visited the tombs of the last direct descendants of Charles I in St Peter's and, according to some accounts, expressed regret that they should have died in exile.

Scott, as Trevelyan emphasises, fired Macaulay to write history that should have the same truth to life. By a fortunate coincidence new material of exactly the kind required began to appear on every hand. The first extracts from Evelyn's *Diary* were published in 1819; the first version of Pépys, bowdlerised, abridged, but still instinct with vitality, in 1825. Before the Victorian age was under way the local and regional antiquarian societies had printed a fair sample of the journals, records and letters that were to flesh out British history with a humanity and an individualism that the seventeenth century would itself have found congenial. Precisely because the age of the two Charleses was a great period of portraiture and of biography and autobiography the characters belonging to it are more apt to engage the interest and the sympathy of the reader. Macaulay took a low view of the two Kings but he was incapable of painting them in a low tone. Charles I is grudgingly allowed 'some of the qualities of a good, and even of a great prince'. But his unfortunate tendency to deviousness and double-dealing becomes, in Macaulay's handling of him, the mainspring of his action: 'He was, in truth, impelled by an incurable propensity to dark and crooked ways. It may seem strange that his conscience, which, on occasions of little moment was sufficiently sensitive, should never have reproached him with this great vice. But there is reason to believe that he was perfidious, not only from constitution and from habit, but also on principle.' The Whig version of English history in the seventeenth century reaches its most powerful expression in Macaulay. Charles I's part in it is more harshly represented than in White Kennet or Burnet.

It is his son however who draws the fire of the heavy guns. Charles I may have been a cheat but Charles II was much worse: a thorough-going cynic, who would not have minded being labelled a cheat because he did not think there was such a thing as honesty. The sternness and force of Macaulay's condemnation is Johnsonian:

> According to him [Charles II], every person was to be bought: but some people haggled more about their price than others; and when this haggling was very obstinate and very skilful it was called by some fine name. The chief trick by which clever men kept up the price of their abilities was called integrity. The chief trick by which handsome women kept up the price of their beauty was called modesty . . . Thinking thus of mankind Charles naturally cared very little what they thought of him . . . His contempt of flattery has been highly commended, but seems, when viewed in connection with the rest of his character, to deserve no commendation. It is possible to be below flattery as well as above it . . .

Having taken every possibility of virtue away with one hand Macaulay skilfully appears to give some of it back with the other:

> It is creditable to Charles's temper that, ill as he thought of his species, he never became a misanthrope. He saw little in men but what was hateful. Yet he did not hate them. Nay, he was so far humane that it was highly disagreeable to him to see their sufferings or to hear their complaints.

What Macaulay has done is to extend the strongly expressed insights of Halifax, Pepys and some other contemporaries into a logical and coherent explanation of the King's character. Totally void of principle, belief, ambition or even idea, Charles appears before us as nothing more than the sum of his abilities and his appetites, dignified by a splendid bearing and beautiful manners. It is a highly effective characterisation, striking in the simplicity of its design and fruitful in explaining his acts and intentions. Perhaps it also represents at least a partial triumph of the King's own projection of himself. If Macaulay in drawing it meant to shock the serious, high-minded reading public of the mid-nineteenth century by exposing Charles's idleness, frivolity and emptiness he also breathed fresh life into the image of the witty, daring, devil-may-care, man of the world. He is far too accomplished a writer to throw away good material, such as the death-bed scene. The King, after enduring agonies that his doctors could only intensify by their horrid meddling, apologises to his attendants for being 'a most unconscionable time dying: but he hoped that they would excuse it'. As the light begins to glimmer round the edges of the curtains he asks that they should be drawn back that he might once more see day. Style and wit and love of life are allowed the last word.

Scott and Macaulay have enriched the historical consciousness of succeeding generations and both have placed the House of Stuart at the centre of English history. Both were attacked with withering scorn, occasionally relieved by a distant recognition of the gifts they had misused, by the third historical Titan of Early Victorian Britain, Thomas Carlyle. Carlyle's mind quivered with a universal rage that could only be soothed by the domination of a master-spirit. Apart from Goethe, the only just persons to be found in the great city of destruction that was the nineteenth century appear to have been his own immediate family. But above the insane triviality and wickedness of the contemporary world and the recorded past towered a few mysterious, massive, awe-inspiring figures who perhaps partook of the divine in which Carlyle so fiercely adjured himself and his readers to believe. One of these was Oliver Cromwell. To Tory historians he had, naturally, appeared as the arch-villain. His very pre-eminence however lent him a certain terrible grandeur. Clarendon insists on this point from the beginning to the end of his famous description of him: '. . . wickedness as great as his could never have accomplished those trophies, without the assistance of a great spirit, an admirable circumspection and sagacity, and a most magnanimous resolution'. Clarendon's successors were less generous and the Whigs from the start fought shy of Cromwell. He was, after all, as much of an embarrassment to them as the theory of Divine Right and Non-resistance was to the Tories. The two positions were comfortably amalgamated in Hume's dismissal of him as a hypocritical fanatic. Carlyle's publication of his Letters and Speeches in 1845 dynamited this. No hostile estimate of Cromwell was left standing that was not based, as Clarendon's had been, on a recognition of his seriousness and his sincerity of purpose. As to his success in dissembling there could hardly be two opinions. The pamphlets and memoirs of his time are loud with the outrage of those whom he had deceived. To accept Cromwell's fundamental honesty did not mean denying his tactical use of trickery and deceit. Carlyle's view of the Stuarts swung between pity and contempt. Charles II was beneath consideration. As for Charles I, the kindest thing was to reject the authenticity of the work Hume had so much admired:

> I struggled through the 'Eikon Basilike' yesterday; one of the paltriest pieces of vapid, shovel-hatted, clear-starched, immaculate falsity and cant I have ever read. It is to me an amazement how any mortal could ever have taken that for a genuine book of King Charles's . . . It remains as an offence to all genuine men—a small minority still—for some time yet.[5]

Nonetheless Carlyle's assertion of Cromwell's greatness elevated rather than depressed the standing of Charles I. Macaulay's central criticism of him, his deceitfulness, was seen to be scarcely if at all less applicable to the great man who had overthrown him.

A tributary stream to the rehabilitation of Charles I was the revival of the Catholic tradition in the Church of England, forever associated with the University of Oxford. In 1845, the year of Carlyle's *Cromwell*, Newman was received into the Church of Rome, to be followed by a number of others. The resentment against the Papacy aroused by these conversions was intensified some five years later by the reconstitution of the Roman Catholic Church in England on a diocesan basis. This clamour obscured the deeper issues. What the Oxford Movement was about was the threat to traditional Christianity delivered by the French Revolution and the Enlightenment. Newman and those who thought like him saw the best defence in the reassertion of the teaching authority of the Church, which in turn required the reassertion of its organic character living and developing in its own right and not simply in the consciousness of its individual members. This concept of churchmanship could trace descent from Laud and Charles I. In Newman's Day it was personified in the venerable President of Magdalen, Dr Routh, whose Oxford career worthily reflected the antiquity of the university. In the High Street, still bridged by the East Gate, he could remember seeing Dr Johnson lumber up the steps of University College. Routh had been born in 1755 and was to die in possession of his office and of all his faculties in 1854, cheated, it was said, of his century by chargrin at the appointment of a Royal Commission to report on the condition of the universities.* It was to him that Newman dedicated in 1837 his *Lectures on the Prophetical Office of the Church*, recalling the continuity he represented in characteristic cadences: 'who has been reserved to report to a forgetful generation what was the theology of their fathers'. In religion and politics Routh belonged to the old Toryism of Church and King that had lost so much of its strength to the Non-jurors and the Jacobites. Jacobitism indeed had been strong in the Oxford of Routh's youth.

In 1823 Routh published an edition of the foundation document of Whig history, Burnet's *History of My Own Time*. '"Why is it, uncle" (once asked his nephew, John Routh) "that you are always working at Burnet, whom you are always attacking?" To whom the President— "A good question, sir! Because I know the man to be a liar; and I am determined to prove him so."'[6] If this was Dr Routh's real opinion of his author he was somewhat hypocritical in defending his general truthfulness in his introduction. But the incidental revelations of opinion are of unusual interest in tracing the fortunes of the Stuart image. Routh, for all his Rip Van Winkledom, describes the doctrine of non-resistance as 'absurd'.[7] Burnet's modified or second state of the character of Charles II he finds 'harsh and hideous'.[8] Yet it is clear that he has largely accepted the version given by White Kennet to which Roger North took such violent exception:

> The disputes, which afterwards arose between an unprincipled, but good-humoured monarch, regardless alike of his own honour and the national interest, and a restless, violent and merciless faction, are subjects of deep concern, on account of their melancholy results.[9]

Behind the rattle of clichés a withdrawal is taking place. Charles II is admitted to be indefensible, though not positively wicked as his opponents are. The citadel of Toryism is the legacy of Charles I. 'The mind feels consolation in the virtues of Ormond, Clarendon and Southampton.' The ground yielded by Carte has been finally abandoned.

A bizarre variant of this view of the Stuarts is to be found in the

---

* Others thought that the sharp fall of his investments occasioned by the Crimean War had more to do with it.

works of the Disraelis, father and son. As Robert Blake shews in his brilliant analysis of *Coningsby* and *Sybil*[10] Disraeli ingeniously pressed the romantic Royalism of his father's *Commentaries on the Life and Reign of Charles I* into the service of his vendetta against Sir Robert Peel. On this reading of history the ancient harmony of English society was destroyed by the greedy profiteers of the Reformation who seized for themselves what the Church had administered for the common good. Charles I—seconded by Strafford and Laud—had tried to remedy this deplorable state of affairs by introducing ship money and other forms of taxation that would hit the rich harder than the poor. The unfortunate results of their pursuit of social justice are only too well known. 'Rightly was King Charles surnamed the Martyr; for he was the holocaust of direct taxation. Never yet did man lay down his heroic life for so great a cause: the cause of the Church and the cause of the Poor.'[11] Politics since that time had consisted of the efforts— generally successful—of the same selfish oligarchy to institutionalise their power and wealth against Crown and People, if necessary by manipulating the one and bamboozling the other. Here again, indeed here especially, Charles I, was the sole beneficiary of such an interpretation. No one, not even Disraeli, could keep a straight face in advancing any such claims for Charles II.

Whether Disraeli ever discussed this panorama of the English past with Queen Victoria may be doubted. The flattery which, we are told, he thought it best to lay on with a trowel is certainly applied with the requisite liberality to the House of Stuart but hardly to the House of Hanover. But quite apart from dynastic questions Disraeli's theory warmly favours the High Church views which Queen Victoria detested with a vehemence beyond even his power to mollify. Charles I's churchmanship and Charles II's sexual morals could hardly have recommended the Stuarts to their successor on the throne. There appears to be no authority for the story that the Queen, when asked which of her predecessors she would choose to take her into dinner, replied Charles II. In the summer of 1851 however, in the middle of the excitements and triumphs of the Great Exhibition she honoured his memory by giving a Court Ball in Restoration costume. Eugene Lami designed it with great magnificence and Winterhalter made some sketches of the Royal couple in their finery. As early as May 8th (the Ball was to be given on June 13th) the Queen and Prince Albert were 'much occupied with our costumes'. As the date approached, the sessions with Lami and the sittings to Winterhalter vied with the almost daily visits to the Exhibition for pleasurable possession of their time and attention. On the great day itself

> We dined together early, and then began dressing for our Bal Costumé. Our dresses, and Charles's [Charles, Prince of Leinigen, Queen Victoria's half-brother] were really beautiful and so correct. Dearest Albert looked very handsome in his, and his admirable wig made him look so young. Our dresses were most exactly carried out from Eugene Lami's drawings. Mine was of grey moire antique, ornamented with gold laces—a very long waist with a berthe of guipure, and sleeves trimmed with old lace. The petticoat, showing under the dress, which was all open in front, was of rich gold and silver brocade (Indian manufacture) richly trimmed with silver lace. Wore diamonds and pearls, and four very large Indian emerald drops were arranged as a 'Sevigné'. In my hair I wore an ornament of pearls and a large emerald—my small diamond crown and pearls twisted in the back of my hair. The shoes and gloves were embroidered to match the dress. Albert's coat was of the richest gold brocade on an orange ground with a little green in it, the manufacture of which did the greatest credit to Spitalfields. The court hose were of crimson velvet & the stockings grey. The silver embroidery of the sleeves and baudelière were quite beautiful. Charles looked extremely well and quite like Charles IInd . . . The Ladies looked extremely well, all improved by the very becoming curls . . . We went into the Throne Room which was empty, and then all the company came by, which was a beautiful sight. The Ladies without exception were much improved by their costumes, some of the dresses being very rich,— the gentlemen wonderfully disguised. . . . It was indeed a magnificent Ball, and I was so proud & pleased to see my beloved Albert looking so handsome, truly royal & distinguished, and so much admired. I must say our costumes were beautifully made and all the accessories well carried out.

Whatever their differences and hers, Charles I and Charles II would surely have approved this attention to dress. So far as can be judged from the entries in her journal the Queen's interest in the period was purely aesthetic. Perhaps the gaiety and glamour popularly associated with the Restoration touched a chord in the ball-giving, opera-going young Victoria that no longer responded in the widowed recluse of the seventies and eighties. Certainly she seems to have taken a sterner line towards Charles II. In 1889 she was only with difficulty prevailed upon to allow the purchase of the famous

portrait of the King in his coronation robes for the Royal Collection.
'The Queen *reluctantly* consents. The Queen does not care for Charles
II.'[12] Perhaps her moral sensibilities had been irritated by the too
well exposed behaviour of her eldest son and heir apparent. The
popularity of Edward VII as Prince and King suggests that her
subjects took a more indulgent view of these matters. It is certain that
as the pendulum swung back from the strict decorum of the high
Victorian age Charles II stood to gain.

In any case both sovereign and nation were agreed in thinking of
the two Kings as persons rather than as emblems. Their politics, from
which their images had been derived, were irrelevant to the concerns
of the late nineteenth century. Whig and Tory no longer existed in any
form recognisable to the age that had spawned them. Like Royalist
and Parliamentarian they had direct descendants in every party. The
only attempt to claim ideological continuity was that based on the
Anglo-Catholic revival, itself essentially liturgical and doctrinal, to
which Disraeli for a time hitched his wagon. It survived to inspire
Christian Socialism and received perhaps its last and most eloquent
formulation in R. H. Tawney's *Religion and the Rise of Capitalism*. Even
here the reader who turns up the index entries under 'Charles I's
social policy' will find that they in fact largely refer to Archbishop
Laud. To identify the Puritan smiting his breast and rolling his eyes
heavenward with the lip-smacking capitalist is one thing. To present
Charles I and the Cavaliers as the forerunners of the Fabian Society is
quite another. Professor Tawney had too strong a sense of humour and
too profound a knowledge of history to do anything of the kind. And
Sergeant Tawney of the Manchester Regiment had more affinities of
spirit with the soldiers of the Eastern Association than with Prince
Rupert's cavalrymen.

The great historians who succeeded the heroic age of Macaulay and
Carlyle were more concerned with the nature of their craft than with
the conclusions to which they themselves had come. The elucidation
and criticism of their sources mattered more to them than whether or
not the Whig dogs got the best of it. Gardiner and Ranke are among
the greatest exponents of modern historical method. They have their
views of Charles I and II but they are much more interested in
analysing, comparing, sifting and testing the materials for forming any
view at all. Ranke subjects Clarendon to the closest scrutiny because
of his part in shaping the image of the persons and the nature of the
issues about which he wrote. 'The view of the event [the Great

Rebellion] in England itself and in the educated world generally has been . . . determined by the book . . . Clarendon belongs to those who have essentially fixed the circle of ideas for the English nation.' He finds him, for all his virtues, too limited, too partial in national and individual loyalties. 'One seldom finds oneself raised to the heights where the real course of events is determined.' But among his partialities, Ranke is careful to point out, could not be numbered the perpetuation of the image that Charles I had laboured to establish. 'The justification of the King . . . was not his object; King Charles always appears in his pages as weak and dependent.'[13] Ranke himself took a kindly view of both monarchs without in the least exaggerating their virtues or their talents. We owe to him the printing of Burnet's earliest, most excoriating draft of his character of Charles II.

With S. R. Gardiner we approach as near to omniscient impartiality as is given to men. The determination to master all the relevant materials, to enter sympathetically into every point of view and to state fully and fairly the findings of such super-human exertion is evident on every one of his many pages. Every subsequent writer on Charles I and on Cromwell (from whom he was directly descended) relies on him. Although he had intended to include the reign of Charles II within the scope of his *History of England* a long life of unbroken labour only brought his volumes to the year 1656. Charles II thus appears only as a marginal and in every sense fugitive figure. Nonetheless it is impossible to think that if Gardiner had been granted the years of Methuselah he would have deepened the conception to support the weight of admiration the King has succeeded in winning from some twentieth-century writers. Painfully just though he strives to be, Gardiner cannot accept any high estimate of either father or son. Both were untrustworthy; and Charles I for all his courage was in no sense large-minded. His fatal defects, in Gardiner's view, were his lack of receptivity, and his want of imagination.

From this temperate judgment delivered by the most sensitive, learned and upright judge few serious historians have since dissented. Many indeed have been much more severe. But the image Charles created and, to pious eyes, consecrated with his own death has outlived the purpose of its making and has acquired an independent significance. The visual arts that Charles I sought to harness to his politics have in the end carried him out of them. To think of him is to most people even faintly conscious of the past to see one or other of the Van Dyck portraits and to remember one of the greatest connoisseurs in the history of English taste. The disasters and dangers of his reign are forgotten, except by those who study the period. The mawkish poem by Lionel Johnson on his statue at Charing Cross is better known than the one on the same subject (but in a very different sense) that is sometimes attributed to Andrew Marvell.

As for his eldest son, he too has profited in escaping from the chain of political and historical reaction. The spirited attempts made in the last fifty years to have him once again taken seriously as a ruler have not altogether succeeded but they have shown once again that the general public are much readier to hear more about him than about any other monarch who died before the opening of the present century. Part of the fascination that he exerts derives from the fact that Charles I and he were father and son: that one of the wittiest and most dissolute of English Kings should be the historical vindicator of one of the most serious and strait-laced: that Royalists, without batting an eyelid, moved at once from rhapsodising over the one to rhapsodising over the other. In human interest there is something for everybody in the Stuarts.

A Note on Sources

Apart from the passage in Queen Victoria's Journal, which is printed here by gracious permission of Her Majesty the Queen, I have not used any manuscript material. I have generally cited my authority where there seemed any need to do so but in a work such as this a full bibliography would be out of place.

The main contemporary authorities such as Clarendon, Burnet, etc are not only cited but discussed in the text. Of others that throw some light on the atmosphere and manners of the Court during these two reigns or on the personality of the two monarchs the following may be mentioned:

The Life of Philip Henry by his son Matthew Henry (1699, reprinted Wordsworth, *Ecclesiastical History*, vi, 107-393). This son of a courtier was a scholar of Christ Church during the Civil War and subsequently became a Presbyterian minister. *The Life of Dr Henry Hammond* by James Fell (Oxford, 1662, reprinted *ibid.* v, 337 ff.). Another divine brought up at Court, where his father was physician to Prince Henry, who remained a pillar of the Church of England. *The Life of Nicholas Ferrar* by Peckard (Cambridge, 1790, but based on contemporary memoirs, reprinted, *ibid.* v, 74-265). This work, together with *The Ferrar Papers*, ed. B. Blackstone (Cambridge, 1938), gives valuable insight into the life and ideas of the community at Little Gidding with which Charles I felt so vivid a sympathy. Izaak Walton's *Lives of Bishop Sanderson* and of *George Herbert* reprinted in the same collection also illuminate the King's personal religion. On the same subject the edition of *Eikon Basilike* that I used is that by Knabel for the Folger Shakespeare Library (Cornell U.P., 1966). Of the various collections of the King's letters *Charles I in 1646. Letters of King Charles I to Queen Henrietta Maria*, ed. Bruce Camden Society (1858), gives far and away the most intimate and self-revealing portrait.

For Charles II the contemporary authorities are extensively discussed in the text. He was not a great correspondent but Sir Arthur Bryant's *The Letters of King Charles II* (1935) and even more vividly *Notes which passed at Meetings of the Privy Council between Charles II and the earl of Clarendon*, ed. Macray. Roxburghe Club (1898), suggest something of his individuality.

Among biographies consulted that may not have been directly referred to in the text or notes are Lister's *Life of Clarendon* (3 vols, 1838), G. V. Bennett, *White Kennet, Bishop of Peterborough* (1957) and C. V. Wedgwood, *Thomas Wentworth, first earl of Strafford : a Revaluation* (1961). Among historical works mention may be made of two not perhaps so widely known as they deserve: Sir Keith Feiling's *History of the Tory Party 1640-1714* (1924) and Pieter Geyl's *Orange and Stuart 1641-72*, trans. Pomerans (1969).

Notes

CHAPTER 1

1 *Reliquiae Woottonianae*, 4th edition (1685), 151.
2 Burnet, *History of My Own Time* (ed. Airy), ii, 178, footnote 3.
3 Clarendon, *Rebellion*, iv, 344.
4 *History of England*, new edition 1774, vii, 153-4.
5 Isaac D'Israeli, *Commentaries on the Life and Reign of Charles I*, i, 417.

CHAPTER 2

1 C. W. Firebrace, *Honest Harry. Sir Henry Firebrace 1619-91* (1932).
2 *Life*.
3 Carte, *Life of James, Duke of Ormond*, new edition (1851), iv, 607.
4 Warwick, *Memoirs*, 65-6.
5 *Brief Lives*, ed. Lawson Dick, 263.
6 J. Bass Mullinger, *Some Cambridge Characteristics in the Seventeenth Century*.
7 *Memoirs*, 64-5.
8 Sir Henry Slingsby, *Diary*, ed. Parsons (1836),
9 Lucy Hutchinson, *Memoirs of the Life of Colonel Hutchinson*, ed. Sutherland
   (1973), 46.
10 *Letters, Speeches and Proclamations of King Charles I*, ed. Petrie (1935), 266.
11 *Reliquiae Wottonianae* (4th edition). The Life and Death of the Duke of Buckingham, 212-13.
12 *Letters, Speeches and Proclamations of King Charles I*, ed. Petrie (1935), 50-7.
13 *Ibid.*, 42-4.
14 See on all this Stephen Orgel and Roy Strong, *Inigo Jones the Theatre of the Stuart
   Court*, 2 vols. (1973).

15 *Ibid.*, 51.
16 *Ibid.*, *Albion's Triumph*, 455.
17 *Ibid.*, *Salmacida Spolia*, 731, 733.

CHAPTER 3

1 *Life of Dr Hammond*, Wordsworth Eccles. Hist., v, 384.
2 *Ibid.*, 381.
3 Izaak Walton, *Life of Bp Sanderson, ibid.*, 477.
4 *Brief Lives*, ed. Dick, 193.
5 *The Duppa-Isham Correspondence*, ed. Sir Gyles Isham, Northants Record Society
    (1955), 14-14.
6 *Ibid.*, 71-2.
7 *Ibid.*, 93.
8 *Ibid.*, 119.
9 *Ibid.*, 69.
10 *Life*, i, 51.
11 *History of My Own Time*, i, 402.
12 Burnet, *Memoirs of the Lives and Actions of James and William* (1673, n.e. Oxford
    1852), i, 10.
13 *Ibid.*, iv, 21.
14 *Clarendon State Papers* (1773), ii, 336-7. Hyde to Nicholas 12 Feb. 47.
15 *Ibid.*, 338-41.
16 *Charles I in 1646. Letters of King Charles I to Queen Henrietta Maria*, ed. Bruce
    (1856), p. 44.
17 Burnet, *Memoirs of the Dukes of Hamilton*, v, 81.
18 I have here followed Sanderson, *A Compleat History of the Life and Raigne of King
    Charles* (1658), quoted in J. D. Jones, *The Royal Prisoner* (1965).
19 C. W. Firebrace, *Honest Harry* (1932), 256-7.

CHAPTER 4

1 Burnet, *Own Time*, i, 86-7.
2 Roger North, *Life of Francis North* (1742), 183.
3 Violet Bonham Carter, *Winston Churchill as I knew him* (1965), 319-20.
4 *Rebellion*, vii, 324-5.
5 *Ibid.*, ix, 18-19.
6 *Diary*, ed. Latham and Matthews, vi, 316.
7 *Charles I in 1646*, 45-6.
8 Quot. Eva Scott *The King in Exile*, 39.
9 *Clar[endon] S[tate] P[apers]*, ii, 227.
10 *Ibid.*, 319.

CHAPTER 5

1 *Clar., S.P.*, ii, 242-4.
2 *Own Time*, i, 90.
3 Carte, *Ormond*, iii, 438-9.
4 *Ibid.*, 480-2.

5 G. R. Balleine, *All for the King: The Life Story of Sir George Carteret* (St Helier, 1976), 83.

6 Bryant (ed.), *The Letters of King Charles II* (1935), p. 37.

CHAPTER 6

1 *Nicholas Papers*, ed. Warner (1886), i, 170-2.

CHAPTER 7

1 *Nicholas Papers*, i, 295.

2 *Memoirs of Sir Stephen Fox* (1717), pp. 19-20.

3 *The Growth of Political Stability in England, 1675-1726* (Peregrine edition 1969), p. 28.

4 *Clar., S.P.*, iii, 297, quot. Eva Scott, *Travels of the King*, 209.

CHAPTER 8

1 Carte, *Ormond*, iv, 572-3.

2 *Ibid.*, 108, 112.

3 *Ibid.*, 111.

4 *Ibid.*

5 Burnet, *Own Time*, i, 464.

6 Plumptre, *Thomas Ken* (1888), i, 157, 158.

7 *Life of Robert Frampton, Bishop of Gloucester*, ed. Simpson Evans (1876), 123.

8 Burnet, i, 464-5.

CHAPTER 9

1 Quot. Eva Scott, *The Travels of the King*, 351.

CHAPTER 10

1 Carte, *Ormond*, iv, 107. It now appears certain that the real architect of the marriage was Sandwich's cousin, the Earl of Manchester. I am obliged for this information to Professor C. R. Boxer, who has recently calendared the despatches of the Portuguese ambassador.

2 Burnet, *Own Time*, ii, 3.

3 Carte, *Ormond*, iv, 351.

4 *Ibid.*, 693.

CHAPTER 11

1 *Diary*, ed. de Beer, iv, 118.

2 Carte, *Ormond*, iv, 693.

CHAPTER 12

1 *Works* (Penguin Books, 1969), p. 22 et seq.

2 *Own Time*, ii, 342.

CHAPTER 13

1 *Examen*, 651.

2 *Ibid.*, 657.

3 *Ibid.*, ii.

4 *Ibid.*, 657.

5 *Life of Lord Keeper Guildford*, 252.

6 *Op. cit.*, 417.

7 *Ormond*, iii, 418.

8 Bulstrode, *op. cit.*, 65.

9 *Walpole Society Journal*, VII (1919). Diary of Nicholas Stone junior, 170ff. I owe this reference to Mr Richard Walker.

10 See on this Hugh Trevor-Roper, *Macaulay* (New York, 1968), pp. xi-xii.

11 Hume, *op. cit.* (new edition, 8 vols., 1774), vi, 196.

12 *Ibid.*, vii, 153-4.

13 *Ibid.*, vii, 146.

14 *Ibid.*

15 *Ibid.*, viii, 209-210.

16 S. R. Gardiner, *Hist. Eng.*, vii, 150-1

17 Lingard, vi, 305.

18 *Ibid.*, 442.

19 *Ibid.*, 545-7, 561-2, 656-62.

20 *Ibid.*, vii, 501.

21 *Ibid.*, viii, 293.

CHAPTER 14

1 *They Asked for a Paper* (1962), 103.

2 Quot. A. O. J. Cockshut, *The Achievement of Walter Scott* (1969), 8.

3 *An Autobiography & Other Essays* (1949), 200-1.

4 *Ibid.*

5 J. A. Froude, *Carlyle's Life in London* (new edition 1897), i, 213.

6 Burgon, *Lives of Twelve Good Men* (new edition 1891), 33.

7 Burnet, i, xiii.

8 *Ibid.*, xvii.

9 *Ibid.*, xxviii.

10 Blake, *Disraeli* (1966), 190ff.

11 *Sybil*, quot. Blake, 195.

12 P.R.O. L.C. 1/S13 part 2 item 7. I owe this reference to Sir Oliver Millar.

13 Ranke, *A History of England,* principally in the seventeenth century (6 vols. 1875), vi, 14, 28-9.

Index